Speaking/Writing
of God

*Jewish Philosophical Reflections
on the Life with Others*

Michael Oppenheim

State University of New York Press

Published by
State University of New York Press, Albany

© 1997 State University of New York

For information, address State University of New York
Press, State University Plaza, Albany, N.Y., 12246

Production by E. Moore
Marketing by Fran Keneston

Library of Congress Cataloging-in-Publication Data
Oppenheim, Michael D., 1946–
    Speaking/writing of God : Jewish philosophical reflections on the
life with others / Michael Oppenheim.
        p.   cm. — (SUNY series in Jewish philosophy)
    Includes bibliographical references and index.
    ISBN 0-7914-3457-5 (alk. paper). — ISBN 0-7914-3458-3 (pbk. :
alk. paper)
    1. Philosophy, Jewish.   2. Rosenzweig, Franz, 1886–1929.
3. Lévinas, Emmanuel   4. Holocaust (Jewish theology)   5. Feminism-
-Religious aspects—Judaism.   6. Religious pluralism—Judaism.
I. Title.   II. Series.
B5800.O77   1997
296.3'092'2—DC20   96-41186
                                                    CIP

10 9 8 7 6 5 4 3 2 1

To Sarah,
David, and Aaron

Contents

Preface

This book represents another stage in my exploration of modern Jewish faith, something which many contemporary Jewish philosophers regard as essential if Judaism is to provide a meaningful orientation in the present. The strengths of the modern Jewish philosophers who are central to this study—Franz Rosenzweig and Emmanuel Levinas—lie in their understanding that the relationship to God is expressed in love for the neighbor and responsibility for the other. They recognized that a sense or trace of the divine—which might be all that is possible for many today—comes, not by directly beseeching God, but in living with and for the other. In addition to the thoughts of these philosophers, I examine the critiques of Judaism by feminist Jewish thinkers and the challenge of religious pluralism. For me, the basic themes in the works of Rosenzweig and Levinas require us to listen to and respect the ideas of feminist Jews and the words of those committed to other religious traditions. I believe that this listening and responding significantly enriches Jewish faith. Feminist Jewish thinkers have brought about a widening of the ways in which the relationship to God can be experienced and expressed. Living with persons from other traditions brings Jews new insights about the life of faith and mystery, commitment and openness, and steadfastness and responsibility.

Almost all of the material in the following chapters is being published here for the first time. An earlier version of chapter 1 appeared in *Judaism* 42:2 (Spring 1993: American Jewish Congress). Quotations taken from Judith Plaskow's *Standing Again at Sinai* (1991) are reprinted with permission of HarperCollins publishers.

While I read significant texts in preparing this work, a number of friends have provided even more guidance and help. Their support has been both scholarly and personal. They have confirmed for me that the most authentic insights emerge from and are tested in dialogue.

My appreciation for the relevance of Rosenzweig's thought has grown out of years of study with the distinguished Rosenzweig scholar, Barbara Galli. I have benefited from her ideas as well as her dedication, carefulness, and intensity. Norma Joseph has been my mentor in studying feminist Jewish thought, and she has shared with me the passion of those working to extend the ways in which Jewish women participate in the life of the community. Marc Lalonde continually surprises, pushes and challenges me as we study together the work of Emmanuel Levinas as well as other modern religious thinkers. Rosemary Hale and other colleagues in the Department of Religion at Concordia University have been marvelously encouraging, always graciously welcoming my new works.

I also want to thank the many students who have read and criticized my work. I have been very lucky in that all of these resources have been available to me in Montreal. While I have learned much from colleagues in the Association for Jewish Studies and the American Academy of Religion, it is those who I am able to see and sit with day-to-day who have most nourished me. I hope that I have sometimes been able to live up to their expectations, and given partial repayment for their abundant gifts.

Introduction:
The Question of Speaking/Writing of God

There has been an effluence of works in the field of modern Jewish philosophy during the past decade. This development reflects a new enthusiasm about the possibility of fulfilling the tasks that Jewish philosophers have set for themselves ever since the appearance of Moses Mendelssohn's book *Jerusalem* in 1783. There are many ways to describe these tasks and I will note three strands. Modern Jewish philosophers have sought to express the nature of the Jewish obligation to the past, commitment to present communal life, and engagement with modernity.[1]

Jewish philosophers recognize that Jews are obligated by the past—that is, by a body of literature, values, and ways of life that have come together to form an ongoing religious tradition. While the nature and extent of this obligation must be explored by these philosophers, they are aware that Jewish life is defined by such events as the call to Abraham, Exodus, Sinai, and Exile. This feeling of obligation toward the Jewish experience also entails that discovering or creating a continuity between the Jewish past and present is immensely important. The commitment to present-day Jewish communities, and to the Jewish people as a whole, is also definitive for the Jewish philosophical endeavor. Modern Jewish philosophers are part of, and participants in, the life of diverse Jewish communities, and they are compelled to help them in their efforts to persist and develop in the contemporary period. Finally, modern Jewish philosophers have affirmed that there is meaning and value in the modern world. They have not repudiated the Emancipation—that is, the Jewish entrance into the stream of Western culture that began for some Jews in the third quarter of the eighteenth century. While noting the difficulties and dangers that beset modern life, they take seriously the impact that such disciplines as comparative religion, philosophy, biblical scholarship, history,

1

psychology, anthropology, sociology, and the natural sciences have had upon our self-understanding. However, one must speak of an engagement with modernity, because these philosophers have not allowed their consciousness of themselves as Jews to be dissipated by their self-understanding as modern persons.

It is striking that contemporary Jewish philosophers are hopeful in the face of these tasks. Despite the tremendous challenges of multifaceted modern social, political, and intellectual forces, Jewish thinkers no longer seem to feel that they are under siege. They believe that they can forcefully speak to Jews about the relevance of their obligations, commitments, and struggles. Further, they are confident that the particular Jewish quest to find meaning can contribute to the efforts of persons in other communities. Studying, drawing upon, and extending the insights of earlier Jewish philosophers—especially those who lived and wrote during the past century—contemporary Jewish philosophers are answering the summons to provide some of the intellectual and emotional resources required by Jews living in freedom.[2]

THE AGENDA

The present work should be seen as an expression of this development in modern Jewish philosophy. *Speaking/Writing of God* is an investigation that focuses on aspects of contemporary Jewish religious language.

I am defining religious language in a way that is both narrow and broad.[3] Narrowly, religious language occurs only when reference to God is made. More widely, the study of religious language is the exploration of the meaning and relevance of the discourse about God's presence and actions. It is the study of all of the ways in which stories, concepts, and categories that revolve around the relationship with God are needed in order to reveal the depth of human existence and, for Jewish thought, the depth of Jewish life. In other words, we revert to religious language when we are confronted with experiences that cannot be encapsulated by our everyday language. On such occasions, we find ourselves forced to understand—that is, to speak and to write—in terms of a transcendent dimension that has broken through into our lives. For Jews, the biblical discourse about God is the basis for their understanding of this transcendent dimension.

Central to this work is the contention that it is imperative for Jewish philosophers to refer to God's presence and actions in discussing the nature of Jewish life and of all our lives as human. This contention has been vigorously confirmed by Jewish philosophers in terms of three of the most significant areas of contemporary Jewish life. Many of them have found it necessary to turn to religious language when confronting the Holocaust, the establishment of the state of Israel, and our life with others.

A number of Jewish philosophers have insisted that the community's struggle with the Holocaust could be meaningfully expressed only in the context of the covenantal relationship with God. Still, except for a few small writings—including those by Martin Buber and Abraham Heschel—the philosophical silence concerning the Holocaust only ended, as it did for Jewish communities throughout the world, with the 1967 Six-Day War. From that time, major works by such innovative Jewish thinkers as Richard Rubenstein (with some earlier pieces), Arthur Cohen, Emil Fackenheim, and, particularly, Elie Wiesel, have appeared and been widely discussed. Fackenheim's clarion call of "If *all present* access to the God of history is *wholly* lost, the God of history is Himself lost" (1972, 79), vividly reflects the place of religious language in confronting the Holocaust. Many of the most powerful insights of Jewish philosophers can be aligned in terms of that statement, with Fackenheim and Wiesel telling stories about a paradoxical and fragmented presence, while Rubenstein and Cohen discuss the ramifications of God's absence.[4]

The establishment of the state of Israel and its ongoing struggle for existence has offered occasions for a more limited and less well-known development of philosophical *midrash*[5] or story about God's presence and action. Fackenheim has described the impact of the 1967 Six-Day War as the experience of "a wonder at a singled out, millennial existence which, after Auschwitz, is still possible and actual" (1972, 95). However, it is Heschel's wrestling with the right words to use in exploring the meaning of the creation of Israel that best exemplifies the wider way in which Jewish philosophers are sometimes forced, as it were, to reach for religious language. He wrote:

> We have not even begun to fathom the meaning of this great event. We do not fully grasp its message for us as a community and as individuals. It has not penetrated our capacity for representing its meaning in our daily lives. . . . For all who read the Hebrew Bible with biblical eyes the State of Israel is a solemn intimation of God's trace in history. It is not fulfillment of the promise, it is not the answer to all the bitter issues. Its spiritual significance, however, is radiant. . . . (Heschel 1969, 219–220)

It is important to note that, in relation to both the Holocaust and the state of Israel, the need to turn to religious language is felt by the wider Jewish community as well as by Jewish philosophers. Jews throughout the world recognize a transcendent dimension—in Heschel's terms, a radiance of meaning—in their attempt to come to terms with these subjects. This is being expressed in the most dramatic forms available within the Jewish communal repertoire. Days are set aside—*Yom Ha Shoah* (Holocaust Day), *Yom Ha Atzmaut* (Israel Independence Day), *Yom Yerushalayim* (Jerusalem Day)—as religious remembrances and celebrations. Many Jews include special references to the Holocaust and Israel in their Passover *Haggada*. There are other liturgic expressions—most strikingly, the Sabbath prayer for the State of Israel that sees the emergence of that nation as marking "the dawn of our deliverance" (Aigen, ed. 1993).

The object of this study is the third area of contemporary Jewish religious language—that is, the relation with other persons. I identify the transcendent dimension—or, alternately, the ways in which religious language, is used—in terms of three features of the relationship with others:

1. the encounter between persons (the self and other);
2. the quest by Jewish women to be accepted—including their distinctiveness/ otherness as women—as full participants in Jewish communal life (Jewish women as both the same and as others); and
3. the dialogue between Jews and non-Jews (the Jew and others).

While these features of the encounter with others have not made an impact upon the religious language of the wider community that compares with the Holocaust and Israel experiences, some Jewish philosophers have powerfully attested to the transcendent dimension of one or another of them. Franz Rosenzweig, Martin Buber, and, more recently, Emmanuel Levinas have all explored the religious, ethical, and phenomenological aspects of the relationships between persons. Feminist Jewish scholars have found that traditional religious language must be transformed in order to open the way for women to fully enter into and express themselves within the Jewish community. The philosophical and religious ramifications of the dialogue with members of other religious traditions have begun to be probed by contemporary Jewish thinkers.

However, the investigation of the role of religious language in these encounters has been limited, even in terms of the Jewish philosophical enterprise. There has been no comprehensive attempt to recognize and detail the different features of these relations with others. The resources for Jewish philosophy, as well as those that Jewish philosophy offers, have not yet been delineated. Serious study needs to be given to the ties between these types of encounters. Finally, it is important to explore the ways in which Jewish religious language as a whole might develop in response to all of them.

This present work attempts to respond to the already mentioned lacunae. It explores the dynamics, with particular interest in how that reference to the transcendent breaks out in their midst; of the relationships between persons, the interaction between feminist Jews and the community, and the dialogue between Jews and non-Jews. It notes some of the traditional Jewish resources from which philosophers have drawn in their attempt to understand these distinct relations. There are inquiries into the processes through which each of these interactions sheds light upon the others. Finally, this work is a contribution to constructive Jewish philosophy. It attempts to expand contemporary Jewish religious language by indicating the manner in which new language develops in answer to the contemporary challenge and promise of all three features of our lives with others.

THE CONTEXT

A major stream of modern Jewish philosophy has focused on the dynamics of the relationships between persons. This area has been variously described as the "interhuman," the "life of dialogue," or the sphere of "the between."[6] It presents, undeniably, one of the richest mines available for contemporary Jewish religious language. The most significant figures in this area are widely recognized as being Franz Rosenzweig, Martin Buber, and Emmanuel Levinas. There have also been serious examinations of them, both separately and in combination with each other.

The work of Martin Buber is the most renowned and thoroughly explored of these three philosophers, although there is an expanding corpus of recent writings about Rosenzweig and Levinas. However, it is the latter two philosophers who are the principal interest of this present work for three reasons.

The first—and primary one—is that this treatment of the interhuman contends that there is a fundamental asymmetry or disproportion in the relationship between the self and the neighbor, the Jewish community and Jewish women, and Jews and those in other religious traditions. The asymmetry appears through the recognition that something is owed by each of the first terms in relationship to those who stand as their partners. Thus, this book explores the obligations that are due to the neighbor, Jewish women, and those of other traditions, by the self, the Jewish community, and Jews who stand before others. Buber has characterized the deepest encounters with others, that is, the relationship of the "I" to a "Thou" in terms of reciprocity and mutuality. However, Rosenzweig and Levinas provide the fundamental vocabulary for this exploration. This is because they portray relationships in terms of asymmetry, particularly as this is expressed through responsibility that we have for others.[7]

The second reason for taking up the work of Rosenzweig and Levinas is that these thinkers vigorously contest the autonomy of the self as a prelude to their description of the life with others. An underlying theme of this book is that the belief in the self's autonomy is one of the major obstacles to realizing the fullness that comes through living with others.

The third reason is that, despite the common point of departure of Rosenzweig and Levinas, there is a pregnant tension between the styles of their religious language. The juxtaposition of their understandings of the breakout of transcendence within the interhuman diagrams the alternating presence and absence of the divine that pervades contemporary Jewish life.

Perhaps the best way to describe the scope and the limits of this inquiry is to place it within the context of Steven Kepnes's discussion of two types of postmodern hermeneutics in his chapter, "Postmodern Interpretations of Judaism" (Kepnes 1996). Following Paul Ricoeur's famous distinction between the hermeneutics of suspicion and retrieval,[8] Kepnes speaks of deconstructive and constructive hermeneutics. The former "attempts to uncover the conditions and processes that lie behind the ostensive meanings of human cultural expressions," and the latter, he finds, "seeks to disclose new possibilities of meaning within the fabric of cultural products themselves" (Kepnes 1996, 5). Kepnes expands upon his understanding of constructive hermeneutics, when he comments on a group of essays which he places under that rubric. He writes that the essays' authors offer

> . . . readings that augment and enlarge the horizon of meanings in their texts and attempt to introduce them as constructive contributors to debates in contemporary academic discourse. (Kepnes 1996, 6)

The label of constructive hermeneutics is equally appropriate to this present work, *Speaking/Writing of God*. It is a study of the nature and role of religious language in the thoughts of Franz Rosenzweig and Emmanuel Levinas. It offers a particular reading, interpretation, or hermeneutical discussion of that dimension in their work and then—reiterating Kepnes's words—"introduce[s]" the insights that emerge from that reading into two of the most compelling "debates in contemporary academic discourse." These "debates" concern the complex challenges that feminist Judaism and religious pluralism present to Jewish life and Jewish philosophy.

The fit of Kepnes's label is further supported by the particular subjects explored in this study. He identifies Rosenzweig as a pivotal figure for Jewish thinkers who pursue constructive ventures. Additionally, he holds that constructive efforts in Jewish thought must be "capable of mounting sustained ethical critique" (Kepnes 1996, 8), and, in this connection he mentions the inclusion of women and the welcoming of non-Jews.

It is also necessary that the limits of this constructive philosophical reading of—and from—the work of Rosenzweig and Levinas be made explicit. First, the present study is not a comprehensive examination of the philosophical oeuvres of Rosenzweig and Levinas. As already indicated, it focuses on the question of religious language, and seeks to highlight the meaning of their work for those concerned with access to the transcendent in our contemporary world. It is also attentive to the impact of ethical and philosophical issues raised by the encounters with feminist Judaism and with persons who are committed to other religious traditions on their works. There are many wider and more detailed discussions of the work of these two Jewish philosophers, including recent books by Paul Mendes-Flohr (1988), Stéphane Mosès (1992), Robert Gibbs (1992), Richard Cohen (1994), and Barbara Galli (1995).

Second, I am not offering a "Philosophy of Judaism," but an engaged inquiry with what I believe is the most dynamic stream of modern Jewish philosophy. The history and meaning of classic Jewish texts—such as the Bible and Talmud—and schools of thought—such as medieval Jewish philosophy and the *Kabbalah,* are not explored on their own nor in a detailed and definitive manner. References to these texts and schools appear only in terms of my interest in how they are understood by the modern philosophers who are the subjects of this study. In light of this, the suggestions offered here in terms of contemporary Jewish religious language need to be supplemented by studies of Jewish history and texts.

AN INVENTORY

The insights of Rosenzweig and Levinas are illuminated and compared in the first two chapters of this book. The first chapter—"Franz Rosenzweig and Emmanuel Levinas: A *Midrash* or Thought-Experiment"—begins with these thinkers' shared attack upon the Cartesian view of the self. This view, which accentuates the rational and autonomous features of life, has dominated modern Western philosophy. In opposition to this understanding, these two Jewish philosophers speak of that meeting with other persons and God that creates meaning, provides orientation, and overcomes both stagnation and death. Their power as philosophers emerges from their affirmation that the deepest things in life are gifts from others. Importantly, Rosenzweig and Levinas believe that this affirmation is both fundamental and distinctive to Judaism.

Chapter 2—"Rosenzweig and Levinas: On Anthropomorphism, the Holocaust, and God's Presence"—begins by seeking to account for the dramatic differences in how these two thinkers speak of God. One small essay from each of them is carefully examined in order to document and understand what lies behind the celebration and joy in Rosenzweig's use of anthropomorphisms, and the supreme austerity in what Levinas believes can be said about the relationship to God. From these two tight analyses surface the views that bring them together and that separate them. Rosenzweig and Levinas indicate the ways in which religious language naturally grows from, and is demanded by, a life dedicated in love and responsibility. However, there is a real tension between the trust in speech, experience, community, God, and ourselves that Rosenzweig believes is still nourished by the Bible and Levinas's intense waiting upon—what he terms—an "empty sky."

The insights of feminist Jews are central concerns of the third and fourth chapters. It has been more than fifteen years since the voices of feminist Jews first appeared in journal articles, edited collections, and a few full monographs. In my view, no Jewish philosopher writing in the decade of the nineties has any excuse to ignore this stream of modern Jewish thought. However, even a brief perusal of works published in the last five years on modern Jewish philosophy indicates that this view is not shared by many male thinkers.[9] Book after book on modern Jewish philosophy—both those that review the past and those that seek to contribute to the future—fail to engage with this reflection.[10]

Modern Jewish philosophers cannot ignore feminist Jewish philosophy by reason of those features that provide its own foundation—that is, obligation to the past, commitment to the present community, and encounter with modernity. Modern Jewish philosophers, who feel obligated to the Jewish past, must also understand that the past, as given to us, is flawed and partial. We do not yet know, as we have not heard from, women in that past. If we agree that this past makes demands upon us, it follows that we must also agree that we are obligated to seek out those voices which were unjustly silenced. The recovery of this unheard past has been one of the major tasks of feminist Jewish writing.

The authenticity of the commitment by modern Jewish philosophers to the Jewish community is also at stake here. Are male Jewish philosophers committed to the whole Jewish community, and to the enhancement of the lives of all Jews? If the answer is "Yes," and no other answer is ethically possible, then, again, we must pay attention to the variety of contemporary voices of Jewish women.

Finally, the honest engagement with feminist Jewish thought arises from the Jewish philosopher's encounter with modernity. One of the most pervasive characteristics of modernity has been the changing role and image of women. The modern history of Judaism—whether one looks at the developments within its different communities, its religious varieties, or Zionism—amply testifies to the impact of these changes. Women outside of Judaism have sought more authentic lives. Women within Judaism have done the same. A major feature of modernity's challenge to Judaism is the summons to ensure that Jewish women are permitted their own effective voices, both within the community and within the academic world.

More than obligations, however, require us to listen to womens' voices, as chapter 3, "To Notice the Color of Her Eyes: Facing the Feminist Jewish Critique," endeavors to attest. By following the argument that the French feminist philosopher Luce Irigaray pursues through the questions that she addresses to Levinas, some of the major challenges of feminist Judaism are illuminated. Feminist Jewish voices—I want to emphasize that feminist Jews voice a great variety of views—are compelling, promising a powerful reviving of Jewish thought in our era. They pose questions about the very foundations of Jewish religious life and culture. In terms of Jewish religious experience and language, they have critiqued and explored the relationships between God and nature, the body, love, and law.

An even more revolutionary path in Jewish thought has been their investigation of the meaning, powers, and limits of the concept of 'monotheism.' Their radical interrogation of monotheism is the result of the recognition that the understanding and place of women in Judaism cannot be changed without a transformation of the perception of the divine. They are asking, in particular, whether monotheism can be purified of the components of exclusion, domination-hierarchy, and dualism that many believe are currently overwhelming it. They fervently search for a transformed monotheism that can affirm the inclusion of the whole community's diverse experiences of the divine; humans' power to be cocreators; and the worth of all persons, as well as all aspects of creation.

The fourth chapter,—"Color II—A Dialogue"—brings together the critique and insights of feminist Jewish thinkers with the themes and lessons of Rosenzweig and Levinas. The metaphor of dialogue is introduced into this exploration, in order to provide a platform for a number of feminist Jewish philosophers to speak about their motivating ideas, concluding reflections, and visions about the future; and then to gauge or envision the responses that might be forthcoming from Rosenzweig and from Levinas. This procedure elucidates areas in which fundamental philosophical concerns coalesce, and it also identifies places where they clash. Through this dynamic of dialogue, I attempt to probe, contest, and even extend insights beyond their original formulations. The interchange has three foci, drawn from feminist Jewish analyses of Judaism:

1. The necessity of female pronouns and metaphors in speaking of God;
2. The ways that feminist insights expand religious experience and expression; and
3. The critique of monotheism.

Especially since the dawn of modern Jewish history, with the entry of Jews into the social, political, and intellectual life of the West, Jewish philosophers have explored the meaning of living in a religiously pluralist world. For most of that time, the relationship between Judaism and Christianity has been the dominant interest. Only now are Jewish philosophers struggling with the ramifications of a pluralism that goes beyond the contact with Christianity, and even Islam. This recent development has made it even more urgent for Jewish thought to explore the relation with persons of other traditions in terms of its impact upon Jewish openness and Jewish commitment.

Chapter 5—"Judaism and Religious Pluralism," and subtitled "Faith and Mystery"—presents a schematic of the positions and themes that punctuate the contemporary Jewish wrestling with the issue of religious pluralism. An understanding that has accrued from the earlier chapters in this study—namely, that our meetings with others will influence our religious language—stands as an additional justification for the discussion of the impact of religious pluralism in this investigation. It is driven by the question, which has also emerged from the preceeding considerations of "What do we owe to the other?"

Chapter 5 also surveys the types of recognition of members of other religious traditions that have been featured by Jewish philosophers, as well as provides its own recommendations. Throughout the discussion, there is an effort to respect the parameters that should inform this particular encounter. Entering into dialogue draws upon Jewish faith, and the conduct of dialogue must honor the mystery of the other's relationship to transcendence.

The conclusion—"What Paths Have Been Opened to Us?"—finds, in Irving Greenberg's depictions of Judaism as a "voluntary covenant" and contemporary life in terms of "holy secularity," a substantial and promising context to evaluate the significance of that transcendence/radiance which arises from the life with others. How does the concept of 'voluntary covenant' challenge our understanding of God's relation to the Jewish people? What role do the encounters with other persons, feminist Judaism, and members of other religious traditions have in a post-Holocaust Judaism that finds the rabbinate and synagogue to be, in Greenberg's words, "too 'sacred' "? Thus, this concluding discussion takes seriously Greenberg's contention, that Judaism is "entering another major phase of the unfolding of the covenant" (Greenberg 1982, 82), as it calls upon contemporary Jewish philosophers to assess anew the nature, powers, and limits of the community's speaking and writing of God.

CHAPTER 1

Franz Rosenzweig
and Emmanuel Levinas:
A Midrash or Thought-Experiment

There is much excitement at this time in the works of two modern Jewish philosophers, Franz Rosenzweig and Emmanuel Levinas. Many contemporary Jewish thinkers see their challenging but potent writings as important examples of the contribution that Jewish philosophy can make to Western thought, and as signposts to speak of the meaning of Jewish existence in the modern or postmodern world. In order to initially explore the insights that they present, I would like to offer some reflections in the form of a narrative that juxtaposes their writings. Obviously, such a juxtaposition gives a distinctive coloring to this inquiry, especially in light of the different ways in which Rosenzweig[1] and Levinas[2] have been read, and the multiple contexts into which their works can be placed.

I have termed my narrative reflections a *midrash* in order to further highlight the selective nature of this treatment. It is not an attempt to list all of the themes or views that Rosenzweig and Levinas share,[3] but to probe certain issues that strike me as relevant and rewarding in the context of contemporary discussions in a variety of disciplines about Jewish philosophy, modern philosophy, language, and the nature of the human.

The point of departure for this narrative—as well as its continual element of orientation—is the criticism by Rosenzweig and Levinas of the notion of the person which philosophers have termed "Cartesian." This notion has its foundation in René Descartes's "cogito," the famous dictum that, "I think, therefore I am." The Cartesian self is a human portrait that accentuates the rational and autonomous features of life. This is not just the notion of the thinking-I, but of the I for which self-consciousness—as well as self-realization through the individual's acts of free choice—are taken to be fundamental.

11

However, an understanding of the work of these Jewish philosophers cannot be divorced from some of their central life-experiences. In light of this, I want to begin with brief biographical portrayals.

Franz Rosenzweig

The major movements in Rosenzweig's life are dramatic and condensed within a few years.[4] Born in 1886 to an acculturated, middle-class Jewish family in Cassel, Germany, Rosenzweig's education was typical of those young Jews who saw it as natural for them to participate in the life of the nation. He studied medicine, history, philosophy and law in various German universities. This personal and academic trajectory was altered by two events in 1913.

The first was a discussion with a passionate Christian, Eugen Rosenstock-Huessy, that brought him to see the relevance of religion—or at least Christianity—for modern life. The second was a religious "conversion" at a synagogue on *Yom Kippur* (the Day of Atonement) in which he, for the first time, experienced the living power of Judaism.

From that time onward, Rosenzweig dedicated his remaining years to studying Judaism and writing about its relevance in the modern world. Importantly, he also concretely endeavored to provide a Jewish foundation for his contemporaries through establishing an adult educational institute—the *Freies Jüdisches Lehrhaus* in Frankfurt—and translating Judaism's past sources. Diagnosed with amyotrophic lateral sclerosis in 1922, he continued to write and to inspire others until his death in 1929.

Emmanuel Levinas

Born in Kovno, Lithuania, in 1906, Levinas received his early education in both Hebrew and Russian at home.[5] During World War I, the family moved to the Ukraine, and Levinas was admitted to a Russian gymnasium there in 1916. In 1920, the family left the Soviet Union and returned to Kovno, where Levinas's education continued in a Hebrew gymnasium. In 1923, he left to attend the University of Strasbourg in France, where he began to study philosophy. His work in that field included study with the famous thinkers Edmund Husserl and Martin Heidegger in Germany.

Levinas fought in the French army during World War II, but was caught by the Germans and taken to Germany as a Jewish prisoner of war. Although he was not held in one of the death camps, he has written in the autobiographical reflection, "Signature," that "the presentiment and the memory of the Nazi horror" (1990, 291) dominated his life history.[6]

After the war, he returned to France. He was an administrator and director of a school for the *Alliance Israélite Universelle*, while also holding a number of university positions. In 1973, he was appointed to the Sorbonne.

After more than six decades of active lecturing and writing about Judaism, philosophy, and the relationship between the two, he died in 1995.

THE CRITIQUE OF PHILOSOPHY

Rosenzweig and Levinas are highly critical of what they hold to be a single philosophic tradition emerging in ancient Greece and continuing through nineteenth-century German lands, or, in their terms, from "Iona to Jena" and beyond.[7] This tradition took the Cartesian self as its true content. They criticize it, not just in the vein that this philosophic endeavor misses something—that is, that it does not see what lies beyond or beneath the panorama of the philosophic vision. They contend that philosophy has ignored—or, better, has not heard—a cry that has its origin outside of the insular totality of the self's world. The nature of this cry, and its ramifications for giving orientation to a person, are central foci for Rosenzweig and Levinas. They speak of how encountering other persons saves the self from the dead end, or the violence, of self-enclosed totality.

For both Rosenzweig and Levinas, there is a natural, but, nevertheless, inauthentic concern or obsession of the self with itself.

Rosenzweig utilized the ancient Greek figure of the tragic hero to express this natural potentiality of human life (1972, 76–79), a potentiality which he believed had, in some sense, been overcome.[8] This tragic figure lives a life of isolation and self-containment which culminates in his or her self-destruction. The hero is driven, from within, by a distinctive character, and remains unrelated to anyone outside. This self trusts only in itself, and, consequently, remains essentially speechless. Rosenzweig characterized the hero's speech with others as frigid, but he has also noted that, for Greek drama, even this limited form of dialogue was less important than the solitary act of soliloquy. The sovereign event of this character's life—that is, the event that fully expresses the nature of the Greek hero and provides whatever meaning there is to that life—is the destined encounter with death.

As for Levinas, throughout his works, he demands that the self be torn from its natural obsession with itself. Prior to being forced to respond to the other, the individual takes himself or herself as the primary value, merely playing with, living on, and enjoying that with which he or she comes into contact. The consequences of this combination of self-absorption and manipulation are many. One of them is ennui. Levinas defined this as an "enchainment to itself, where the ego . . . ceaselessly seeks after the distraction of games and sleep" (1981, 124).

Both Rosenzweig and Levinas portray the individual as seeking to incorporate all that is different from the self, all alterity, into a single total system of thought and life that is coterminous with himself or herself. Levinas noted that a fundamental critique of this totality bound his work to Rosenzweig's when, in his first major book, *Totality and Infinity*, he wrote that "[w]e were impressed by the opposition to the idea of totality in Franz Rosenzweig's *Stern der Erlösung*, a work too often present in this book to be cited" (1988, 28).[9] For the two authors, not only is the self the originator of this idea, but the traditional philosophic endeavor constitutes its clearest expression.

In the Introduction to part 1 of his *The Star of Redemption*, Rosenzweig provides a critique of the idea of totality, which he depicts in terms of the cognition of the All (1972, 3–22). He holds that cognition of the All is the individual's response to the threat of death—that is, the threat that one's particular life will cease. The history of philosophy is animated by an answer to this fear. From Greek times to its modern culmination with Hegel, philosophy has sought a so-called "one thing" that forms the basis of everything else in the universe. Because philosophy is fundamentally idealistic, according to Rosenzweig, this one thing has been the thinking-I. Philosophy maintains that the thinking-I is the essential I—that is, the only real and permanent part of the person—and that this essence is identical with both God and the world. It concludes that death is an illusion, because what is ultimately real in the individual cannot die. The essential I continues to be part of the All of the universe, regardless of what happens to the body.

In "The New Thinking"—an essay which Rosenzweig allowed to appear at the beginning of a later edition of *The Star*—the interrelationship of self, philosophy, and totality reappears. However, it is not the threat of death that animates this depiction of philosophy's identification of self with *das All*. Rather, Rosenzweig speaks of philosophy's fundamental reductive method, which insists on collapsing the human experience of persons, the world, and God back into the self (1970, 190–192). He once again states that what emerges in the modern period under the label of "Idealism" is a perennial philosophic theme.[10]

The connections among self, philosophy, and totality are also very prominent in Levinas's work.[11] In broad outline, Levinas holds that philosophy, as ontology, expresses a fundamental feature of humans—namely, the urge toward totality. By this, he means that philosophy, through the exposition of that which exists or Being, incorporates all that is different from the self—that is, alterity, into a single universal system.

Levinas insists that, despite first impressions, the basic absorption of everything into the self, or the solitude of the self, is not broken even through the act of knowing (1989, 76–78). Through knowledge, a system of interrelationships binds all things together into an identity with the self. For Levinas, Western philosophy, from Parmenides to Hegel, can be properly characterized as monist. The totalizing spirit of this endeavor necessarily brought it to deny all that lay outside of the self—that is, all transcendence.

Levinas's work draws much of its energy and eloquence from an ethical protest against the political ramifications of, or correspondence with, the egocentricism of traditional philosophy. His opposition to the philosophy of being is his rejection of a system of thought that he believed supported and justified the chauvinism, arrogance, and violence of the West. He speaks of this philosophical underpinning as a "philosophy of power" (1988, 46). He sees it as issuing in a notion of the State, as well as real states, in which opposition and difference are systematically, but usually quietly, crushed. The "tyranny of the State" is just this "non-violence of the totality," this violent nonviolence (1988, 46).[12] Levinas has in mind the domination and murder committed by Europe against the "other," whether that so-called "other" consisted of "foreign" communities close by or "barbaric" peoples in distant lands.

The notion that traditional philosophy is at an end is shared by Rosenzweig and Levinas, as well as many other thinkers today. Rosenzweig contrasted the "old thinking" of traditional philosophy to the "new thinking" of the "speaking-thinker" (1970, 196–201). The former builds mathematical and logical systems out of reason, while the latter uses speech as his or her medium and gives prominence to both time and other persons. Rosenzweig designated the old thinking as "logical," while the latter he saw as "grammatical."

A central focus of an important essay that Levinas wrote on Rosenzweig is the idea that philosophy has reached a dead end (1990, 185–186). Their treatments of this theme mirror each other so closely that, in the first pages of the essay, it is extremely difficult to disentangle Levinas's views from his presentation of Rosenzweig's position. Levinas holds that the end of philosophy is the end of thinkers who stay within themselves—that is, who think as an isolated and isolating occupation. Rather, philosophers must turn to life, to the recognition that they are persons who live with other persons. While this is still a form of thinking—and not just individual, idiosyncratic rantings—it is a thinking built upon life. Only it can "escape the totalitarianism of philosophy" (1990, 186).

Thus, both philosophers share the view that a wider notion of reason must be the basis for a new type of philosophy. In addition, they see language as the new organon for this endeavor. Levinas writes that "if the face to face founds language . . . then language does not only serve reason, but is reason" (1988, 207). By this, he means that reason should not be understood as impersonal structures or laws. Reason or rationality is constituted by, or arises out of, the dynamics of human interaction.

The view that traditional philosophy has come to an end is vividly reflected in the variety of genre and philosophic styles utilized by these two men. Although philosophers have experimented with writing styles throughout the modern period—Kierkegaard and Nietzsche stand as notable examples—none, perhaps, went further than Rosenzweig. After his two-volume dissertation on the political philosophy of Hegel and *The Star*, Rosenzweig recognized that he could no longer write books. Even this *Star* is a strange piece. The central section was composed as letters (love letters?) to the wife of his friend, Eugen Rosenstock-Huessy.[13] Rosenzweig said that he needed to "see the 'other' " in order to write (1970, 91). Most of his later work consists of long letters and some essays. His small book, *Understanding the Sick and the Healthy*, is in the form of letters from a doctor describing the treatment of a patient struck down by a special case of paralysis, *apoplexia philosophica.* The writing, to which Rosenzweig dedicated much of his time during his last years, was a translation and notes on the poems of the medieval Jewish poet and philosopher, Jehuda Halevi. The notes to poetry were seen by him as the "practical application" of the new philosophic method of speech/thinking (1970, 201). In his commentary on these powerful religious poems, Rosenzweig addresses both the poet and his own readers.[14]

Levinas has often reflected upon his own startling style of writing. It follows upon his understanding of the betrayal, by both philosophy and most writing, of the responsibility for other persons. While many of his books and essays utilize some of the structures and terms of phenomenology, there are frequent twists or interruptions.[15] Levinas speaks of ethical language as the interruption of phenomenology (1981, 193).[16] The repetition that hammers, but never flattens, is well illustrated by the following sentence.

> The most passive, unassumable, passivity, the subjectivity or the very subjection of the subject, is due to my being obsessed with responsibility for the oppressed who is other than myself. (1981, 55)

Some of his phenomenological descriptions of the caress are fully poetic in their power and sensuality. Equally important are those philosophic excursions by way of interpretation of Talmudic texts.

MEETING THE OTHER

It is only through the encounter with the other that meaning is created, and stagnation and death are overcome. Not only is life hollow without other persons, but the "new" would be an impossible category if there were only that which the self can give birth to from within itself. Rosenzweig affirms this insight in a number of different contexts. He holds that the isolated self—that self of the tragic hero—becomes an eloquent, speech-filled soul only through the transforming love by God and the neighbor.[17] As *The Star* puts it,

> Only the soul beloved of God can receive the commandment to love its neighbor and fulfill it. Ere man can turn himself over to God's will, God must first have turned to man. (1972, 215)

> . . . where someone or something has become neighbor to a soul, there a piece of world has become something which it was not previously: soul. (1972, 235)

Rosenzweig believes that a person becomes fully human through the transforming powers—that is, the divine powers, inherent in language. For example, it is upon hearing one's name and responding that the self becomes visible, even to itself (1972, 174–175).

Levinas is equally expressive about the way in which relationship brings health to the isolated self. He tries to construct an understanding of the individual human that is not just a duplication of the Cartesian story of the ego. It is not self-consciousness that brings authenticity, according to Levinas, but, rather, it is "my inescapable and incontrovertible answerability to the other that makes me an individual 'I' " (1986, 27). He refers to discourse as a "traumatism of astonishment," that ruptures the self and introduces the new (1988, 73).

Levinas agrees with Rosenzweig that the deepest things in life—those which found the possibility for our existence—are gifts from others. The confidence that one has in truth, as well as the sense of the meaningfulness of one's own life, derive from meeting others and being responsible for others. Similarly, according to Levinas, the uniqueness of the self is confirmed by the realization that there are responsibilities that only I can fulfill (1985, 101; 1986, 27).

However, there are noteworthy variations in the two thinkers' treatments of the need to step beyond the self, or have the self transformed. In most places, the setting aside of the self or ego is not the focal point of Rosenzweig's interest. Rather, the interhuman phenomena of speech and love hold his attention, and the transcending of the ego which results from these events is of secondary interest. The self is forgotten through participating in the life of speaking to others and loving others.[18]

With Levinas, the issue of the overcoming of the self is fully emergent. He sees an intense conflict between the individual's natural love of the self and the demands of ethics. For example, he has written that "No one is good voluntarily" (1981, 11); and that, for ethical thought, "*the self* as this primacy of what is mine, is *hateful*" (1986, 26). Levinas believes, perhaps, that the ramifications of self-absorption/projection are more dire than does Rosenzweig. Reflecting this concern, he utilizes more forceful language, as it were, to describe this process. For him, the overturning of the ego requires an acute rupture or tearing open of the self. As he puts it, it is as if the alterity of the other "devastates its site [the self] like a devouring fire, catastrophying its site" (1989, 176).[19]

There is a philosophic step or presupposition that precedes the reconstitution of the self through the encounter with the other. This is the recognition that, to be a self is to be separate—namely, separate from all totalities. The view that the recognition of a distinct self, including a sense of boundaries and a limited autonomy, as a foundation for the later development of the self through relationship, is something that Rosenzweig and Levinas share with some current clinical psychological theorists.[20]

Part 1 of *The Star* has the principal purpose of combatting the monism of Idealism by insisting on the separateness and autonomy of the philosophic elements of "God, man, and world."[21] Rosenzweig writes that "the premise of separate existence" is necessary in order for us to see how these separate elements are spanned (1970, 198). For him, our life is made up of experiences of such spanning.

The necessity for an understanding of the person that respects the integrity of both the human and particular humans is argued in an additional way in *The Star*. Early on in his discussion, Rosenzweig proposes a "metaethical" theory of "man" (1972, 62–82).[22] This position treats the human on its own terms, liberating a philosophic anthropology from the domination of any rational or ethical system.

The importance of separation for Levinas's argument is well illustrated by three early section headings in *Totality and Infinity*: "Separation and Discourse," "Separation and the Absolute," and "Separation as Life." In these sections, Levinas gives special attention to features of the individual's life that rest upon the premise of separation—namely, the experience of time, the idea of Infinity, and the solitude of enjoyment. He also utilizes the term *atheism* to refer to the self's autonomy (1988, 53). By this, he means an understanding of the human individual as someone who stands outside of the divine totality or any other systematic whole.

To be human is to be there for another—to say, as Abraham said, "Here I am." It is important to emphasize that, for Rosenzweig and Levinas, the transformative encounter in human life is not with nature, but with persons. Even the so-called "dialogue" with sacred texts is modeled upon the exchange between persons.[23] They also share an understanding that the fullest expositions of the interhuman realm require[24] the use of religious midrash, that is, the utilization of religious language or terms such as *God, commandment, neighbor,* and *soul.*[25] These terms permeate Rosenzweig's *The Star* as well as Levinas's *Totality and Infinity* and *Otherwise Than Being.*

Thus, both Rosenzweig and Levinas describe the overcoming of the individual's innate isolation and self-obsession through the life with others. Further, what makes life with other persons possible is the divine action prior to or behind, as it were, these relations. For Rosenzweig, God's revelation is experienced in the divine/human powers of speech and love (1972, 156–204). For Levinas, God's concern for the other that gives substance and form to all human interaction is felt immediately in the turning of one person to another (1985, 109; 1986, 24–25).

Thus, more pointedly, for both, there are no authentic ethics that arise naturally from the individual's reason, for this is suspect. Every legitimate ethic, the realm of relations between humans, reveals at least a trace of God's revelation. This is, for Rosenzweig, God's revelation that is already immanent within our speech and acts of love (Rosenzweig 1972, 201). With Levinas, the commandment not to kill is God's shattering message that bursts through the face-to-face encounter (1985, 89).

Rosenzweig and Levinas hold that language or speech is the key for understanding the interhuman realm. With Rosenzweig, there is an excitement and an amazement about the powers of language as living speech or *parole*, and not as mere structure, that carries through all of his work.[26] He believed that language was as natural and as necessary to human life as oxygen was to living things. He did not regard language as some ill-shaped foreign implement, but the medium into which individuals are born and through which they live and grow. Without language there is no human life.

For Rosenzweig, the study of language was the study of all the social processes that surround speech. The speech act thus uncovered, and also developed, the basic trust that persons have for one another, as well as the ways in which individuals draw out or create each other.[27] He spoke of the transcending of self-concern through the call of another and of the maturation that appears when responsibility is given and accepted.

Of all of the activities of speech, Rosenzweig was most fascinated by the function of names—that is, proper names (1972, 186–188; 1995, 216–218). He considered allowing the statement already in *The Star* that "For name is in truth word and fire, and not sound and fury" (1972, 188) to stand as the motto for the whole book.[28] The calling of a person's name by another was, according to him, a paradigm of transformation. Through such a call, the two persons are tied together and plunged into the world. In the call, the caller wills to put herself or himself into relation through question or through request. The life of the one called is also obviously transformed, because some type of response cannot be avoided.

Rosenzweig's love of language brought him to see its liberating powers. Freedom was not lost, in his view, by a request or imperative. Rather, it was created.[29] For him, new possibilities arise as a consequence of being called, and the free life is the one in which such interactions or opportunities continually arise. He had no ear for a discussion of freedom that limited the individual's life to the expression of the isolated self's own determinations and choices.

Although I will discuss the use of religious categories further on in this book, the theme of the divine character of language naturally arises here. Rosenzweig saw language as nothing less than a divine gift. Its potency or creativeness is an extension of God's first act. For Rosenzweig, God is revealed in words, and redeems humans through the process of our address and response. In this sense, all language is revelation. He found that the biblical love poem, *The Song of Songs,* provided the validation for his insight into the divine nature of speech (1972, 199–204). *The Song of Songs* is the story of the exchange of "I" and "Thou" between God and humans, just because it is fully a sensual love poem. Rosenzweig believed that, in such language, the dichotomy between transcendence and immanence evaporates. He could not separate the words of love between persons, from lover to beloved, or friend to friend, or neighbor to neighbor, from the words of love that are addressed by God (1972, 199).

Rosenzweig had a deep trust in language (1972, 151). He was more interested in all the ways in which language works, than in the few times when it seems either to fail or to distort.[30] While it is misleading to think that Rosenzweig did not recognize that language can be manipulated or distorted, I find that his primary concern was to testify to its powers.[31]

There are some strong parallels between Levinas's reflections on language and what we have just discussed. This is especially evident in the sense that, for both philosophers, the social processes that surround speech are more important than are the analyses of linguistic structures. More significantly, they agree in giving priority to speech over writing, and to criticizing those who see language as deriving from thought rather than the other way around. However, there are some marked differences between the view-points of the two philosophers.

First, the theme of the distortion of language is prominent in Levinas's writings, particularly in the work, *Otherwise Than Being or Beyond Essence.* Second, with Levinas, the treatment of language is often located within a wider discussion of "the face."

For Levinas, language pierces the individual's armor of self-concern. It uproots this natural attitude and brings the person to experience responsibility for, and to come to the aid of, the other. Language is creative. Not only does it awaken responsibility, it creates the power to respond (1988, 178). Levinas describes some of the features of human interaction that language awakens as the power of welcome, of gift, full hands, and hospitality (1988, 205).

In that fundamental encounter with the other that is language, the new appears. We learn something from our meetings with other people. We are given insights, orientations, and ideas that we did not possess before. "Teaching" is the term which Levinas uses to denote the fact that something new emerges from human interaction (1988, 180). He is quite insistent that we recognize that teaching is more than maieutics—namely, the technique of helping the student to recall the truth that is latent within himself or herself (1988, 51,180). Without the notion of teaching—which is based on receiving something from the outside—we would be assigned the terrible destiny of living from our own resources alone. There would be nothing in our lives but that which we found within.

The issue of the corruption of language is most clearly introduced through Levinas's distinction between "the saying" and "the said." As far as I have understood it, this is a distinction between the ideal possibilities of encounter or language on the one hand, and the reality of the ways in which these possibilities are often limited or subverted (1981, 45–51; 1989, 183). Again, "the saying" is not literally limited to spoken language (1981, 48). It also includes the whole situation of being in relationship, of approach, of giving, and other aspects, that precede or, alternatively, are the foundations for the possibility of speech occurring between persons. "The said" is the limiting of real speech by linguistic structures that inevitably reflect the self's attempt to erase everything that cannot be one with itself. Through the category of "the said," Levinas is suggesting that the actual encounter between persons must be understood in the context of the particular social and political structures of the time. These structures or systems are, to some extent, expressions of the powerful urge toward totality or the domination over what is not "the same."[32]

Readers of Levinas's works recognize that, compared to the eloquence and dramatic effect of his discussion of the impact of the face, every interpretation or commentary appears hollow. The face stands for the whole human body (1985, 97). It is just that Levinas has discovered that the poverty, and vulnerability, as well as the wealth of the human, is contained in the face. In particular, he speaks of the face of the poor and the stranger that overcomes every defense that the self might erect (1988, 213). Confronted by the face of another, silence is impossible, for one cannot be otherwise than responsive and responsible (1985, 88).

All that is found in the encounter with another that, at times, is discussed in the context of language, is depicted at other times by Levinas in terms of standing before another person's face. As he writes, "meaning is the face of the Other, and all recourse to words takes place already within the primordial face-to-face of language" (1988, 206).[33]

The theme of the face is not as prominent in Rosenzweig's work, but it is also not totally absent.[34] The human face appears at the climax of *The*

Star (1972, 422–424). He sees it as mirroring our understanding of the interaction of God, man, and world that gives orientation to everyday life. While
the face of which he speaks is human, he believes that it provides a reminder
of God. Thus, for Rosenzweig, in living with other persons, the individual is
continually made aware that she or he also lives before the divine countenance.

More importantly, it seems to me that Rosenzweig shares with Levinas
a positive attitude toward the body. For both of them, erotic love is a valuable
topic for the philosophical understanding of the human. This is illustrated, in
the case of Rosenzweig, by the prominent places given in *The Star* to *The
Song of Songs* (1972, 199–204) and to a discussion of the kiss (1972, 423).
In addition to the theme of the face, the poetic/philosophic description of the
sensuous discovery of the other through caress is another testimony to Levinas's
view of the philosophic importance of the body (1981, 89–94).

The use of religious categories and terms is an essential feature of the
description of the encounter between persons, especially in reflections upon
language for Rosenzweig, and the face for Levinas. They share the view that
the interhuman realm reveals a trace of the divine. They do not believe that
human relationships exist for the sake of the divine, or that religious story
diminishes the importance of the human in any way. Yet, their work powerfully implies that an understanding of the relationship between persons requires religious story.

The divine nature of speech is one theme that illustrates Rosenzweig's
use of religious story. In his view, speech is human—fully human—because
it continually and effortlessly, as it were, brings out the highest in human
lives (1972, 202). Yet, precisely for this reason, it is divine. The fullness of
the human comes only through a power that stands beyond all humans and
draws them upward. The interhuman—Martin Buber's "the between"—is the
miraculous place where traces of the divine can best be sensed.[35]

In other words, Rosenzweig believed that the word is recognized as
both human and divine, when we acquire an appreciation for how persons are
brought to life through speech. God's relationship to speech might be seen in
two forms: first, as the origin or source of the trust that enables persons to
throw themselves into speech; and second, as the power that transforms persons once they begin speaking. For example, Rosenzweig saw the acceptance
of words from a speaker—including our belief that the other is sincere—as
being based upon a trust in speech. No explanation can account for this trust,
but Rosenzweig found that a religious story about God's creation of language
points to the elemental nature of this trust, and to its source in terms of a
"person" prior to all human persons. Rosenzweig wrote

And language is easily trusted, for it is within us and about us; as it
reaches us from "without," it is no different from language as it echoes

the "without" from our "within." The word as heard and as spoken is one and the same. The ways of God are different from the ways of man, but the word of God and the word of man are the same. What man hears in his heart as his own human speech is the very word which comes out of God's mouth. (1972, 151)

Second, Rosenzweig saw the need to use a religious midrash when speaking of the dramatic ways that other persons empower an individual to change, and the incredible ways that speech allows someone to reach beyond herself or himself—that is, to transcend the self. He spoke of the act of being touched by God's love, often through the speech of one's neighbor, as the transformation of the individual from a defiant and fearful self into an eloquent soul.

As noted earlier, for Levinas, the act of looking into a human face embodies the whole encounter between persons (1985, 85–92).[36] Looking into the face of the person that is next to one exposes the vulnerability of the other, along with the direct, if unspoken, command not to kill the other.[37] Face-to-face with the other is the stance that first engenders responsibility. Yet, this face-to-face requires religious story in order to be fully described. The vulnerability of the other is both heightened and made more concrete by discussing it in the light of standing before the poor, the orphan, and the stranger of whom the Bible speaks. The recognition that one must not kill the other who stands nearby is more than the result of some vague feeling not to harm. It is the acknowledgement of the commandment of "Thou shalt not kill!"

While Rosenzweig and Levinas recognize the necessity of utilizing religious story or midrash to illuminate the relationship between persons, they are careful that God does not, thereby, become a philosophical theme. For them, God is not a term in an argument. Story or midrash is suggestive. It does not prove anything, but points to the wondrous elements that lie within the interhuman realm. In other words, the term *God* is not part of some system of the self. The word is used because it allows the responsibility that the individual has for another to be expressed or pronounced in the most forceful way. This responsibility just cannot be communicated outside of the context of such terms as *commandment, neighbor, stranger,* or even *creation.* Levinas wrote in the essay, "God and Philosophy," that

The religious discourse that precedes all religious discourse is not dialogue. It is the "here I am" said to a neighbour to whom I am given over, by which I announce peace, that is, my responsibility for the other. "Creating . . . the fruit of the lips. Peace, peace to the far and to the near, says the Lord." (1989, 184)[38]

TWO JEWISH PHILOSOPHERS

There are other dimensions of the works of Rosenzweig and Levinas that might prove to be valuable to explore, and many of the topics discussed here require more analysis. However, as a conclusion, let us reexamine a few elements that have already emerged, and suggest that these might be distinctive to modern Jewish philosophy.[39]

Rosenzweig and Levinas were trained in philosophy, and their works take their point of departure from such pivotal thinkers as Hegel for Rosenzweig, and Husserl and Heidegger for Levinas.[40] However, they stand apart from the major philosophical streams. Both of them offer an ethical critique of earlier—and contemporary—philosophy by insisting on the centrality of the relationship to other persons. As we have seen, this ethical critique incorporates religious story into its philosophical discussion.

At least in terms of their notions of the self, Rosenzweig and Levinas do not represent a purely modern nor postmodern position. They do not speak of the alienated modern self that must battle the outside world, while discovering some hidden meaning within. Yet, they also do not give prominence to the postmodern notion that the self's basic problem is that it is without a center or that it is fragmented and discontinuous. Many postmoderns prominently feature a self trying to recapture or reincorporate the missing, the erroneous, what is unthought, or "the bastard."[41] However, Rosenzweig and Levinas maintain that the healing of the self does not occur through some type of individual contortions. Rather, it comes from the outside. The new— namely, "teaching," is the gift that only another can bestow upon the self. There is no truth more fundamental nor instructive than that children are born out of two.[42]

Unlike much of modern philosophy, Rosenzweig and Levinas do not offer the encounter with one's own death as a criterion of authenticity. The confrontation with death is still just the act of a single person, and an act of solitude. In the work of some thinkers, especially Heidegger, the encounter with death seems to bring the self to denounce an essential relationship to another.[43]

However, Levinas's treatment of death heightens one's responsibility for others. It is this concern for other persons rather than the turning of the self upon itself that is exemplified in the treatment of death in the following lines:

> Always future and unknown it [death] gives rise to fear or flight from responsibilities. Courage exists in spite of it. It has its ideal elsewhere; it commits me to life. Death, source of all myths, is *present* only in the Other, and only in him does it summon me urgently to my final essence, to my responsibility. (1989, 179)

While Rosenzweig does begin *The Star* with a discussion of the individual's fear of death, the facing of death is important for him primarily because it shatters philosophy's pretension to have included or subdued everything in its system.[44] He does not believe that authenticity arises out of the confrontation with death. For Rosenzweig, facing the future death of the self makes one death/like or mute. It is only within the meeting with the other that speech and life well up.

Often in surprising ways, both philosophers' discussions turn toward the theme that the encounter with the other overcomes death. While neither Rosenzweig nor Levinas believes that a person can escape his or her concrete death, they hold that, through the life of speech/love and responsibility,[45] death is not permitted to wipe away all meaning. Rosenzweig begins the core of *The Star*—Book 2: Revelation—with a quotation from *The Song of Songs.* "Love is strong as death" (1972, 156). Later, he adds

> Death, the conqueror of all, and the netherworld that zealously imprisons all the deceased, collapse before the strength of love and the hardness of its zeal. . . . The living soul, loved by God, triumphs over all that is mortal, and that is all that can be objectively stated about it. (1972, 202)

Levinas has written in *Otherwise Than Being* that

> In it [the approach to the other] life is no longer measured by being, and death can no longer introduce the absurd into it. . . . No one is so hypocritical as to claim that he has taken from death its sting. . . . But we can have responsibilities and attachments through which death takes on a meaning. (1981, 129)

Thus, despite the truth that the individual will some day die, the relationship between persons and with God builds up things that death cannot overcome.

In their work, there is a fascination with language. They trust in speech, seeing it as having a source, origin, or foundation that is beyond humans. They are also very positive about the body. Just as language is not some kind of clumsy instrument, they do not have an instrumental view of the body. The body is more than an apparatus of the mind. The body—especially the human face or countenance—is the window to the soul or the whole being of a person.

I think that there is a link between these attitudes toward language, body, and other persons. Rosenzweig and Levinas are critical of views that insist that language is a derivative of—or an almost unnecessary dimension of—thinking. They are equally opposed to the position that the body is a

crude and almost expendable extension of mind. What they are excited by is
the concrete world of the everyday. This is the world of interaction—that is,
of persons who are encountered precisely through the specificity of their
speech and bodies.

In this world, other people are very important because they liberate the
individual from the cage of the self. If this is the case, then the concrete other
is not important because she or he is similar to me, or capable of being
assimilated into a rational, abstract, and universal system of the same.
Rosenzweig and Levinas maintain a pluralism that is not just tolerant of the
other, but requires the other as different.[46]

I would like to suggest that the positions of Rosenzweig and Levinas
which have just been outlined in terms of death, human interaction, speech,
responsibility, the body, and pluralism, are positions common to many modern Jewish philosophers. Some of these views can be found in works by
Martin Buber, Abraham Heschel, Emil Fackenheim, and others. For example,
Fackenheim once linked the pivotal role of the theme of death in modern
philosophy to the influence of Christianity. He contended that, on the other
hand, the portrait of humans that views the interaction between persons as an
essential feature of existence was a position more in harmony with basic
features of Judaism (1973, 215–216).

Finally, despite these pronounced areas of similarity between Rosenzweig
and Levinas, it is precisely with reference to religious story that a major
difference appears. For both of them, it is vital that God be understood as
person. Only the language of person provides them with the resources, for
example, to speak of God's concern for the neighbor and the stranger. Yet,
with Rosenzweig, there is a celebration of, and joy in, biblical anthropomorphisms. These offer him the means to compose story after story about all of
the ways in which God lives with people. In one of the last articles that he
composed—on biblical anthropomorphism—he wrote that, behind the biblical stories about the encounters between humans and God, there lies the
double assumption of the Bible as a whole.

> . . . namely that God is capable of what he wills (thus even of meeting
> the creature from time to time in fully bodily and spiritual reality) and
> that the creature is capable of what he should be (thus even of fully
> understanding and recognizing God's self-embodying or self-spiritual-
> ization turning toward him from time to time). (1937, 532)[47]

By contrast, with Levinas there is a supreme austerity in terms of what
can be said directly about the human relationship to God. Beneath his linguistic hesitancy or carefulness is the fear of appropriating God into a system of

the same, of affirming a *"Gott mit uns"* (God with us). However, this austerity exhibits its own type of grandeur. Levinas has written

> It is not by superlatives that we can think of God, but by trying to
> identify the particular interhuman events that open towards transcen-
> dence and reveal the traces where God has passed. (1986, 32)

I am intrigued by the reasons that lie behind this difference, as well as
by the powers and limits of each of these paths. Chapter 2 will discuss these
matters.

Is it legitimate to suggest that the opposition to the notion of the self
that is tied to the Cartesian "cogito" brings together writings of Rosenzweig
and Levinas? Despite the differences between them, it is through a midrash
that focuses on this opposition that two central features of their work have
been illuminated—the critique of philosophy, and the transformation of the
self that arises from the encounter with the other.

CHAPTER 2

Rosenzweig and Levinas:
On Anthropomorphism, the Holocaust,
and God's Presence

Is it possible for Jews who experience all of the questions, challenges, and suspicions that characterize modern life to use the word *God* in their speech and writing? Even if this word can somehow be spoken, what meaning does it have for the speaker, or for those addressed? While these questions are neither new nor unique to the modern Jew, Jews do have special resources in seeking answers. The writings of Franz Rosenzweig and Emmanuel Levinas resound as such resources.

There is a profound combination of sophisticated philosophical understanding with a powerful, immediate commitment to Jewish religious experience in the works of Rosenzweig and Levinas. One area that best reflects this combination is their use of religious language. Language about the relationship or encounter with God has a place in all of their work, extending beyond their specifically religious writings.[1] However, despite some fundamental areas of agreement in their understanding of this relationship between God and humans, there are dramatic differences in the way in which they speak of God. With Rosenzweig, there is a celebration of and joy in the use of anthropomorphisms. With Levinas there is a majestic restraint in terms of what can be said about the relationship to God.[2] This inquiry will attempt to grapple with these areas of agreement and disagreement, with the aim of identifying the insights which they present today.

In light of a number of concerns, even this second examination of Rosenzweig and Levinas ought to be understood as offering only preliminary remarks. The literary corpus of each is large and diverse. As we saw, the diversity, and the experimenting with genre are essential characteristics of their work. Additionally, the power and precision of their thought—as well as the play with expression—can be lost when specific texts and statements are not given sufficient attention in the interests of some systematic goal. Further, the richness of their insights can be touched upon only by an individual critic at any particular time. Thus, any offering or reflection is at most a partial *midrash*.

In the case of each thinker, I will focus initially on one relatively short text. Pieces that I have selected reflect what I believe are diagnostic of recurring themes, while still having special perspectives to offer in themselves. Thus, my presentation will attempt to carefully explore the argument and language of specific texts, while also commenting upon the significance or place of each of these writings within the overall oeuvres.

In 1928, a small note or essay—taking up less than eight pages in a later collection—was published by Rosenzweig that comments on an article on anthropomorphism that had recently appeared in the *Encyclopedia Judaica*.[3] Rosenzweig's piece, which I will refer to as "On Anthropomorphism," is recognized by scholars of his work as an unparalleled gem. However, it is not well-known, and a partial translation into English and commentary by Barbara Galli appeared only as recently as 1993.[4] Levinas's essay, "Loving Torah More Than God," is also a very compact statement. It was delivered as an address in 1955 and first translated into English in 1979.[5] While the essay might not be the most detailed expression of Levinas's attitude toward religious language, from the provocative title to its last words, it beautifully conveys that paradoxical mixture of austerity and passion that characterizes much of his writing about persons and God.

THE BOUNDLESS TRUST

Rosenzweig's review of the *Encyclopedia Judaica* article was one of the last pieces that he composed. Together with his on-going translation of and notes on the poems of Jehuda Halevi, it demonstrates the maturity, fullness, and strength of his language. Years of being silent as a result of paralysis, seem to have given him the power to turn the written word into living speech.

Rosenzweig begins his essay "On Anthropomorphism" by quoting a paragraph from the article that expresses the ambivalence—that mixture of embarrassment and confidence—of modern Jews who acknowledge biblical stories as part of their heritage, but believe their sophisticated age has gone further.[6] He quotes

A distinction is to be made between formal anthropomorphism, which adheres to the absolute spirituality of God and uses anthropomorphic modes of expression only to demonstrate God's being and works, and the material anthropomorphism of, for instance, the ancient Greeks and other pagan peoples. The former, which is not anthropomorphism proper, has its roots not merely in the inadequacy of human language . . . but also in the limitation of human thought. (1937, 526–527)

On the one hand, biblical anthropomorphisms were distinguished from "pagan" efforts to speak of the gods. However, on the other hand, they were regarded as stylistic anachronisms. The language of anthropomorphisms in the Bible was dissipated by means of two explanations—human limitations in experiencing and expressing the spiritual and transcendent, and the misdirected tendency to project upon God the highest human attributes.

Rosenzweig quickly disposes with the issue of the purported defectiveness of experience, language, and thought by asking exactly what other experience, language, and thought are being referred to here in order to arrive at a judgment about the weaknesses of our human ones. The second issue—the psychological reduction through an allusion to projection of the experience of God—required a more elaborate response from Rosenzweig. There are few contentions more important for Rosenzweig than that experiences of God are real. It represents the foundation for his understanding of the nature of Judaism, its role in the modern world, as well as his whole philosophical anthropology. The main work of his essay is to argue for the reality of religious experience, and to describe the way in which anthropomorphisms in the Bible shape our understanding of this realm.

Rosenzweig claims that arguments can be brought forward to question any realm of experience, not just those that are theological. In his words:

> But there is no argument against the possibility of theological experience that could not be validated with the same authority also against the possibility of biological or psychological (or any other) experience as well. (1937, 527)

The matter can be decided only by examining the nature of those experiences under question. The shift from language—that is, the nature of anthropomorphic expressions—to the experiences that ground the language is first nature for Rosenzweig, who continually spoke of the need for a philosophy based on experience—*erfahrende Philosophie* (1970, 192)—and of his own work as absolute empiricism (1970, 207).

The exploration of the nature of biblical anthropomorphisms in terms of the human experiences that ground them stands in diametrical opposition to all the reductionist exercises, whether ethical, psychological, sociological, or those of demythologizing the text that have been standard fare throughout the nineteenth and twentieth centuries. Rosenzweig respects the authenticity and power of this biblical feature. He understands that they cannot be replaced, nor—explained away, which amounts to the same thing. There is also no standpoint beyond them, for they arise from and reflect immediate, genuine experiences.

The nature of theological experience is described in the following lines:

> Theological experiences, as long as they are genuine experiences and not phantoms, have just this in common: they are experiences of meetings, not experiences of an objective kind like experiences of the world, not a mixture of both, like experiences between human beings. Therefore, to remain here within the precinct of experience one does not want to assert something either about God or about man, but only about an event between the two. And the Bible offers the best guide precisely to this. (1937, 528)

The first part of this quotation insists that theological experiences be understood as "meetings." Experiences of God are not reducible to the intrahuman or interhuman realm. For Rosenzweig, all legitimate theological experiences are real meetings between separate persons—God and humans.

Rosenzweig elucidates what theological experiences have in common with other experiences, and also what is distinctive to them. He speaks of three classes of experience. There are experiences of the world that he sees as "objective" and there are experiences between humans that he labels as a mixture of both the "objective" with something else. However, he does not specify the nature of that "something else." Meetings between humans and God share this "something else" with those experiences that are purely interhuman. However, unlike the latter events, theological experiences have no objective element.

The point of departure for discussing the nature of theological experiences is Rosenzweig's proposal that there are three categories of human experience. He states that humans have experiences of things, experiences of other persons, and experiences of God.

In differentiating these three types, Rosenzweig is, first of all, proposing that there is not just one model of experience. Unlike positivists, Rosenzweig argues that one cannot understand every experience in terms of bumping into or utilizing things. Meetings between persons are not like this first class of experiences, they have a feature that is not objective. By noting that there is a feature of the experience of other persons that is not objective, Rosenzweig opens the way for depicting theological experiences as nonobjective, but not as being totally sui generis. While this method of discussing theological experience will not convince someone that theological experiences are authentic, it is effective in reminding the reader that not only purported meetings with the divine have aspects that are not objective.

Rosenzweig does not explain in the essay what is meant by the objective (*gegenstandlich*) feature in experiences of the world and in encounters between persons. In another writing, he examines what can be communicated about religious experience (cited in Glatzer, ed. 1970, 242–247). He again introduces an analogy from interhuman experience—in this case, "the daily and hourly reality of marriage," and uses the adjective objective (1970, 243). In this instance, objective seems to refer to what can be communicated to a third person (1970, 243), who is not part of the original human exchange, and also what might be confirmed by such a third person.

Extrapolating from the other writing, the differences in the three types of experiences might be put in this way. In terms of both experiences of things and experiences of other humans, there is an objective element. There is something "objective" that can be passed on—such as pictures, sound recordings, and the like—to a person who is not an original participant. In other words, a third-party is able to confirm aspects of the event.

This objective element dominates experiences of things, but there are dimensions of encounters between humans that cannot be objectively passed on to nor confirmed by a third party. One might say that the meaning and impact of the encounter for the human parties cannot be fully captured even with pictures and recordings. Further, while theological experiences share with interhuman experiences the feature of being real meetings, they differ from the latter in that there is nothing that can be objectively passed on to nor confirmed by a third person. The reality, meaning, and impact of the divine/human encounter cannot be objectively expressed nor confirmed.

There are other considerations about the nature of theological experiences that are appropriate to note here. The comparison of interhuman and theological experiences is extremely significant. Even if a third person cannot verify the latter experiences, the fact that they are similar to interhuman encounters means that the third person can have a range of experiences to draw upon to gain some insight into the former. It means that, in describing theological experiences, our understanding of interhuman meetings provides helpful and meaningful resources. Finally, it means that, for Rosenzweig, the metaphor of God as person is not replaceable by something else. It is precisely that relationship with other persons and not with things in the world, that shares features with the encounter with the divine.

Rosenzweig's long quotation cited earlier in this chapter began with the statement that theological experiences, "as long as they are genuine experiences and not phantoms," have something in common. Thus, Rosenzweig is suggesting that a distinction can be made between genuine theological experiences and phantom experiences. The term *phantom* might point in the direction of a mere imagining of a meeting. However, as we will see later, he employs the word again to refer to a case in which particular language about God is used, but no specific experience lies behind it.

Finally, Rosenzweig affirms the value—indeed, the necessity—of critical examination of these meetings. Earlier in the text, when discussing theological along with biological and psychological experience, he adds that, "the necessity for critical examination and consideration of collected experiences is, for theology, no different than it is for every other science" (1937, 528). Thus, although they are not objective, religious experiences can be examined and compared, and statements can be made about how they follow, or fail to follow, certain norms. In this sense, theological experience can constitute a realm of "scientific inquiry." Perhaps, the discussion to follow on the meaning of anthropomorphisms in the Bible exemplifies the lines of such an investigation.

Rosenzweig will next turn to a discussion of the meaning of the anthropomorphisms that are found in the Bible. He insists that biblical anthropomorphisms are not descriptions of God but "assertions about meetings between God and man" (1937, 528). Nothing is ascribed to God, nor are divine attributes characterized. The Bible consists, not of lists of God's features, but expressions of the ways in which the encounter with God is experienced. The human environment, or the experiential frame—that is, the context, event itself, and the impact that it has on the human partners—are boldly portrayed through the anthropomorphisms. In discussing an example from one of the *Psalms,* he writes that

.... every single declaration [about God] is only the one end of a line at whose other end stands the one praying, calling full of fear for help and who sees how God draws near to him and storms down upon his afflicters. (1937, 529)

Rosenzweig displays the context within the biblical text for the anthropomorphisms in order to illuminate the human situation that lies behind them. His analysis indicates two things. First, that real, human experiences give rise to this language. They are not just the result of imagination. Second, he shows that the Bible itself refers to the experience that produced the metaphors.

A shift from analysis to declaration about present reality is found in the statement

This basic law of the biblical style [of providing frame and not attribute], and of style only because of the biblical way of thinking, is now confirmed in the living experience that is open to everybody today,

as indeed it can hardly be otherwise if the Bible has more than historical value. (1937, 529)

For Rosenzweig, the style of anthropomorphisms communicates the essence
of biblical thinking itself. The living experience of the divine which is the
kernel of such anthropomorphisms is also the core concern of the whole
Bible. The Bible illuminates the paths through which God was available for
His[7] creatures—paths that are equally accessible today.

Whenever humans seek God, God will be found, and whither humans
may try to flee the demanding word, the word will penetrate. Anthropomorphisms embody, endorse, and enliven this lesson through lines about the God
who speaks and hears, draws near, searches out, and steps forth. Thus, what
the Bible provides is

> . . . a boundless trust in His unboundable powers, always, and every
> moment, to meet our and all creation's momentary bodiliness and spiri-
> tuality, bodily and spiritually, in the body and in the soul. (1937, 530)

The thoroughness of the analysis—that is, the fit between style and
lesson, is emphasized in Rosenzweig's quick parry against those attributes,
such as omnipotence and omnipresence, that seem more respectable to many
critics. First, these are attributes, as nice as they might seem, and, thus, they
stand outside of "the biblical way of thinking." Second—and more importantly—they have no experiential frame. These attributes are examples of
those, non-experienced "phantoms," of which Rosenzweig spoke earlier in
the article. As he writes, "What do I know of 'all'!" as in all-powerful or all-
knowing. "What I have experienced and do experience is presence, power,
knowledge, goodness—each in its and my hour" (1937, 530).

Rosenzweig then weaves another piece into his argument. Characteris-
tically, he dispatches an opponent by refusing defense and taking up offense.
The usual objection against anthropomorphisms arises from the vague feeling
that they somehow undermine monotheism, the understanding that God is
One. Rosenzweig contends, however, that God's uniqueness is jeopardized,
not when anthropomorphisms abound, but when they are suppressed. Anthropomorphisms indicate that the living God is ever present. When these are
missing, and God appears only as a distant power, humans will search for
something to mediate that distance. Rosenzweig points to Philo's category
"Logos," Christianity's "Spirit," and the theosophical speculations of the late
Kabbalah as exemplifying such quests. This shows, for Rosenzweig, that the
anthropomorphisms are "the protective armor" of monotheism (1937, 531).

Within the argument about anthropomorphism as the protective armor,
the notion of trust (*trauen*) in experience appears twice. The first time this is

expressed as "the courage to trust that the really experienced experiences of God also come really and immediately from God" (1937, 531). The second time, it is "the certainty, firm as a rock, that everything that we experience of God comes from Him Himself" (1937, 531). In this short, carefully crafted essay, this repetition is highly significant. In these cases, Rosenzweig ties the anthropomorphisms to trust or certainty. In this way, he both reiterates and pushes forward his discussion. Rosenzweig is saying, as we have seen, that the anthropomorphisms emerge from meetings between humans and God. They are not imaginative descriptions nor rational characterizations of the divine. Instead they refer to the way that the encounter with the divine was experienced and understood. Because this is the underlying presupposition of the style or thinking of the Bible, we are assured by the appearance of these metaphors that experiences of the divine were seen as real. Again, the presence of the metaphors indicates that the authors and hearers of the biblical narrative trusted in the reality of these meetings with the divine.

Rosenzweig attaches to the second statement the bold declaration that "we are indebted to this certainty," that what we experience comes from God Himself, "next to the Law and the Prophets, for our continued existence as Jews" (1937, 531). Through this assertion, Rosenzweig is, first of all, placing the biblical and Talmudic anthropomorphisms on the same level with the Law and Prophets. Given the central place that the Law and Prophets have had in Jewish tradition and consciousness since the ancient period, Rosenzweig's juxtaposition of the three is innovative and telling, to say the least. Second, the significance of the anthropomorphisms is further enhanced by proposing that they, along with the Law and Prophets, are responsible for the continued existence of the Jewish people. While the latter two elements are the source of those ways of life and understandings that express the covenant between God and the Jewish people, the anthropomorphisms evidence the people's trust that God was present and continues to be present for them.

The essay ends with Rosenzweig proposing an alternate paragraph to the one that stands as the introduction in the *Encyclopedia Judaica*. A new feature of this paragraph is a discussion, from what he terms a *psychological* perspective, of the possibility of "backsliding into polytheism" (1937, 532). He attributes this backsliding to the "consolidation of a genuine present revelation of the real God to a lasting image of God precisely by . . . resisting the ever-new will of God's revelation" (1937, 532–533). This awkward sentence does clarify some of Rosenzweig's earlier reflections. It appears that polytheism is not, for him, the result of pure imagination. It could reflect an actual encounter with God, but a mistake is made in interpretation. The encounter becomes the basis for making a permanent image of God. In contrast to—and as protection from—such a polytheistic image, biblical anthropomorphisms consistently depict the different experiential contexts and understandings of encounters with the divine.

Going further, Rosenzweig adds that the encounter with God is rightly understood as a revelation of an "ever-new will." He is affirming that the God who is ever present to humans cannot be confined nor limited beforehand. Revelation not only reflects and speaks to the concrete life of persons, but it also opens them to the new. Additionally, Rosenzweig might have in mind a point that Emil Fackenheim once suggested, which is that, because God appears at specific moments in history through meetings with particular persons and groups, each appearance will have some new and unique features (Morgan, ed. 1987, 93). Rosenzweig's somewhat oblique reference to a Talmudic statement that "in each case God dispatches none of his messengers with more than one message" (1937, 533), seems to have this in mind.

Rosenzweig's substitute paragraph proceeds to affirm that the metaphors reflect in the most steadfast way the biblical trust in both God and humans. They maintain, according to Rosenzweig that

> God is capable of what he wills (thus even of meeting the creature from time to time in fully bodily and spiritual reality) and that the creature is capable of what he should be (thus even of fully understanding and recognizing God's self-embodying or self-spiritualization turning toward him from time to time). (1937, 532)

Rosenzweig's essay leaves the reader with no doubt of the importance that he attributed to these biblical features. Beginning with a few hints within the essay itself, let us explore some of the reasons for the prominence that he gives to them.

It is not accidental that the substitute paragraph, previously discussed, in which the basic themes of the essay are powerfully restated, is introduced by Rosenzweig through an allusion to his "new thinking" (1937, 532). The new thinking is the philosophical method or approach which bases itself upon concerns for speech, time, and the other person. It constitutes both his attack upon earlier systematic, and idealistic philosophies as well as the essence of much of what is most constructive and innovative in his work. Although the basic features of this approach were developed and expressed in many of Rosenzweig's early writings, they were not fully formulated until the appearance of his famous essay in 1925, *"Das Neue Denken"* ("The New Thinking"). The question of the importance of biblical anthropomorphisms for Rosenzweig will first be pursued by following upon the connection to the new thinking that he himself expressed.

Perhaps the most significant quality of the new thinking is its trust in life—that is, its trust in specific common-sense features, as well as in the overall meaningfulness of life.[8] Trust is also the leitmotiv that permeates the essay on anthropomorphisms, appearing explicitly or implicitly throughout. Dimensions of this trust featured in the essay are trust in speech or language, experience, community, God, and in humans themselves.

Rosenzweig demonstrates his faith in the trustworthiness of speech or language very early in this essay, when he questions the assumption of the author of the encyclopedia article that anthropomorphisms were the unfortunate result of the "inadequacy of language" in expressing the spiritual or transcendent. Rosenzweig argues that genuine experiences, and not phantoms, lie behind the anthropomorphisms. These metaphors reflect, with striking precision, the ways in which God is met by humans. By means of words about God seeing, calling, responding, and even stretching out His hand to touch the penitent, the anthropomorphisms communicate the experiential matrix from which humans speak. Anthropomorphisms are not a consequence of the limits of language. Rather, they indicate its richness.

Rosenzweig affirmed that "in the new thinking, the method of speech replaces the method of thinking maintained in all earlier philosophies" (1970, 198). The view that language is a faulty, inadequate instrument is one which Rosenzweig found endemic to more than just the author of the encyclopedia article. Actually, it has haunted the writings of philosophers from the Greek times until the present.[9] Philosophy consistently trusted logic and mathematics over speech as instruments for arriving at and communicating truth. Thus, the defense of the meaningfulness of biblical anthropomorphisms was vital to Rosenzweig's wider philosophic agenda. How could he affirm a trust in speech and language, if these biblical words—written so long ago and repeated over millennia during moments of joy and trial—were now to be jettisoned as meaningless?

The issue of trust in experience—and, in particular, in what he designates as theological experience—dominates this essay on anthropomorphisms. Rosenzweig writes of "the courage to trust that the really experienced experiences of God also come really and immediately from God" (1937, 531). In terms of the argument itself, it is insufficient for Rosenzweig to ground biblical anthropomorphisms in experience—that is, in meetings between humans and God. He must contest the view that is triumphant in the modern West that such meetings are illusions. We have already explored the way in which Rosenzweig accomplishes this—first, by insisting that there are three classes of experience and not just one all-purpose, "objective" model; and second, by comparing theological experience with interhuman meetings.

The contentions of Rosenzweig's essay on anthropomorphism that there are three classes of experience, and that the experiences within these realms can be trusted, echo also throughout "The New Thinking." In opposition to Philosophy, which Rosenzweig characterized as fundamentally reductive, the new thinking does not try to collapse the experiences of God, humans, and world into each other. By taking "each separately," he insisted, "we have exact knowledge, the immediate knowledge of experience, of what God, man, and the world are" (1970, 193). Yet, underlying everything, remains that trust in experience. In his words, "faith in experience might constitute the formulable element in the new thinking" (1970, 207).

In the essay, trust in the meaningfulness of the biblical anthropomorphisms—that is, in the way they testify to authentic meetings between God and humans—also grounds the Jew's trust in her or his community. The anthropomorphisms in the Bible record God's call that constituted the Jewish community, the revelation of a particular way of life given at Sinai, and God's ongoing concern and direction for the Jewish people. What meaning would there be in living as Jews if this testimony could no longer be accepted as valid? Perhaps this link between the biblical metaphors and the Jewish community is the reason why Rosenzweig provocatively declared that the anthropomorphisms stood on the same plane with the Law and the Prophets. As long as the axial encounters with God are kept alive—both as memories and as the pattern/guarantor for new meetings—the continuity of Jewish existence is assured.

One of the primary foci of the new thinking is life within community. Rosenzweig critiques the modern notion of the autonomous individual who lives exclusively from his or her own resources. In Rosenzweig's view, it is life within community that provides orientation to the world. In "The New Thinking," two communities, the Jewish and the Christian, are treated, because Rosenzweig believes that only these provide full portraits of God, humans, and world, and also introduce the eternal into the present. Further, through their ritual, they allow humans to act out the elemental relationships. "In their God, their world and their man, the secret of God, of the world and of man, which can only be experienced but not expressed in the course of life, can be expressed" (1970, 203).

The last two features of that trust embodied in Rosenzweig's essay are mutually supportive—a trust in God's power and concern to meet humans, and one in the human ability to recognize and respond to such approaches. As we have seen, Rosenzweig puts these together and labels them as the *double assumption* of the Bible. The assumption of the Bible is that, first, there is no dimension of our lives into which God cannot penetrate. They elicit from us a "boundless trust in his unboundable powers, always, every moment" (1937, 530) to meet us wherever we are.

God's will and capacity to search out every person is graphically presented through these metaphors. They leave the reader—more than that, the recipient of Torah—with the knowledge that God's concern for His creature is everlasting as is His strength limitless. There is no darkness, within or without, into which God's gaze does not penetrate, nor is there a silence into which His voice does not call.

The second part of the biblical assumption refers to a trust in humans, that "the creature is capable of what he should be . . . of fully understanding and recognizing God's . . . turning toward him" (1937, 532). Rosenzweig understands that the ability to recognize God's call and, perhaps, to respond, is not something to be taken for granted. Many of the challenges to faith in the modern period—particularly those that explain away the possibility of revelation—directly undermine one's confidence in these abilities.[10] The earlier discussed confidence in experience is similar to this trust in the capacity of humans, but Rosenzweig gives special attention to it because he seems to find that the biblical anthropomorphisms target it directly. Every example of such metaphors thus demonstrates not only that God can be everywhere, but that humans have recognized—and still can recognize—each of God's searchings for them.

While all three categories of creation, revelation, and redemption are used in the new thinking to illustrate the wider relationships among God, world, and man, it is revelation which is the pivot of Rosenzweig's approach. The experience of God's turning toward humans grounds the belief in creation and the hope for redemption. This experience, in turn, requires that two-sided confidence in God's power to meet and in humans' power to acknowledge such meetings, that Rosenzweig found expressed in the anthropomorphisms of the Bible.

Thus, the biblical anthropomorphisms that many persons regard as archaic, insignificant, and inaccessible, are, for Rosenzweig, the very embodiment and guarantor of some of the most profound dimensions of human life. The issue of the meaningfulness of the anthropomorphisms is directly tied to the confidence that we can have in the trustworthiness of speech, experience, community, God, and ourselves. Through the indivisible link between the anthropomorphisms and trust, this essay places itself at the core of Rosenzweig's writings as much as does his acclaimed masterpiece, *The Star of Redemption*. While the essay is an astonishingly compact account, *The Star* is, more than anything else, an extended panegyric about trust. It begins with death's threat to trust, and ends by pointing the individual into life, sustained by the prophet Micah's words that all that is needed is "to do justice and to love mercy and to walk humbly with Thy God" (1972, 424).

Rosenzweig's treatment of biblical anthropomorphisms also illuminates the significance of the notion of God as person in his thought. Anthropomorphisms would, indeed, be only a literary device—perhaps due to the limitations of speech and thought—unless God must necessarily be encountered as person. If God is a ground of being, a force imminent in nature or humans, or a void, then "It" does not have concern, seek out, and speak. Experiences of God could, only with the most inexcusable latitude, be spoken of as meetings, and these would be meetings to which no other experience offers a parallel. In this case, the whole concrete life of humans with the divine upon which Judaism is based is lost—the words; the experiences; and the understandings of tradition, of God, and of human nature.

However, anthropomorphisms are more than devices for Rosenzweig, because God is encountered as person. As the essay insists, this is not a statement about God's nature nor about His essence. Anthropomorphisms point to the existential matrix which surrounds experience. We do not know what God is in-Himself, but we do know how God has been and still is encountered. How important is this notion that God is encountered as person? Again, it is only as important to Rosenzweig as the categories of creation, revelation, and redemption. We can trust in ourselves, our experience, and speech and community because we have met and still meet this God of the Bible as someone who can be trusted.

After all of this analysis, have we unlocked the secret of the appeal of the anthropomorphisms for Rosenzweig?

Much of their attraction for him—and for many of us today—is heard in their proclamation about God's ability and willingness to meet us. Throughout the essay, Rosenzweig celebrates, as it were, in these metaphors. He is fascinated by their simplicity, concreteness, and limitless variety. Why? The unselfconsciousness and simplicity bespeak the Bible's confidence in God. The concreteness and variety are the highest demonstrations that God can be found everywhere. If Rosenzweig almost revels in the multiplicity of the metaphors; God sees, hears, speaks, finds, and so on, it is because, through each one of these, we have biblical assurance of God's power and love. If this is the case, then, no amount of instances of anthropomorphic language is too many. Every example must be treasured.

Their appeal resides in the special word in Rosenzweig's essay that rivals that of *trust* in terms of its prominence, the word *today, (heute)*.[11] Actually, there is no rivalry between them. They stand together as both a present trust and as a trust in the present. Rosenzweig writes of "the living experience that is open to everybody today" (1937, 529), and "the meeting with creation or creature today as ever" (1937, 529). Although the essay is purportedly about a feature of the biblical literature, it is, in fact, about the possibility of encounters with the divine today. The Bible is not of interest to Rosenzweig because of some "historical value" (1937, 529), but because it teaches of how God is encountered *today*.

The legacy of Rosenzweig—which can be explored from so many perspectives—is found at least in part, in the two-dimensional secret contained in his treatment of anthropomorphisms. What characterizes Rosenzweig's overall thought—the element that he shares with Martin Buber and Abraham Heschel, and which was passed on to such contemporary thinkers as Eliezer Schweid and Emil Fackenheim—is just this firm trust that the God who spoke in the past speaks continually into the present. This trust is reconfirmed every time we face the biblical text, or hear the biblical word, through the concrete, simple, but overpowering language of God's encounters.

The Bible is the basis for the ability to speak to and write about God. The words used to express the encounter with God are both fully ours, reflecting genuine experience, and more than ours, speaking through the biblical text. This correspondence between our word and the biblical word is one of the bases for Rosenzweig's statements that language has a divine origin, and that speech is more than purely human.

THE INTIMACY OF THE CRY

Taking up but five pages in *Difficult Freedom,* "Loving Torah More Than God" offers a passionate entrée to the richness of Levinas's discussions of the relationship with God. Its strengths as an introduction are many.

"Loving Torah" takes its place among the author's Jewish writings, in contrast to his attempts to give philosophic—which he designates as "Greek"—expression to his ideas.[12] As a Jewish writing it has a vividness and directness that is unavailable in those "Greek" works that must struggle to unsay philosophy—that is, to force philosophic language against itself to speak ethically of what cannot, but must, be said. Additionally, the essay takes its point of departure from the story of a person living through the last hours of the Warsaw Ghetto uprising. The shock of this antiworld underlies everything in Levinas's essay, which might be less manifest in—but not less true of—his other writings. As the autobiographical statement "Signature" attests, the authorship—as well as his life as a whole—are "dominated by the presentiment and the memory of the Nazi horror" (1990, 291). Finally, Levinas's essay searches for the meaning of Jewish suffering, suggesting, in the process, the religious category for which Israel stands.

There is, however, a significant limitation in the use of this essay as an introduction to the resources that Levinas presents for Jewish religious language. Written in 1955, it predates the two mature philosophic works for which the author is best known, *Totality and Infinity* and *Otherwise Than Being or Beyond Essence*, which originally appeared in 1961 and 1974, respectively. These later works reflect important and distinctive developments in the author's insights. In order to call upon some of these insights—that is, to selectively explore a few of the most prominent strands in his later work—we will briefly examine some of his statements given in a series of interviews of 1981, which was later published under the title *Ethics and Infinity*.

Levinas begins "Loving Torah More Than God" by stating that, although there is no lack of recent "beautiful texts" about Judaism in the West, these fail to convey to readers that Judaism has something to do with "spiritual matters." This lacuna—the result of Jews not having contact with Hebrew studies, and of, thus, losing sight of their "origins" is addressed by a "true" piece of fiction which Levinas had just come upon (1990, 142).

The anonymous story—"Yossel, Son of Yossel Rakover from Tarnopol, Speaks of God"—first appeared in an Israeli journal. Levinas contrasts its "deep and genuine experience of spiritual life" (1990, 142) with what is all the rage in the eyes of Parisian intellectuals—namely, the religious outpouring of Simone Weil. While Levinas is circumspect about turning this story about God and the Holocaust into some kind of spectacle, he believes that this subject is tremendously important. Although the world has forgotten the event, the cries of the victims "continue to resound and reverberate down the centuries" (1990, 143). Levinas commences, for the manifold reasons of testimony: of himself as one "who survived," of those who cried out, and of the spiritual in Judaism.

Levinas raises the question of theodicy. What could "this suffering of innocents" tell about God, and about good and evil? He notes and critiques the "simplest and most common answer" to the Holocaust—namely, that there is no God. Atheism is the obvious response for those who presuppose that God is someone who "dishes out prizes," someone who rewards and punishes. However, this notion of God entails that persons are to be treated "as children." Further, Levinas speculates that if this childish God has been banished by the Holocaust, people will continue to believe in "a good and sensible world," and will consequently fill their empty heaven with some other being, perhaps a "lesser demon or strange magician" (1990, 143).[13]

Trust in God is not surrendered by the story's protagonist, Yossel, to "an empty sky" *(un ciel vide)*. God's absence brings each individual to experience the full force of human responsibility for justice. Equally, it means that persons who accept responsibility for justice will inevitably be the "first victims" of the savageness of those who rule the world (1990, 143).

In this essay, Levinas seems to hold that savageness by some and suffering by others is characteristic of the world. We live in "a disordered world—that is to say, in a world where good does not triumph." Neither God nor human institutions intervene to contest or right injustice. Again, those who are just are left to struggle and suffer with "a justice that has no sense of triumph" (1990, 143).

Yet, according to Levinas, it is precisely from this sense of abandonment—"the God who hides His face is not, I believe, a theological abstraction or a poetic image"—and suffering that God's presence emerges. The distinctly "Jewish sense of suffering" which follows upon the struggle against injustice brings an intimacy with God. "By belonging to the suffering Jewish people, the distant God becomes *my God*." Israel is thus both a historical people and a "religious category," taking its sustenance from the Torah that teaches a life of law and morality (1990, 143–144).

What is the nature of this intimacy with God? It is not born of some atonement for the sins of others, nor is it a paradox that requires faith to overcome reason. For Jews, the relationship to God is not the "emotional communion" with the God incarnate. It is a "spiritual or intellectual relationship" which the words of Torah elicit. God is a close God—that is, a living God present for Jews educated by the Torah. Levinas writes, "confidence in a God who is not made manifest through any worldly authority can rely only on the internal evidence and the values of an education" in Torah (1990, 144).

Levinas recognizes that this is a "difficult path." However, he is deeply suspicious of some of the alternatives. A spirituality that teaches a direct contact with God "unmediated by reason" is referred to by him as "madness." He is wary of the inspiration that evokes God's "sacred mystery." At the very least, the path of Torah is a "protection" against the possible abuses of a religiousness that leaps beyond the realm of ethics (1990, 144–145).

More positively, the difficult path is nothing less than the "heroic situation" of faith. Levinas explores the route whereby the presence of God is prepared by God's absence through the metaphor of debt. A God who is always manifest to correct human wrongs is one who does not allow humans to be responsible and also keeps them in debt to the divine. In contrast to this, the God absent from the world, but present through the Torah echoing within, educates mature adults and is placed in the debt of those who live, unaided, by the divine injunctions. In Levinas's words

> . . . to hide one's face so as to demand the superhuman of man, to create a man who can approach God and speak to Him without always being in His debt—that is a truly divine mark of greatness! (1990, 145; 192–193)

Further, this absence allows room for and it succours faith, because only faith can describe the attitude that does not owe something to the other, but has credit and waits. By acting in the world for God, and waiting upon God, the individual remains expectantly in faith. Here exists an active faith namely, the refusal of resignation and of being deferred by the debtor.

While the adult can still evaluate and "judge his own sense of weakness," she or he now has the right to call upon God. The call is activated by faith's confidence that, ultimately, "God must show His face, justice and power must join, just institutions must reign on earth" (1990, 145). Thus, although the fundamental "disproportion" between humans and God continues, there is also some sense of an "equality" between them. This is what it means to carry Torah into the world where God is absent, and where justice is without triumph. Here is an intimacy that can "love Him in spite of all of God's attempts to discourage such love," "demand that He show Himself," and "reproaches God for His inordinate Greatness and excessive demands" (1990, 145).[14]

Levinas completes the portrait of this stance of "difficult adoration," by affirming that, only in this way—that is, through ethics—is a personal relationship with the personal God established. He concludes, "loving Torah even more than God means precisely having access to a personal God against Whom one may rebel—that is to say, for Whom one may die" (1990, 145;193).

Levinas's words are arresting and appealing. There is a refrain of phrases that capture clearly and poignantly our feelings and reflections concerning life as a whole: "an empty sky," "a disordered world," and "justice has no sense of triumph." Some persons recognize and almost remember these words, because of the encounter with the shock of the Holocaust. The shock is the double one of the unimaginable horror together with the knowledge that no one came to save the innocents. Levinas's words haunt others who stand further from the Holocaust, but are daily reminded that this is not a "good and sensible world." Despite efforts at justice and hope in its victory, we hesitatingly but finally acknowledge that this is a world where "good does not triumph." After such shock and disillusionment, does religious language—that is, language about the relationship to God—have any place? It is precisely Levinas's ability to give meaning to religious language in this context that reveals his significance for us.

The goal of Levinas's essay/commentary is not to find meaning in the Holocaust. He is neither trying to turn the Holocaust into a "spectacle," with overpowering examples of its barbarity—the dreadful details of what occurred are well-known—nor is he endeavoring to conjure up a direct connection between it and God. While the cries of its innocents reverberate in their particularity, they also remind us of the nature of human history. For Levinas, then, to struggle with the Holocaust is to remember that for which Israel throughout its history testifies.

The paragraph on the option of atheism speaks tomes. He rejects the notion that atheism is the necessary response to the Holocaust. Atheism is a logical response, only if a person is first committed to a particular belief about God's relationship to the world. If God is a being who rewards and punishes on earth in perfect measure with human understandings and expectations of justice, then the Holocaust utterly shatters belief in God. However, according to Levinas, this is a notion of God that views humans as children, a notion neither desiring nor requiring religious and ethical maturity.

Levinas provocatively adds that, if God is rejected because of this expectation of justice prevailing on earth—that is, the expectation of "a good and sensible world" (1990, 143), then heaven will not remain empty for long. As long as the expectation survives that justice rules the world, a new ruler or pretender cannot be far behind. Levinas might here have in mind varieties of nationalism, fascism, and communism. These promise truth and justice in the here and now. Although they proclaim that heaven is empty, they enshrine the nation or the people as the ultimate force that will somehow right all wrongs of the past and present. Levinas contends that the Torah knows nothing of such magic tricks.

Levinas endeavors to indicate the place or value of religious language today by taking up the traditional notion of "the God who hides His face."[15] For him, the Holocaust brings to the fore a millennial Jewish sensibility. God is not found in the world, because He "renounces all aids to manifestation." Yet, these stark words concerning God's absence identify only part of our complex and ambivalent religious awareness. Thus, Levinas writes that, even though God is absent in the world, the person who takes up Torah in the struggle for justice finds God "within" (1990, 143).

What does it mean to say that something is carried "within?" Levinas is saying that we have testimony—almost against ourselves—to God's existence through some of the knowledge, values, and passions that orient our lives. I find that he does not say too much by this.

What, precisely, is found within? The author points first to sensibilities tied to one's life as a Jew. There is the "pride" of being part of the Jewish people. For Levinas, this pride is not in some natural priority or superiority, but develops from the identification with the particular destiny of the Jewish people. That destiny is to carry Torah—that is, justice—into the world. There is also an element of pride attached to the experience and appropriation of the suffering that such a destiny makes inevitable. Levinas is saying that, to belong to the Jewish people, in living and suffering for justice, one testifies to the divine, even though it is to the One who hides His face.

Torah itself is another reminder that is carried within. This is the evidence of conscience, of the values taught by Torah. Other writings of Levinas offer that the commandments not to kill, to love the neighbor, and the words of the prophets are examples of such values. When these are recalled into one's life, although our own "sense of weakness" cannot be forgotten, a contact with the divine is sensed.

Faith, faith in God as the ultimate author of justice is also an inner dimension that testifies to the divine. This faith refuses to resign itself to the world's injustice. It continues to fight. Further, it refuses to acquiesce in God's absence, because it fully believes that God will someday set things right—"God must show His face."

Thus, the relationship to God which Levinas describes is not one of some mysterious contact with the sacred. Reason and conscience are not left behind. Yet, Levinas does not hesitate to speak of the intensity of this relationship. He believes that the suffering and dedication to justice that Torah seeks to instill transforms God from some distant concept into a present reality. The acute ordeal of suffering leads to an intense experience—and perhaps an incontrovertible one—of the close God.

While there is often an austerity to Levinas's words, it is the term "*intimacy*" (*intimité*) that overpowers the final sections of the essay. He writes, for example, that "the intimacy of the strong God is won through a terrible ordeal" (1990, 144). The secret of the relationship with God becomes illuminated through the rhythm of the verbs of intimacy. What relationship is closer, or more intimate, than the one in which a person can demand of, reproach, rebel against, cry out to, but still truly love the other? This is a closeness that allows the ultimate act of love for God—"for Whom one may die."[16]

Still, in our time, this is a conflicted intimacy—that is, an intimacy of the cry.[17] The cry in Yossel's words, "do not bend the bow too far," expresses the dismay at God's seeming efforts to "discourage" our love of Him. Levinas reminds us that the cry that summons God's presence, at first within and ultimately manifestly in the world, requires a price. "But only the man who has recognized the hidden God can demand that He show Himself." As we see, there is a terrible ordeal that lies behind the adult relationship to God (1990, 145).

In Levinas's commentary, we are offered a midrash to help express seemingly contradictory experiences of God. At times, we feel abandoned, much like Job.[18] At other times, perhaps, we experience God's companionship. All evidence in the world points to the former, but Levinas persuades us that some things carried within speak of God's reality, and possibly indicate God's presence. Even the dialectic between absence and presence, so difficult to describe, uncovers another dimension of our religious predicament. We ask: Because the feeling of being abandoned requires a prior belief that someone was there, is God's return actually prepared by this absence?

Levinas is able to demonstrate the powers within the language of God as person for our time, "under an empty sky." A notion of God as person, or the metaphor of God as person, is the prerequisite for the whole preceeding discussion. This metaphor does not lose its power because we experience an absence. God's presence in the world does not have to somehow be conjured up for the resiliency of this language to be felt. The presence of the personal God is found within. It is also only to a person, and not to a ground of being or a void, that we can have access. Only to such a One does the word intimacy apply for, we cry out to, reproach, demand of, but still love only another.

There is much development in Levinas's work from the time of the writing of "Loving Torah More Than God" of 1955. Two primary concerns might be identified in his later work, especially in *Otherwise Than Being or Beyond Essence*, which deeply effected his use of religious language. There is a sustained wakefulness, an intense carefulness dedicated to preventing God both from being identified with one's own desires and from being turned into a piece of knowledge or theme within an overall philosophic system. Actually, these concerns are linked integrally in Levinas's understanding, because, as explained in the preceding chapter, he holds that philosophy traditionally provides systematic expression to—not to mention justification for—the interests of both self and society—that is, the same.

In order to prevent such appropriations, Levinas speaks of God only ethically—that is, in relation with other persons. He writes about God only indirectly. He writes in such a way that no direct content or knowledge of God is offered. In essays such as, "Jewish Thought Today" and "Revelation in the Jewish Tradition," these concerns are summarized.

> Ethics is an optics of the divine. Henceforth, no relation with God is direct or immediate. The Divine can be manifested only through my neighbour. (1990, 159)

> The Revelation, described in terms of the ethical relation or the relation with the Other, is a mode of the relation with God and discredits both the figure of the Same and knowledge in their claim to be the only site of meaning [signification]. (1989, 208)

Only a very lengthy discussion would adequately present the factors behind these developments in Levinas's religious language, but it is worthwhile to present a partial sketch here. In terms of the philosophic dimension, there is his own growing sensitivity, as well as the important critiques of his work by Derrida[19] and others, to the necessary—albeit extremely difficult—operation of writing about God in a way that inhibits rather than fosters philosophic appropriation.

It seems to me that the impact of the Holocaust on his work is also increasingly intense. The deep suspicion of attempts to ally God with the self certainly reflects his knowledge of the way that the perpetrators of the Holocaust appropriated God as their own, inscribing *"Gott mit uns"* on the buckles of their belts (1989, 291).

The section of *Ethics and Infinity* under the heading "The Glory of Testimony," presents a good example of the way in which religious language is used in Levinas's later work. At the beginning of this section of the interview, he responds to a question by affirming that he is not reticent to use the word *God* in his writings, or as he said; "I am not afraid of the word God, which appears quite often in my essays" (1985, 105). Despite Levinas's awareness of the difficulty in using this word without appropriation, he recognizes its importance for his thought.

Still, the word *God* or *the Infinite* does not have a place in any statement about the self. It is not juxtaposed with terms such as *self, mine,* or *I,* but with the word *other.* Levinas powerfully speaks of God and the face of the other person.

> To my mind the Infinite comes in the signifyingness of the face. The face *signifies* the Infinite. It never appears as a theme, but in this ethical signifyingness itself; that is, in the fact that the more I am just the more I am responsible; one is never quits with regard to the Other. (1985, 105)

As we have seen, the encounter with the face of the other person, face-to-face, as it were, is a famous motif in Levinas's philosophy. Standing before the face of the other encompasses the fullness of the ethical relationship to another. The face does not represent nor present a piece of knowledge to be put into a system. It cannot be understood in a context, but remains uncontainable. The poverty and vulnerability of the other that demands an ethical response by the self appears through the face. Even more strongly, the face overcomes the self's natural defenses and interests, appearing ethically from a position of height above oneself. First of all, the face commands, "Thou shalt not kill."

Confronting the face of the other brings access to God. In the paragraph previously quoted, this is stated as, "the face *signifies* the Infinite." The ethical relationship to another person provides one with a trace of God—that same God who commands not to kill and calls each person to care for the poor, the orphan, the stranger, and the widow.

Further on in the interview, Levinas provides another perspective on the way in which God, or the Infinite, accompanies the appearance of the other. He writes

> When in the presence of the Other, I say "Here I am!", this "Here I am!" is the place through which the Infinite enters into language, but without giving itself to be seen. . . . I will say that the subject who says "Here I am!" *testifies* to the Infinite. It is through this testimony, whose truth is not the truth of representation or perception, that the revelation of the Infinite occurs. It is through this testimony that the very glory of the Infinite glorifies *itself.* (1985, 106–107)

This reference to the Infinite or God is even more sensitive to the danger of speaking of a direct relationship that can be made into a recipe or a piece of knowledge. Here, it is not the face that signifies directly, but the response that the face elicits is what signifies or provides a trace of the divine.

An almost overwhelmingly beautiful insight into revelation is expressed in Levinas's words. He writes that the ethical response to the vulnerability of the neighbor "testifies" to—that means gives evidence of—the presence of God. Even more than that, testifying introduces or brings a trace of that divine presence, or, as Levinas states it, "through this testimony . . . the revelation of the Infinite occurs" (1985, 106).

The giving over of oneself in ethical concern—the "Here I am!" said to the person who stands next to you, or the neighbor—invites the presence of God. Here, it is not a matter of finding God within the self or even in the other, but of testifying to God's presence by indicating its impact upon human life through acts of responsibility—acts which arise from the ethical thoughts and feelings inspired by God and Torah.

The same insight can effectively be presented in terms of the place of religious language in our lives. When does the word *God* appear? The word *God* appears in its most authentic way in describing both the call that is felt before the face of the other, and the response to that call. In other words, Levinas teaches that authentic religious language accompanies a life of ethical action dedicated to the neighbor and inspired or directed by God.

Up to this point, we hear what might be a lesson with four ways of expressing the relationship to God. First, the face of the other gives access to God. Second, the response that the face elicits testifies to the presence of the Infinite. Third, the divine is introduced or made present through the active response to the call of the other. Fourth and more generally, the word *God* appears in terms of a life of ethical action.

However, it must be remembered that this relationship to God takes place in a world where "justice does not triumph." In such a world, God's presence can only be a secret held "within." Still, Levinas makes the case for the significance of religious language by demonstrating that only such language reveals the true human situation. Only such language, therefore, can bring us to act. Through his words, we recognize that "difficult adoration" of God which he sees as synonymous with Judaism, but also open to all persons.[20]

WALKING WITH AND WAITING UPON GOD

In this concluding section, we continue to follow the question of what resources for Jewish religious language we find in these two modern Jewish philosophers. I believe that this might best be accomplished by identifying what they share, and also what is distinctive to each of them.

The writings of Rosenzweig and Levinas offer three affirmations that are vital for contemporary Jewish life. These are:

1. God is present;
2. The relationship to God is tied to the interhuman realm; and
3. God is encountered as person.

While there are important differences in emphasis and expression between Rosenzweig and Levinas in terms of these shared insights, their affirmations provide us with an irreplaceable orientation.

Revelation is not just a category of the past for Rosenzweig and Levinas. In other words, it is not just past treasures—that is, encounters and promises given to the patriarchs—that nourish Jewish life for them. God's presence— at least a trace of that presence—is available today. Rosenzweig's passionate interest in the anthropomorphisms of the Bible cannot be explained in terms of some sentimental or historical value that he attributed to them. The attraction lay precisely in their assurance that God's love is accessible for us. They express and guide our encounter with God, the "living experience that is open to everybody today."[21]

While Levinas is unable to write with the same unreservedness about God's presence as Rosenzweig often, but not always,[22] does, there is no doubt that, for him, also God's revelation continues into our time. We remember his words that the person who takes up Torah finds God "within," and also that the "glory" of God becomes manifest in those who testify to it through ethical action. The austerity that sometimes characterizes Levinas's discussions of God's presence does not diminish the significance of the belief that he shares with Rosenzweig about a Jewish life that continues to be touched by God.

The insight that a trace of God appears by way of the relationship with other persons reverberates throughout Levinas's writings. He held that "the divine can be manifested only through my neighbor" (1990, 159), and that in the response to the other, the "very glory of the Infinite glorifies itself" (1985, 107).

This understanding that the relationship to God arises from the interaction with the other also plays a major role in Rosenzweig's work, although the specific texts explored above do not take it up directly. In the essay on anthropomorphisms, Rosenzweig does describe the parallel between meetings with humans and the encounter with God, but we have seen that it is in other places that the junction between the two relationships is voiced. In the second book of the *The Star of Redemption*, for example, Rosenzweig defines the process of redemption in terms of the love of neighbor which transforms the other by bringing him or her into contact with God's love. Human love and human speaking are the instruments of, or the occasions for, the appearance of God's love. He writes

> Love simply cannot be "purely human." It must speak. . . . And by speaking, love already becomes superhuman, for the sensuality of the word is brimful with its divine supersense. (1972, 201)

Or, in the letter of 1920, he clearly voices the way that giving aid to the neighbor is the basis for or that which elicits support "from above."

> . . . each of us is only held up by the neighborly hands grasping him by the scruff [of the neck], with the result that we are each held up by the next man. . . . All of this mutual upholding . . . becomes possible only because the great hand from above supports all these holding human hands by their wrists. (cited in Glatzer, ed. 1970, 92)

Together, Rosenzweig and Levinas teach that the word *God* arises naturally from a life dedicated in love and responsibility to the neighbor.[23] Seen from another angle, they seem to suggest that the self's inhibitions in using religious language are overcome, when the self is given over in responsibility for the neighbor.

What I find most striking in Rosenzweig's and Levinas's statements about the relationship to the neighbor is this portrayal of the dynamic between human action and God's presence. It is not that God's presence evokes human response, but that human action in terms of answering to the call of the neighbor introduces God's presence.[24]

One of the most attractive qualities of the work of these Jewish philosophers is that the nature of that witnessing is presented. They speak of the witnessing, or the testimony of love and responsibility—that is, of ethical action toward the other. God is present for me, not prior to my action, but through my love of the neighbor. Both Rosenzweig and Levinas recognize that, in loving the neighbor, a person testifies to—that is, makes manifest—the love and the presence of God.

The foundation of or presupposition for the two affirmations about God's continued presence, and the relationship to the neighbor as the instrument for that presence, is a third assertion, that God must be understood as person. The metaphor of God as person is the sine qua non for their religious language. The tremendous power of this religious language demonstrates the vibrancy of the metaphor. In other words, the language of God as person gives wings to all of their insights into the relationship with God. Rosenzweig's language about meeting, loving, and trusting God requires the notion of person. The "boundless trust in His unboundable powers" (1937, 530), is a trust in the powers of that person to seek us out, speak with us, and love us. With

Levinas, the metaphor is equally irreplaceable. The verbs about intimately demanding, reproaching, and crying out to God—even the image of absence, or of God's hiding His face—require the metaphor. The God who becomes my God through human suffering must be a God about whom it makes sense to say that He shares my suffering. In all, Rosenzweig and Levinas eloquently demonstrate the limitless resources in Jewish religious language through opening the richness of the metaphor of God as person for us.

However, there are distinctive features to their religious language that also have much to teach us. In the selections that we have seen of Rosenzweig it is the matter of trust that is all pervasive. In particular, the anthropomorphisms in the Bible nourish the trust in speech or language, experience, community, God, and in ourselves. For him, the anthropomorphisms communicate directly with us in order to ground our trust. They convey that immediacy of the relationship with God from which they arose so that we are enabled today to speak of and to write about God.

With Levinas, there is no escape from the haunting sense of "the empty sky." The Holocaust deeply wounded us. While Levinas sees the Holocaust as underlining a religious sensibility that was always essential to Judaism, it is impossible to ignore the unique influence of that event upon his words. For him, although we might experience moments with or traces of God, the divine absence is not overcome. Although Levinas speaks of the interhuman realm as the place where God is found, it might be his statements about the suffering that inevitably accompanies this realm that have the most power over us. Through the ethical life that often must witness alone, the individual learns of that suffering of faith and for others that is Israel's destiny.

In addition to the resources for religious language that Rosenzweig and Levinas each give, it is, together, that we might find them most relevant. They teach of dimensions of that intimacy with God that constitutes the divine covenant with the Jewish people. Rosenzweig shows how the words of that intimacy of mutual trust, written long ago, are also our words. Levinas helps to formulate a language of the intimacy of the cry that demands, but, at the same time, loves. Together, Rosenzweig and Levinas help by providing the words to understand and express our trusting, walking with, and, at other times, our intense waiting upon, God.

Finally, what direction do they give for Jewish religious language? They have told us that these words still have meaning, that they naturally arise out of human interaction, and that they are about the relationship to God as person. Most of all, they insist that religious language is both possible and desperately needed.

Rosenzweig is at his most powerful in showing that the words are alive, that they can still be said. Levinas teaches that, despite our justifiable reticence in this "disordered world" we must speak/act, for God requires witnesses—especially now.

CHAPTER 3

To Notice the Color of Her Eyes: Facing the Feminist Jewish Critique

The critique and challenge by feminist Jewish philosophers and theologians of Jewish history, institutions, practices, and thought are both radical and liberating. It is radical, for it poses questions about the very foundations of Jewish religious life and culture. It is liberating for it envisions a flowering and fullness to this life and culture, beyond the inequities and limits that presently bind us all. As is argued in the introduction to this book, contemporary Jewish philosophers can no longer ignore this compelling stream of Jewish thought without, at the same time, abandoning the tasks that constitute their raison d'être—obligation to the past, commitment to present Jewish communities, and the encounter with modernity.

The scope of this chapter is wide, surveying and outlining the basic features of the philosophic challenge that feminist Jews pose. It will set the stage for a more focused examination of the issue of religious language that will appear in the following fourth chapter. Thus, the movement from general treatment to intensive exploration of religious language, that characterizes the relationship of the third and fourth chapters in terms of feminist Judaism, mirrors the path taken in the first and second chapters that probed the work of Franz Rosenzweig and Emmanuel Levinas.

The point of departure for this chapter will be an essay by the French feminist, Luce Irigaray, that analyzes major elements of the work of Levinas. Irigaray is not a Jewish feminist. However, the incisive questions that this philosopher poses to Levinas bring together, in condensed form, many of the essential features of the wider feminist Jewish critique of Judaism.

"Questions to Emmanuel Levinas: On the Divinity of Love" was first presented at Essex University in 1987. It followed an earlier reflection, "The Fecundity of the Caress," that Irigaray wrote on Levinas's phenomenology of the caress.[1] Totalling less than nine full pages, the "Questions" interweaves suggestive queries with terse arguments in ten sections. In the essay, major elements of Irigaray's overall philosophical oeuvre are presented—the (im)possibility of philosophy recognizing the subjectivity of the other (woman), the importance of sexual difference,[2] the banishing to darkness of women's sexuality, the appropriation of women's desire by male *jouissance* and thought, the lack of images and symbols for women to express themselves independent of men, and the exclusive control of divine power by male gods.

My suggestion that Irigaray's "Questions to Emmanuel Levinas: On the Divinity of Love," might be an appropriate entrée to the feminist Jewish critique rests upon a number of considerations. First, Luce Irigaray is a philosopher and psychoanalyst whose writings spanning the last two decades have brought her recognition as one of the most important "radical French feminists." Her quest to provide a place and voice for women—the "others" of Western culture—is seen in writings that blend complex methods of analysis with inspiring imaginative vision. The appreciative, albeit provocative, examination of Levinas can be seen as part of her interrogation of pivotal Western philosophers, from Plato to Nietzsche, Heidegger, and Derrida, who have relegated woman to the "status of appearance, non-truth" or subjected them to other forms of philosophic banishment.[3]

Second, Levinas is not, however, just another Western philosopher. He seeks to undo philosophy by way of a passionate ethical protest. As we have seen, the core of this protest lies in his presentation of the face-to-face encounter between the self and the other as an event that overturns both the individual's and the state's natural tendency to appropriate or efface those who are different. Thus, Irigaray's clash with Levinas is not over what constitutes first philosophy.[4] Actually, they agree that ethics should provide the foundation for philosophy. However, the clash arises over the most effective way of ethically testifying to the other—the poor, orphan, widow and stranger.

Levinas once said, "The best way of encountering the Other is not even to notice the color of his eyes!" (1985, 85). In light of the place of this encounter in his work, his statement about "the best way" of entering into this relation is significant and telling. Can there be an encounter with the other, if the body is overlooked, and the male gender is assumed? Irigaray's own question is framed in terms of whether, despite Levinas's regard for the other, "the feminine other is left without her own specific face" (1991, 113).

Third, Levinas insists that the infinite duty to the other that grounds his work has its source in Judaism's sacred texts—Torah and Talmud. Consequently, the ramifications of Irigaray's questions resound beyond Levinas's philosophical reflections, confronting some of the fundamental principles of Jewish life and self-understanding. Her inquiry probes the effects of what she contends is a male-centered vision in Judaism. It examines, among other issues, the ways in which God is understood, the notion of God as a transcendent Other, and the relationships between God and nature, the body, love, and law.[5]

This essay will repeatedly shift its focus from Irigaray's analysis and criticism to the positions of feminist Jewish philosophers and theologians. The order of my treatment here will repeat the eight-section format that Irigaray utilizes in her "Questions to Emmanuel Levinas." I will isolate specific issues that Irigaray pursues with Levinas and the Jewish tradition, and then follow each presentation with statements by scholars who identify themselves with feminist Judaism. These scholars include Judith Plaskow, Lynn Gottlieb, Sylvia Fishman, Rita Gross, Cynthia Ozick, Ellen Umansky, Marcia Falk, and others.[6]

Irigaray's questions lead off, providing a powerful and unique combination of critique and vision that, when seen together, constitute an intriguing systematic. Statements by feminist Jews that amplify, modify, or reformulate then follow. The excitingly diverse group of voices of feminist Jews is brought together by the understanding that there is a reciprocal relationship between cultural images (which live in language) of God, the body, and woman, on the one hand; and the everyday social and political place and treatment of women, on the other hand.

It is impossible to do justice to all of the issues that appear in Irigaray's essay or, to a much greater extent, in the expansive literature of feminist Jewish philosophers and theologians. The elements that I pick up or hear— and the way in which I discuss them—will reflect my own positions and understandings as one male Jewish philosopher. This is not an apology, just a reminder concerning the nature of hearing. I hope that an attentive and responsible hearing will bring out the new and surprising, the unexpected, and even the unwanted.

Finally, it is not my intention to include a defense of Levinas or Judaism here. Offering responses is not part of the effort of noticing "her" eyes and listening to what Irigaray describes as "her song" (1986, 249). Levinas's notion of the "feminine" has been analyzed by a number of writers in addition to Irigaray.[7] The matter of the accuracy of feminist understandings of Judaism and Jewish history—whether by Irigaray or feminist Jews—is beyond the scope of this treatment, just as was the case in the preceeding chapters with Rosenzweig's and Levinas's conceptions of Judaism.

OTHER BUT NOT OUTSIDER

"Is there otherness outside of sexual difference?" (1991, 109), the first line in Irigaray's text, introduces its major theme and method of approach. Irigaray maintains that Levinas does not characterize "the feminine" in his work as "other than himself." She finds that the feminine is the "underside or reverse side"—that is, the "negative" of the male longing for light. The feminine is defined as "modesty" by Levinas. It shuns the light. In this way, the feminine does not exist for itself, and female sexuality is left in darkness, without representation.[8]

Irigaray explores the causal and historical background of the denial of women's sexuality by alluding to the homologous fit between the social under-standing and position of women, and a society's images of the divine. She maintains that, when there is a male culture of "men-amongst-themselves" with its corresponding "monopoly of divine power by male gods" (1991, 109), female sexuality is made invisible, and female sexual organs are no longer represented in images of the divine. She holds that, at an early period in "the history of women," when there were goddesses, female sexual organs were always indicated in the depiction of women's bodies and also those of the goddesses. As goddesses later became associated solely with motherhood, the sexual organs—and the acknowledgement of women's sexual desire—gave way to representations of the womb.

For Irigaray the biblical love poem, "the Song of Solomon" (*The Song of Songs*) represents a transition stage in this development, while still being able to affirm female desire, and, thus, to boldly present physical love be-tween the lovers. It describes "the sensual delight of the lovers who wed each other with all their senses, with their whole body" (1991, 110). She contrasts this acknowledgement of woman as an active subject through her desire for another to Levinas's phenomenology of "the caress," in his *Time and the Other*. In the latter treatment, woman's pleasure and subjectivity have disap-peared, for "the feminine merely represents that which sustains [male] desire, that which rekindles [male] pleasure" (1991, 110).

Further, Irigaray claims that the philosophic author of "the caress"—that is, Levinas—is not really interested in making contact with the body of the other through the power of touch. She quotes Levinas that the "intention-ality [the purpose and goal] of pleasure," is "directed purely and simply toward the future itself" (Levinas 1987, 89), and she adds that this under-standing transforms the concrete body of the other (woman) into a dimension of the male subject's life in the future. Irigaray concludes that, in this betrayal of woman's desire, her body, and the sensual present, "the masculine subject loses the feminine as other" (1991, 110).

Irigaray proposes two reasons for the fact that "the other sex as an alterity irreducible to myself eludes Levinas" (1991, 110). First, he does not know of the "communion in pleasure," or that immediate ecstasy of love in which the self is transcended and transformed.[9] She raises the issue of sexual difference by pondering whether his being a man might account for this lack of awareness

... of pleasures neither mine or thine, pleasure transcendent and immanent to one and to the other, and which gives birth to a third, a mediator
between us thanks to which we return to ourselves other than we were?
(1991, 111)

She asks, from the other side, whether it is only her experience as a woman
that unveils this "pleasure with the lover of my flesh." Most importantly,
this act of love teaches her that persons are not interchangeable, "in so far
as he is a man and I am a woman, and in so far as he is he and I am I"
(1991, 110). Thus, the pleasure of and between lovers concretely puts into
abeyance theories that proclaim the possible substitution of one for the
other, or that conceive of pleasure as somehow being a mere dimension of
the self.

The second reason for Levinas's inability to recognize the other sex as
an independent subject is that he "substitutes the son for the feminine" (1991,
111). Instead of focusing on the present reality of love between two in their
difference/otherness, the telos is shifted to the future male child and its relationship to the self/same/father. The failure of this treatment is radical. It does
not recognize the otherness of woman. It takes up the child as an aspect of
the self rather than as someone independent, and it "does not recognize God
in love" (1991, 112).

Many of the issues and themes that Irigaray entices through her questions about the failure to recognize women as subjects also appear in the
writings of feminist Jewish thinkers. These thinkers have examined such
problems as women as nonsubjects, women as tied to male desire, the anoma-
lous attitude toward women's bodies, the son's displacement of the woman,
and the equation of women with motherhood.

The understanding that women do not stand as authentic subjects in
Judaism—along with the contention that the norm in Judaism is male—are
basic to feminist Jewish positions. These two sides constitute a single theme
under the rubric of *women as outsiders*. The theme is most dramatically and
poignantly articulated by Judith Plaskow as the leitmotiv for her book, *Standing Again at Sinai*. She writes

Entry into the covenant at Sinai is the root experience of Judaism, the
central event that established the Jewish people. Given the importance
of this event, there can be no verse in the Torah more disturbing to
the feminist than Moses' warning to his people in Exodus 19:15. "Be
ready for the third day; do not go near a woman." For here, at
the very moment that the Jewish people stands at Sinai ready to re-
ceive the covenant . . . Moses addresses the community only as men.
(1991, 25)

There are many other instances of this as being an outsider, peripheral, and the exception in religious practice and community life which are cited in feminist texts. There are haunting reminiscences about "not being a Jew in the synagogue" (Ozick 1983, 125) and of being "forever banished to the women's section, where they could only peek over or through the *mekhitzah* [wall] to view the central activities of the prayer service" (Fishman 1993, 148). This experience is vividly characterized by Thena Kendall as "like being expelled from paradise" (1983, 96).

The view that men are the subjects of Jewish history, and that women's voices have been silenced and suppressed, is forcefully put by Lynn Gottlieb. She writes

> After all, since the beginnings of Jewish history most of the official interpreters of Jewish religion have been men. Men have recorded their laws, commentaries, legends, prayers, theologies, mystical testimonies, and politics in thousands upon thousands of volumes. Until recently women's words have not found life on the written page. . . . Our names have been unrecorded, glossed over, or suppressed. Our contributions have been devalued or forgotten. (1995, 4)

Still, it is in terms of the area of Jewish law, *Halakhah*, that the feeling of being an outsider is most often expressed. It is important to remember that Halakhah was the primary foundation for religious life and communal and individual identity until the modern period. It retains all or much of its influence among the different communities of Jews today, and, thus, continues to have great impact upon the lives of Jewish women. Cynthia Ozick summarizes the findings of many feminist Jews in the following lines:

> Under *halakhah,* the male is the norm, and the female is a class apart. For instance, there is a Tractate entitled *Nashim,* "Women"; but there is no corresponding Tractate called "Men"—because clearly all that does not apply to women falls to men. Men are the rule, and women the exceptions to the rule. (1983, 124)

Julie Greenberg turns to the Talmud to demonstrate the way that men are normative and women only outsiders. She argues that

> Men are the ones making the rules, men are the ones addressed; and the system, even at its most sensitive and humane, is controlled by men to protect and perpetuate their interests, which they see as synonymous with God's and the Jewish people's interests. (1986, 181)

Rachel Biale understands the condition of being an outsider in terms of lacking "halakhic power." She writes that women "have been silent recipients, outsiders to the [halakhic] process" (1984, 8).

Finally, Rachel Adler, in the essay, "The Jew Who Wasn't There: Halakhah and the Jewish Woman," describes this problem in terms of women being "peripheral Jews." She notes that "the category in which we are generally placed includes women, children, and Canaanite slaves" (1983, 13).

Offering a somewhat different tone, Sylvia Fishman provides a voice that is both critical and appreciative of the place of women in the Jewish tradition. She agrees that Judaism has been predominately male centered. She writes that

> ... the assumptions and the language of Judaism, its narratives, laws, and liturgy—with a number of noteworthy and deeply significant exceptions—have largely been framed in the language of men to reflect the experiences of men. (1993, 143)

Yet, Fishman also believes that by building upon "the biblical, rabbinic, and historical wellsprings of Judaism," Jewish women can both uncover what is latent in the tradition and develop new roles and possibilities of experience (1993, 144).

Recently, new ways of theorizing feminist Judaism have been offered that take Irigaray's argument about women as other with utmost seriousness. These views reject an understanding of the Jewish past that is fixated upon male domination and female powerlessness. Such thinkers as Maurie Sacks and Lori Lefkovitz believe that the opposition domination/powerlessness is, itself, based upon male norms and models.[10] Sacks notes that Chava Weissler and other scholars attempt to explore "the concept of an independent female mode of experiencing Judaism" that highlights women's experiences (1995, 298). She cites the work of Annette Weiner who redefines what constitutes power "to include influential behavior in reproducing the relationships that constitute society" (1995, 298–299). Sacks also indicates that feminists have questioned the ruling notion that the private sphere is inferior to the public realm, and speaks of "women's material wealth in the form of ritual objects, heirlooms, even control over daily expenses and food" as a frequently ignored "source of power" (1995, 299).

Lori Lefkovitz—who, along with Sacks, acknowledges the influence of French feminist thought—discusses the importance of exploring Jewish women's experience through new categories. She argues that

> When Jewish feminists strain to locate women using classification systems typically associated with the study of Judaism (with categories

such as law, ritual, and theology) to the exclusion of classifications that may offer the figure of Woman a more comfortable fit (and here I have talked about laughter as one such possibility), we may miss opportunities to reread woman in the Jewish tradition in ways that are finally recuperative, empowering, and even redemptive. (1995, 165–166)

Male and female desire are not a major line of exploration for most feminist Jews. Irigaray's view that male desire defines the female as well as her depiction of the process by which female desire is left unacknowledged is certainly more detailed than appears in their texts. Male desire does come into focus, however, when the topic of women as *temptresses* is explored. It has been noted that, in Jewish law and practice, women are sometimes regarded as dangerous, because they tempt men to turn away from the higher spiritual pursuits (Adler 1983, 16). As Judith Plaskow relates, women's "gait, their voices, their natural beauty are all regarded as snares and temptations and subjected to elaborate precautions" (1991, 191). This supposed danger was used to impose limits on general social interaction between the sexes, and to restrict women to peripheral places, outside of male vision or desire. In this way, the guarding of male desire is permitted to define social life and women's place.

Another element in Irigaray's critique—that the female body is never acknowledged in its concreteness—is somewhat mirrored in the statement by Rita Gross that, within the Jewish tradition there is a "fear and rejection of our embodied condition, particularly the female body" (1983, 245). Yet, what is more characteristic of feminist Jewish literature is that the attitude toward the female body is explored in terms of prescriptions in Halakhah, particularly the laws of *niddah* (menstruation). They portray the menstruating woman as ritually impure (Plaskow 1991, 177).[11] Thus, rather than ignoring women's bodies, feminist Jews find, in the words of Judith Plaskow, that "women's very bodily functions are devalued and made the center of a complex of taboos" (1991, 191).

Is there a contention within feminist Jewish texts that corresponds to Irigaray's suggestion that, in Levinas's description of the caress, the son displaces woman? Not exactly, but the theme of the preeminence of the son within the Jewish tradition is omnipresent in this literature. The son's centrality is expressed in numerous ways, according to feminist thinkers, but, most importantly, in the ritual of circumcision as defining the covenant community. It is interesting that in Judith Plaskow's discussion of the traditional male ritual, she speaks of the marginalization of women (1991, 82), which is somewhat reminiscent of Irigaray's charge of the woman's displacement by the son.

Significantly, feminist critiques acknowledge that the Jewish tradition does not see the body and sexuality as having value only in terms of procreation. There are references to the halakhic laws of *onah* which regulate a husband's sexual obligations to his wife. Judith Plaskow speaks of this positive view of sex.

> The laws are formulated from the perspective of women's gratification (of course, as men perceived it), and they represent an understanding of marital sex as more than procreational. Having children is one primary purpose of marital relations, and men (again, the laws of sexuality are addressed to men) are required to be fruitful and multiply—that is, have at least two children. But *onah* is an independent value, a commandment alongside procreation that applies if a woman is pregnant, barren, or past childbearing age. (1991, 180)

There is a large literature that explores another way in which women's subjectivity has been denied—that is, the equation of women with motherhood, and the stereotype of the Jewish mother. For example, Erika Duncan, in "The Hungry Jewish Mother," reviews recent efforts by feminist Jews through fiction to critique the image of the "all-engulfing nurturer" (1983, 27). She writes that "through learning to suckle herself and other women has the hungry Jewish mother been transformed" from the emptiness of only being for men (1983, 37).

It is important to summarize some of the similarities and differences between the attempt of Irigaray to have women regarded as true subjects, and the parallel effort of feminist Jews. Especially in this section, Irigaray is attacking what she sees as the male appropriation of women into the thought and world of men, into the domain of the same. In order for women to be acknowledged as full subjects, she believes that men must come to understand the *otherness* of sexual difference. Feminist Jews make their case that women have been refused recognition as autonomous subjects, primarily by uncovering the traditional ways in which women have been treated as *outsiders*. To be seen as an outsider means that women are not counted as part of the community of Jews. The history and dynamic by which Jewish women have been excluded as outsiders from the loci of power of the community is a fundamental issue for them. However, the understanding that women are also other than men—in terms of different experiences of their bodies, the world, and the divine—does play an important role in feminist Jewish writings, as will be illustrated later in this chapter. Irigaray's insistence that women be regarded as independent subjects is reiterated by feminist Jews through their questioning of the practice of assuming only one norm (of course, that of men); their critique of male notions of power and powerlessness, and their rejection of the equation of women with motherhood, which undermines women's autonomy by subsuming them within the male concern for progeny.

In the second section of Irigaray's essay, the content of Levinas's category of "the other" is probed. The definition of the other appears to be self-evident to him, which leads Irigaray to suspect that it must come from somewhere, "as a postulate, the projection or the remnant of a system, a hermeneutic locus of crystallization of meaning, etc." (1991, 112). She queries whether behind the "mask or lure" (of the female?) lies the male subject.

Irigaray's suspicion about the nature of the other is heightened because of the major place which paternity has in Levinas's philosophic system (1991, 112). His privileging the father's generation of the son, and taking this as a model of the relationship to the other, increases the invisibility of women. This also covers over the relationship—including the maternal one—between mothers and daughters,[12] which Irigaray holds was not the case at the time when there were goddesses.

Among the other features of this section is an intensive interrogation from two different directions of the nature of that ethics that constitutes the heart of Levinas's philosophy (1991, 112).

First, Irigaray argues that, without the recognition of sexual difference, the other has no irreducible difference from the self. It has no independent identity. Each person can then, be reduced to, or substituted for, another—a situation which Irigaray insists is incompatible with a true ethics.

Second, she finds that, within Levinas's ethics, there is a distorted definition of the ideal, at least in terms of women. Because men are the only real subjects, the ideal that women are to strive for is one "defined in relation to the ideal of the other genus"—that is, men (1991, 112). According to Irigaray, this ethical distortion mirrors, and perhaps reinforces, the centuries-long subjection of women to an alien ideal in Western societies.

We have already explored the parallel between Irigaray's view, and that of feminist Jewish thinkers, that the assumed subject is male, whether in Levinas's treatment of the caress, or the Jewish tradition as a whole. Feminist Jews have also identified and sought to overcome the failure of the Jewish tradition to value the mother-daughter relationship, and other relationships between women. In response to this situation they point to the reinstitution of old rituals, and the development of new ones for women—including birth/naming ceremonies for girls and the *bat mitzvah* for young women—and the creation of new forms of communities of women (Ackelsberg 1986; Fishman 1993, 124–127; Plaskow 1991, 57–58).

Lynn Gottlieb has diligently researched "women's ceremonial history," uncovering "rituals and customs that women created around birth and pregnancy, weaning, the onset of menstruation, marriage and death, and holy day celebrations, including *Rosh Hodesh* [the appearance of the new moon]" (1995, 8). Her book, *She Who Dwells Within*, offers new ceremonies to "affirm women's lives" (1995, 8) by widening their experience of the sacred.

These ceremonies include "rituals for the initiation of young Jewish women into their womanhood, a prayer for mothers, and two ceremonies honoring elder women" (1995, 9).

However, I have not yet located an argument that could be compared with Irigaray's specific critique of ethics (in terms of a foreign ideal that is forced upon women) in the queries of feminist Jewish philosophers.

In the third section, Irigaray inquires about another missing element, "the face of the natural universe" (1991, 113). Her question gains strength by being pared down to a minimum. "Who is the other if it is not rooted and situated in the natural universe?" (1991, 113). She affirms that human identity and the human universe must be understood in its "irreducible incarnation," in the "natural universe, in the body" (1991, 113).[13]

A new attention to the natural world (and the body) is an extensive feature of feminist Jewish philosophy. Actually, this interest is a pervasive one in feminist literature in general, which traces many faults in Western culture to the repudiation of humans as embodied natural creatures.[14] Feminist Jews have offered many intense and multilayered discussions of the devaluation of the body, nature, and the overall relationship between the human and the natural world. One of the most outstanding examples of the creative efforts to redress these faults is Marcia Falk's fashioning of new *brachot* (blessings) to express the sense of the sacred in Jewish life.[15] In drawing metaphors for God within these blessings "from all aspects of creation," Falk both critiques the androcentric language of the divine and reestablishes the connection between human life and nature. She explains her reworking of the blessing over wine in this way:

> Thus the power I wished to invoke at the moment of my blessing—that flow connecting the divine with the realms of nature and humanity—was not a force that came down from above to command the fruit of the vine into being. Rather, it was a nurturance that enabled the vine's fruits to grow, sustaining them from within, allowing them to ripen. (1989, 135)

Judith Plaskow contended that her concern to reimage/imagine the divine implied a new consciousness that she found in much feminist literature, that "human beings are not the acme and end of creation but participants in a broad and complex web of life all of which is sacred" (1991, 145). Finally, Rita Gross has examined the parallel between the "rebellion against the closed round of our natural existence" (1983, 246), and the refusal to attribute any higher meaning to that which constitutes our link with that existence—namely, sexuality.

The fourth section examines the tension in Levinas's work between, what Irigaray characterizes as, the "phenomenological approach" and the "metaphysical tradition" (1991, 113). The first is descriptive, and includes the caress, sexual love, and the "alterity" of the feminine, while the second is ontological and theological, according to Irigaray. With the second, one finds the language of the father, the father-son, and man-God relations, as well as the foundations of the ethical. This division between the phenomenological and the metaphysical results in the feminine being separated from the realm of the ethical and from the divine. In addition, the two sides are not equal in power, because the phenomenological is ultimately subordinated to the metaphysical. In Irigaray's eyes, the feminine other—jettisoned from the realm of ethics, responsibility, "human freedom and human identity"—is left to represent the underside of the male—that is, "animality, perversity, childhood" (1991, 113).[16]

Irigaray laments that, while there are positive elements in the phenomenological reaching out to the other (woman)—"after having been so far—or so close—in the approach to the other sex . . . to the mystery of the other," Levinas eventually "clings once more to this rock of patriarchy in the very place of carnal love" (1991, 113). Consequently, his philosophy does not fulfill the imperatives of a real ethics, which would mean "to leave the woman her face, and even to assist her to discover it and to keep it" (1991, 114).

Irigaray's understanding that women have been removed from the realm of ethics and responsibility finds confirmation in the analysis of women's (non)role in Halakhah. Apologists for the way in which Halakhah has traditionally applied more *mitzvoth* (obligations) to men than women, have seen this difference as positive for women. However, feminist Jews have recognized that this division exempts/extracts women from the realm of both the responsible and the sacred. In not obligating them to fulfill positive *mitzvoth*, excluding them from the *minyan* (the basic prayer unit) and not allowing as admissible their testimony in court, Jewish women are made "peripheral" to the life of the community (Adler 1983, 13–14). Although the explicit charge that women have been split from the ethical does not appear in this literature, feminist Jewish investigations certainly make this conclusion unavoidable.

Irigaray's second charge that women are made the underside of the male, through their identification with "animality, perversity, childhood," does find echoes within feminist Jewish analyses. The image of woman as "temptress," in addition to illustrating the way women are defined in terms of male desire, is an example of the projection upon women of the denied, underside of men. Rachel Adler in her study of this image within early Rabbinic literature gives substance to this point. She writes

> The Talmudic sages viewed the female mind as frivolous and the female sexual appetite as insatiable. Unless strictly guarded and given plenty of busywork, all women were potential adulteresses. (1983, 16)

Just as Irigaray identifies two processes by which women have had their subjectivity taken from them—either ignored as subjects or labeled as animal, and so forth, the feminist Jewish critique has uncovered similar strategies. These critics find that women are either ignored—not addressed at Sinai—or depicted as temptresses. We have also seen women's otherness—meaning here, their being seen as outsiders, that is, not as Jews—expressed and enforced by the taboos formulated upon their bodies. In fact, Judith Plaskow holds that the association between women and sexuality is "the chief manifestation of women's Otherness" (1991, 170). However, rather than having women's desire taken away, as Irigaray sometimes discovers, the image of the temptress that feminist Jews discuss depicts women's desire as beyond all limits, as insatiable.

THE CRITIQUE OF MONOTHEISM

The brief references to the interrelationship between the understanding of God and the recognition of women, which punctuate the early sections of Irigaray's text, expand to become the major theme of those that remain. Irigaray holds that, before philosophy or "the phenomenological" and theology or "the metaphysical" can be integrated in the way that Levinas attempts, the whole notion of "monotheism" must be examined. Her query is, not uncharacteristically, striking. "Is monotheism wisdom or a patriarchal and masculine passion?" (1991, 114). She demands a "radical interrogation" in terms of the ethical implications of

> . . . the sexual attribution of their [monotheistic religions] paradigms, whether these be of God, the ways in which God is referred to (in particular the masculine gender used by language, when he is not represented pictorially), God's commandments, etc. (1991, 114)

No less profound, forceful, and unsettling than Irigaray's questions to Levinas about the effects of monotheism on Jewish life and thought are the challenges to this paramount feature of Judaism by feminist Jews. They are embarking on a revolutionary path in Jewish thought, exploring the meaning, powers, and limits of this concept.

The radical interrogation of monotheism is the result of the recognition that the understanding and place of women in Judaism cannot be changed without a transformation of the perception of the divine.[17] Judith Plaskow, for example, has written that "the equality of women in the Jewish community requires the radical transformation of our religious language" (1983, 229). Rita Gross expresses her recognition of the correlation between religious

language and everyday life in noting that, "if it is daring, degrading or alienating to speak of God using female pronouns and imagery, that perhaps
indicates something about the way women and the feminine are valued" by
the community (1992, 168). In a more positive vein, Marcia Falk remarks
that

> . . . recognizing the enormous power of God-talk to educate and shape
> our lives, feminist Jews in our time are taking back the power of nam-
> ing, addressing divinity in our own voices, using language that reflects
> our own experiences. (1989, 128)

While a major focus of the feminist "wrestling"[18] with God-language is
a critique of male language, and an exploration of female language, it goes
well beyond this. They are asking whether monotheism, itself, can be purified
of the components of exclusion, domination/hierarchy, and dualism that they
find currently inhere in it. They fervently search for a transformed monotheism that can affirm: inclusion of the whole community's diverse experiences
of the divine; humans' power to be co-creators; and the worth of all persons
as well as of all aspects of creation.

Feminist Jews have sought to teach the community that monotheism as
the worship of one God must be able to incorporate diverse notions and
experiences of the infinite. Marcia Falk's discussion well illustrates this point.

> What is it we are affirming with a monotheistic creed? I believe mono-
> theism means that, *with all our differences*, I am more like you than I
> am unlike you. It means that we share the same source, that one prin-
> ciple of justice must govern us equally. Thus, monotheism would seem
> to imply that if we are all created in the image of divinity, the images
> with which we point toward divinity must reflect us all. . . . It would
> seem, then, that the authentic expression of an authentic monotheism is
> not a singularity of image but an embracing *unity* of a *multiplicity of
> images*, as many as are needed to express and reflect the diversity of
> our individual lives. (1989, 129)

Rita Gross bases her argument for the inclusivity of divine images on
a discussion of the limitations of our religious language. She labels as "unrealistic, self-aggrandizing, and fundamentally idolatrous" (1983, 235) the
belief that a particular set of (male) images corresponds to the true reality of
the divine. This exclusive attachment to males' images has, Gross contends,
undermined the "thorough awareness of the inherent limitations of any theological or religious language" (1983, 235), which she insists is the prerequisite for an authentic monotheism. Drorah Setel noted the mistake of thinking

that only one image of God defines monotheism, and reflected upon the wider questions that this initial point touches. She writes

> Contemporary Judaism is plagued by vulgar monotheism, a confusion between a belief in one God/dess and the belief in one *image* of God/ dess. I believe that the unity of God/dess is an important theological issue for the development of feminist Judaism in representing an alternative, relational system of holiness within the tradition. It is also an important issue for all feminist theologians because it raises questions of unity, diversity, and difference which are becoming increasingly significant in feminist thinking. (1986, 117)

The possible connection between monotheism and domination is a second issue raised. Examining such traditional attributes as lordship and kingship, feminist Jews have asked whether the association of these terms with domination might sanction the authority and power of some individuals and groups over others. They have in mind, not only men over women, but Israel over other peoples (Plaskow 1991, 132–133; Falk 1989, 129). Marcia Falk discussed the awareness of this issue in colorful language. She said that feminists have discovered that more is needed than just "feminizing the male God"; "For a feminized patriarchal image is still patriarchal, though now in transvestite masquerade" (1989, 129). Even more widely, Judith Plaskow has questioned whether these images of God's power over humans might both "encourage human passivity" and foster "self-abnegation" (1991, 133).

Sensitivity to the way that attributes of domination might inhere in traditional Jewish monotheism is reflected in the examination of a third dimension—the notion of God as transcendent. Some feminist Jews have queried whether God is better understood, or should also be understood, as a power within the individual and community, and not just as a force "out there" (Falk 1989, 130). As Judith Plaskow writes, "attempting to link the reimagining of God to a new vision of community, feminists repeatedly choose metaphors that picture divine power, not as something above and over us, but in and around" (1991, 140). Lynn Gottlieb's emphasis on the Shekhinah as "She Who Dwells Within" belongs to this endeavor to think of God as imminent.

A fourth obstacle uncovered within Jewish monotheism is dualism. While Judith Plaskow links this problem with the issue of domination through the phrase, "hierarchical dualisms" (1991, 132; 1994, 69), it is not always treated this way. There is a recognition by some that, when the tradition incorporated male images into the divine and excluded female ones, a dualism was created that substantiated the inferior social place and image of women. More widely, Plaskow believes that the "critique of hierarchical dualisms has been central to the entire feminist project from its beginnings," and cites Drorah Setel in support of her view (1994, 69).

The diversity of views of feminist Jews is well attested by the clarity and force with which Sylvia Fishman directly opposes Plaskow's position concerning dualisms, even hierarchical ones. Fishman warned that

> The hierarchies represented by the division between God and humanity, Sabbath and weekday, are the bedrock of Judaism, beyond which it cannot be reduced and still remain itself. Intrinsic to the Jewish vision of the universe is the belief that physical and moral order are created by separating the elements and creating for them complementary but distinctive roles. Without distinctions, the earth—and human life—is chaotic and formless. . . . The desire for a life undemarcated by hierarchies may well be feminist, but it is antithetical to historic Judaism as a religion and a culture. (1993, 235)

The understanding of God as person constitutes another, and fifth, ingredient of monotheism that feminist Jews have explored. Anthropomorphic metaphors for God have had a central place in Jewish literature, worship, and texts from the emergence of this tradition. However, the exclusive use of masculine metaphors has brought feminists to ask about the legitimacy of this aspect of God-language. Marcia Falk has argued that the relationship to all of nature is deprecated when the metaphors for God are limited to the realm of the anthropomorphic. She writes

> For as long as we image divinity exclusively as a person, whether female or male, we tend to forget that human beings are not the sole, not even the "primary," life-bearing creatures on the planet. We allow our intelligence and our unique linguistic capabilities to deceive us into believing that we are "godlier" than the rest of creation. And in so doing, we neglect the real responsibility attendant upon the gift of human consciousness: to care for the earth in ways that respect all human and nonhuman life upon it. (1989, 132)

From another perspective, Rita Gross believes that the understanding of God as person might be too much a part of Judaism's foundations for anthropomorphic metaphors to be devalued at this time. She finds that for many Jews

> The whole *siddur*, most of *halakhah* and *aggadah*, in short, almost everything that makes the Jewish religious enterprise distinctively *Jewish* becomes non-sensical without the metaphor of a divine Person in a

covenant relationship of mutual responsibility and love with human persons. (1983, 236)

Sylvia Fishman agrees with the position that regards anthropomorphic images, or what she calls "gender-specific imagery," as intrinsic to Judaism. She holds that

> ... utilizing balanced, gender-specific imagery may in the end be a more effective, sensitive, and meaningful use of language than eliminating gender altogether. The balancing of gender-specific language and imagery is in some ways implicit in the structure of traditional Jewish Sabbath and holiday readings of the Hebrew scriptures. (1993, 240)

Finally, Judith Plaskow works to both amplify the current array of personal metaphors for God—an effort that she shares with others—but also argues that wider metaphors will still be needed in our attempt to express the relationship to the divine. In her writings she explores images of God as "lover, friend, companion, cocreator" (1991, 164), but also shows these must still be augmented. For her,

> Anthropomorphic images must thus be supplemented by a second kind of language that can evoke the creative and sustaining power of God present throughout the world and in ever-widening circles of relation. This stratum of language will encompass an even wider range of images than the first—from natural and impersonal metaphors to conceptual terms that express God's relation to all being and becoming.
>   Images of God as fountain, source, wellspring, or ground of life and being remind us that God loves and befriends us as one who brings forth all being and sustains it in existence. (1991, 164–165)

The most pervasive concern of feminist Jewish theology in terms of the reevaluation of monotheism has been to critique the use of masculine metaphors and pronouns that dominate traditional Jewish religious language, and to seek remedies for this situation. Judith Plaskow shares with many other thinkers the insight, which, in her words, is that

> Our language about divinity is first of all male language; it is selective and partial. The God who supposedly transcends sexuality, who is presumably one and whole, comes to us through language that is incomplete and narrow. The images we use to describe God, the qualities we

attribute to God, draw on male pronouns and experience and convey a sense of power and authority that is clearly male. (1991, 6–7)

The minimalist answer following upon this critique has been to insist upon the addition of female images of God. Rita Gross, for example, introduces two reasons for such a change. First, "female God language compels us to overcome the idolatrous equation of God with androcentric notions of humanity in a way that no other linguistic device can" (1992, 171–172). Second, she looks at the function of religious language, not just in theology, but in prayer, and adds that "the only way that we can simultaneously retain the language of address, and overcome the problems of exclusive male God language, is by adopting female forms of address *in addition to* male forms" (1992, 172).

In the next, or sixth, section, Irigaray pursues her argument about the imperative of recognizing sexual difference. She uncovers the radical consequences of the male notion of the divine by asking us to contemplate what a reversal of this notion might mean. "Are the peoples of monotheism ready to assert that their God is a woman?" (1991, 115). She contends, against those who believe that the male deity is somehow sociologically neutral, that with such a reversal of the male paradigm the "entire socioreligious economy" and "the symbolic order" would be in "upheaval" (1991, 115).

The issue of "the Goddess" in Judaism—which is the way in which the question of God as a woman is often raised—is very charged. Feminist Jewish theologians do work with this term, but they are also aware of the powerful negative associations that it has in Judaism. Worship of God exclusively as a Goddess, or of a Goddess alongside a male deity, is not what these thinkers are discussing. As Judith Plaskow writes

> ... the overwhelming majority of Jewish feminists who have experimented with religious language in no way see themselves as imaging or worshipping a Goddess; they are trying to enrich the range of metaphors Jews use in talking about God. (1991, 150)

The positions that these thinkers take in terms of utilizing the language or metaphors of the Goddess is wide-ranging. The most positive and extensive treatment of this issue is to be found in the reflections of Rita Gross. She, as well as Lynn Gottlieb (1995, 36), have even argued that, in order to meet the need to elaborate female concepts and metaphors for God, Jews ought not to be reticent to examine such images in other religious traditions, and to adopt those that are appropriate. Gross summarizes her insights about the ramifications of utilizing the language of the Goddess in the following manner:

My remarks on the imagery of Goddess, which I think takes us far beyond the simple insertion of female pronouns into familiar contexts, seem to have stressed two points over and over. One is that we need Goddess because She breaks stereotypes of the feminine and thus frees women from the limitations of that stereotype. Women can be strong *and* beautiful, feminine *and* wise teachers, mothers *and* participants in culture. If Goddess provided that much it would have been enough. But it seems that She brings much more. Dimensions of deity that have been lost or severely attenuated during the long centuries when we spoke of God as if S/He were only a male are restored. They seem to have to do with acceptance and immanence, with nature and the cyclic round. Metaphors of enclosure, inner spaces, curved lines seem to predominate. What a relief from the partial truth of intervention and transcendence; of history and linear time; of going forth, exposure and straight lines! (1983, 246)

Judith Plaskow shares some of these views about the positive results of introducing the language of the Goddess into Judaism. She particularly refers to the need for images of female power, and for a reexamination of our tie to body, earth, and sexuality, which this image can further. She adds that, to recognize "the many names of the Goddess among the names of God becomes a measure of our ability to incorporate the feminine and women into a monotheistic framework" (quoted in Umansky 1989, 190).

The position of Ellen Umansky is more complex. She acknowledges the advantages of introducing Goddess language into Judaism, but also recognizes that this task is not simple, given Judaism's historical prohibition about worshipping a Goddess. Thus, for her,

Before Jewish feminist theologians can reappropriate the Goddess within the monotheistic framework of Judaism, they need to explore ways in which this appropriation can be accomplished. More specifically, they need to suggest a naming of the Goddess that would address her as the feminine aspect of the Divine and not as a separate and idolatrous Being. (1989, 191)

Among the creative linguistic "paths" that Umansky examines are coining a new Hebrew word for Goddess, taking an existing Hebrew word that refers to the divine, and utilize it to speak of a Goddess, "retain *Elah*, a word that already means Goddess; yet deny the identification of *Elah* (Goddess) with *Elilah* (a female idol)," and reexploring traditional Hebrew religious language (1989, 191–192). She refers to Lynn Gottlieb, who attempts to uncover new meanings in these terms. She notes Gottlieb's serious play with Hebrew terms for God:

> Her experience of *Elohim* as Creator is that of all-spirits who, in a "time before time . . . birthed creation". . . . the image of *lilah* as female creative process emerges out of her own vision of Lilith as the "motherbed of creation" and the "progenitor of light". . . . *Adonai* is not "Lord" but the "I" as the ground of experience and the door to the mystery of life. . . . *Shaddai* is transformed from "the Almighty" to "my breasts" . . . alternately imaged by Gottlieb as "the many breasted woman." She also finds meaning in *Shechinah* . . . as She-Who-Dwells-Within. . . . *Shechinah*, for her, is "immanent Presence," a crystal generating light. She is active, the source of vitality, through whom we discover our own energy and vision. (1989, 193)

Still, the language of the Goddess to express the feminine aspect of, or feminine metaphors for God, is not universally valued by feminist Jews. Julie Spitzer strongly warns against utilizing the word *Goddess*, believing that it "conjures up pagan imagery" (cited in Fishman 1993, 239). At one time, Cynthia Ozick held that the "resurrection" of such language, and its accompanying concepts and images "slanders and sullies monotheism" (1983, 121). Margaret Meyer, while acknowledging the need for reinterpretation of features within the Jewish tradition, opposes incorporating images from fertility goddesses. She asks, "Do we want to get rid of an old man only to substitute for him a fertility goddess or a nursing mother?" (cited in Fishman 1993, 231).

Jewish thinkers have assiduously pursued the query that Irigaray introduces, about the possible social and symbolic consequences of new female imagery for the divine. We have already explored the deleterious effects that most feminist Jews regard as resulting from an exclusively male language of the divine. In contrast to this, the transformation of Jewish religious language through the inclusion of feminine metaphors and concepts, that is, "the ability to say 'God-She' is the sign," in the words of Rita Gross,

> . . . of Jewish women's authentic entrance in their own right into the ritual covenant community of Israel, as well as the unexpected resource for Jewish self-understanding that comes with that entrance. (1992, 172)

Testimony to the profound way that experiencing God as "She" can transform one's self-understanding and experience of the divine is movingly given by Amy Eilberg. Eilberg writes about the singular event of the birth of her child as bringing her to experience "the feminine God." She writes

> This God fully shared with me the overwhelming joyousness and miraculousness of my daughter's birth, and celebrated my own rebirth, as a mother. . . . This feminine God, after all, was the model of all human acts of creativity and caregiving. . . . I am, I now know, forever transformed by that moment of encounter with the other dimension of God, the feminine God, for whom love and nurturing are of ultimate value. (cited in Fishman 1993, 177)

Lynn Gottlieb reinforces the views already surveyed. She insists that, by developing a feminine language for God, women can "finally picture ourselves created in God's image" (1995, 22). She illustrates this through a personal note, relating that, one time after she began to replace the traditional divine appellation *Adonai* (Lord) with the term *Shekhinah*, a woman came to her and said that only now did she find "herself in the center of theological metaphors," no longer "the other" (1995, 23).

The multifaceted effects on the Jewish symbolic order that follow upon the integration of the feminine into the divine have also been described. Gross's inventory of these effects included the acceptance of humans as embodied and sexual beings; the understanding that there is an order of existence which includes the things that limit, as death and destruction, as well as those that are positive, such as birth and creation; and the rupturing of the familiar feminine stereotype in order to express images of women as powerful, trustworthy, and creative in both the natural and cultural domains (1983, 243–246).

However, there is no clearly corresponding treatment in this literature to Irigaray's probing of the eclipsing of the worship of goddesses by the male divine. There are two reasons for this.

First, there is scepticism about the accuracy of the premise that there was a worship of the Goddess that preceded the introduction of Israelite religion.[19] Judith Plaskow criticizes the view that "the ancient Hebrews invented patriarchy: that before them the goddess reigned in matriarchal glory" (1989, 298; also see Daum).

Second, most feminist Jews share the belief that, at the time of the emergence of Judaism—or at least Israelite religion—the opposition to the worshipping of female, along with male, deities was set as one of the fundamental demarcations of monotheism. Thus, there is no call for the reemergence of a Goddess alongside a male God. Yet, as we have seen, this does not mean that the traditional notions attached to pre-Israelite religion (or so-called "paganism") and to monotheism have been exempted from critique. It has been argued that some of the concepts usually associated with pre-Israelite religion need to be taken back into Judaism—including the positive valuing of the ties to earth, body, and sexuality, and that some of the concepts often found in conjunction with monotheism must be rejected—including exclusion, domination, and dualism.

THE EROTIC, LAW, AND THE DIVINE

In the seventh section of "Questions to Emmanuel Levinas," Irigaray again turns her attention to the portrayal of women as active subjects and amplifies her view of the way in which the prevailing masculine divine inhibits this attribution. She repeats the contention that women, who usually are portrayed as the passive objects of male desire, must be recognized as equal partners "in reciprocity as subjects" (1991, 115), for the full powers of love to be released. However, Irigaray affirms that, only through women's links with a "Mother God"[20] can they find release from "the genealogical economy of patriarchy"—that is, the subjection of women to men's "Father God" (1991, 115). She writes

> Without relationships between both natural and spiritual mothers and daughters, that are relationships between subjects, without cultural recognition of the divinity of this genealogy, how can a woman remain the lover *(l'amante)* of a man who belongs to the line of a Father God. (1991, 115)

Within the juxtapositioning of questions and affirmations that focus on the "genealogical economy," Irigaray touches upon "scenarios of temptation and fall" (1991, 115). She sees Levinas's depiction of women as passive, able only to entice or seduce men, as belonging within such scenarios. For her, this characterization of women as passive constitutes "the Fall," and the way out envisions a world in which a mutually creative sexual love can become both "spiritual and divine" (1991, 115).

We have already explored the effort of feminist Jews to provide vehicles for expressing the value of relations between women, including between mothers and daughters. The treatment of sex and the erotic by these philosophers will be taken up in the next chapter of this book. The category of the Fall does not attain the significance in feminist Jewish reflection that it has for Irigaray. Even while the feminist critique has demanded changes in the association of women, sexuality, and evil, it does not, on the whole, see the story of the Fall as the principle focus of this complex of notions. Still, there are some references to it (Blu Greenberg 1987, 1040–1041).

The understanding of and value attributed to sexual love in Levinas's thought is the starting point for Irigaray's eighth section. She notes that the religious or theological realm seems to provide the platform for Levinas's evaluation of sexual love, and believes that it is, therefore, appropriate to query "how are God's commandments brought to bear in the relationship between lovers?" (1991, 116). Another question follows, but through it, Irigaray seems to point beyond Levinas as well as offer her own position. She writes,

> If this relationship [between lovers] is not divinized, does that not pervert any divinity, any ethics, any society which does not recognize God in carnality? (1991, 116)

Further, she wonders about the understanding of both humans and God, if acts of love, "these gestures of ultimate relations between living humans," are not acknowledged as "a privileged approach to God" (1991, 116).

One of the axiomatic features of feminist literature is the critique of the ways in which sex and sexuality have been understood in Western culture. Feminist Jews have applied this critique to the Jewish tradition as well as sought a new perception of the place of the erotic in understanding our lives as humans and in relationship to God. We have already seen that feminist Jews note a deep ambivalence within the tradition toward sex and sexuality. The association of women with sexuality is an important element in the portrayal of women's otherness within the Jewish tradition. Yet, sex is not regarded as an evil, because it is recognized as a positive and creative part of family life, even an obligation under biblical and Rabbinic law (for pro-creation—*p'u ur'vu* and *onah*—man's conjugal duties to his wife).

Judith Plaskow has made the exploration of the erotic a central focus of her creative theological work. While the treatment of this topic extends to all of her writings, it is most developed in *Standing Again At Sinai*, in the chapter, "Toward a New Theology of Sexuality." She refers very positively to Beverly Harrison's understanding of a new sexual ethics in terms of a "spirituality of sensuality" (1991, 207). Plaskow expresses her ideas through a series of questions:

> The question becomes, then: Can we affirm our sexuality as the gift it is, making it sacred not by cordoning off pieces of it, but by increasing our awareness of the ways in which it connects us to all things? Can we stop evicting our sexuality from the synagogue . . . and instead bring it in, offering it to God in the experience of full spiritual/physical connection? Dare we trust our capacity for joy—knowing it is related to our sexuality—to point the direction toward new and different ways of structuring communal life? (1991, 205)

The new recognition of the creative and positive role of the erotic in human life has many ramifications within feminist Jewish thought. It has been explored in terms of the change in status and images for women within the community, the reevaluation of our lives as embodied, new patterns of personal and communal interaction, and transformations in the understanding of and relationship to the divine. For example, Rita Gross links the refusal to allow sexuality as a metaphor for the divine with the tradition's rejection of feminine metaphors for God, the scorning of human embodiment, and the fear of the natural rhythms of life and death. In her words:

> Once we begin to speak of deity in both female and male terms, sexuality reemerges as a significant metaphor for imaging both intradivine relating and the divine-human relationship. . . . The rejection of sexuality as an acceptable religious symbol is, I believe, closely connected with fear and rejection of our embodied condition, particularly the female body. . . . Rebellion against the closed round of our natural existence and our attempts to identify with a nontemporal principle transcending that closed round necessarily deny any ultimate significance to the primary method of continuity within that round—sexuality. (1983, 245–246)

In particular, Irigaray's question about the act of love as a vehicle for experiencing the divine finds echoes within the Jewish literature. Feminist Jews recognize that the transformation of religious and communal life that they demand requires not only new images of the divine, but an expansion of the ways in which God can be met. Norma Joseph is one writer who has commented on this. Love is a major approach which she articulates for knowing God, in addition to acts of compassion, justice, righteousness, and faithfulness. She speaks of some lines of Hosea as being her "favorite example of the power of human love as a vehicle for *expressing and experiencing* God's love" (1992, 170). Many of the Jewish writers explore the erotic as a religious experience through references to either Jewish mysticism or *The Song of Songs*. We will explore these reflections further.

Irigaray's penultimate section takes up the issue of mysticism. The author notes that mysticism is not an element in Levinas's work, but she raises the question of "is mysticism not linked to the flesh in its sexual dimension?" (1991, 116). Irigaray ponders how God can be understood outside of mysticism. More pertinent to her major argument, she suggests, through another question, that there might be a connection between this deficiency and the devaluation of both "the flesh" and women. When the flesh is cut off from the divine, she queries, is not "the woman reduced to animality, perversity, or a kind of pseudochildhood?" (1991, 116). Are not women deprived of their subjectivity/desire and seen as reproducer, passive object of men's sexuality, or even worse when mystic experience is ignored?

Although present throughout this essay, it is at this juncture that Irigaray most clearly expresses her appreciation for Levinas's concern for the other, as well as her disappointment about the manner in which his intentions fall short.

> He certainly aspires to something else and to the Other (*Autrui*). But the other, woman, he does not notice her existence. And what other or Other (*Autre*) is possible outside of this realization? Except for that or those which are substituted by authority. (1991, 116)

The possible role of mysticism in a renewed Jewish religious and communal life is an important issue within feminist Jewish writings. Some authors believe that Jewish mysticism embodies essential resources, from within the tradition, for these transformations. For example, Judith Plaskow sees in the mystical tradition a "source of some of the more positive strands in Jewish attitudes toward marital sexuality" (1991, 188). She cites a popular thirteenth-century mystical tract, *Iggeret Ha-Kodesh*, which depicts sexual intercourse as an "act of great holiness" and argues for the powerful cosmic effects of this act upon both human and divine realms. Plaskow also refers to contemporary Jewish reliance on the concept of *tikkun*, which is associated with repairing, healing, and redeeming. While *tikkun* is not exclusive to the mystic streams of Judaism, its use today is primarily in connection with these. Plaskow utilizes it as a strand to include social responsibility and ecological concern in her theological work (1991, 220).

There is a pronounced use of mysticism within this literature as a resource for reimagining the divine and for new expressions of religious experience. Susannah Heschel has written that "interest in female images of God is leading to greater exploration of the Jewish mystical tradition, generally neglected or even denigrated by modern Judaism's rationalist bias" (1983, 217). A major area of focus in the quest for new understandings of God has been that aspect of God closest to humans, the *Shekhinah*. This term has had uses in Jewish history outside of mysticism, but, once again, feminist Jews are primarily interested in its utilization within this context.

According to Plaskow, mystics conceived the Shekhinah to be the feminine element of the divine. She finds that, in the medieval development of Jewish mysticism, *Kabbalah*,[21] the Shekhinah was called the "bride" of God and a language was developed to describe the "marriage" of the bride with the more hidden, masculine aspect of God. Although this feminine dimension of the divine never gained the prominence in the liturgy as did the masculine characterization of God, a number of Shekhinah images were developed including "princess, daughter, queen, mother, matron, moon, sea, faith, wisdom, community of Israel, mother Rachel" (Plaskow 1991, 138). Drorah Setel writes of her fascination with the Shekhinah, which she defines as "She-Who-Dwells-Among-Us," as "the one explicitly female metaphor preserved in the tradition" (1986, 117). She notes that this "Divine Presence in relationship . . . is experienced in learning, communal gathering, making love and other relationships of human intimacy and connection" (1986, 117). Judith Plaskow refers to others who have utilized this mystic concept, including Rachel Adler and Penina Villenchik.

However, some Jewish thinkers are more circumspect about the utilization of the Shekhinah. Judith Plaskow recognizes that while there are positive features of this image—its association with divine immanence, and with relationship to God as nonhierarchical, as well as some negative ones—it is still subordinate to the masculine image of God (1991, 139–140). Marcia Falk contends that "far from redeeming women, the image of the Shekhinah has, until now, only supported the male-centred vision" and calls for "autonomous female images," rather than ones that reinforce this subordination or women's otherness (1989, 130).

Lynn Gottlieb is both critical of the way in which the image of the Shekhinah has reinforced negative stereotypes of women, and she believes that it possesses great potential for expressing women's encounter with the divine. She finds that, in Jewish history, the Shekhinah has been "linked to the material world, the negative commandments, stern judgment, the side of evil, passivity, and exile" (1995, 22). It has also served as the repository for "male projections of women as overly emotional, earthbound, and sexually dangerous beings" (1995, 22). Still, Gottlieb writes that, when women begin "interpreting and composing Shekhinah texts for themselves" (1995, 20), "the many images associated with the Shekhinah can become a source for women's encounter with the divine today as well as a bridge to our past" (1995, 22).

Overall, it is fair to conclude that, despite the prominence of mystic concepts and terms in the work of feminist Jews, they still do not afford this feature the importance that Irigaray does in her critique of Levinas and Judaism. In particular, the link between mysticism and a more positive attitude toward what Irigaray described as "the flesh in its sexual dimension" (1991, 116), does not attain the same centrality in feminist Jewish reflection that it does for her.

Irigaray's "last question," concerns the notion of God as lawgiver. She asks us to speculate upon the fact that God is revealed through law and is not available to be seen. In her words, "What radical difference distinguishes the God who makes his presence known in the law from the one who gives himself, through his presence, as nourishment, including nourishment of the senses?" (1991, 116). She adds, is this movement from the God who is seen to one who imposes His will through law tied to the breaking away from "more feminine cultures?" (1991, 117).

Not only God's invisibility, but the whole seeming separation of the sensible from the divine is a matter for Irigaray's exploration (1991, 117). The divine law, neither figuratively written nor immediately legible, represents God's dictates. These are imposed upon the sensible, both man and flesh. Irigaray reflects upon the bifurcation of the divine and sensible, which she regards as analogous to another division, that of hearing and seeing.[22]

As far as I know, Irigaray's query about the lack of the sensible in Jewish images of God is not repeated by feminist Jews. However, her probing of the understanding of God as lawgiver, and of the place of law in Judaism, highlights another significant area of feminist Jewish reflection.

Judith Plaskow is probably the person closest to Irigaray in terms of finding very problematic both this attribute of God and the overall place of the law. While she does not explicitly repudiate the notion of God as Lawgiver, she does consider this as one aspect of God's image as "dominating Other" against which she is rebelling (1991, 128). The related notion of God as partner in covenant is, however, taken up in a very positive way. Plaskow frankly raises but leaves open for the present the "deeper question of the compatibility of feminism and law" (1991, 73). At the very least—and here she stands in the company of many other feminists—she calls for the recognition of the human part in determination of *Halakhah*, its past changes and responsiveness to alterations in the community and outside world, an acknowledgement of Halakhah's prejudiced image of and damaging effects upon women, and, finally, the absolute imperative that women participate in its decision and creation process.

The fact that there has been so much writing by Jewish feminists about the present faults and needed corrections within Halakhah implies that this dimension of Jewish life is not regarded as a dead end by many. One of the more eloquent and passionate appeals is by Cynthia Ozick. Ozick weaves together a critique of the areas in which Halakhah codifies injustice against women with Torah's own fundamental commitment to justice. Thus, she calls, in the name of Torah, for changes to be made.

> The relation of Torah to women calls Torah itself into question. Where is the missing Commandment that sits in judgment on the world? Where is the Commandment that will say, from the beginning of history until now, *Thou shalt not lessen the humanity of women?* (1983, 150)

Blu Greenberg also believes that the "wider principles of Torah" (1981, 45) make it incumbent upon Halakhah to redress its failure to grant full equality to women. She writes, "Halakhah, the Jewish way, cries out for reinterpretation in the light of the new awareness of feminine equality, feminine potential" (1981, 46).

As did so many others, Rachel Adler is not ready to ask women to step outside of the framework of the law nor for Jewish feminists alone, or, on their own, to make changes to Halakhah. After isolating the negative image of women and the types of changes that must occur, she writes that

> The halakhic scholars must examine our problem anew, right now, with open minds and with empathy. They must make it possible for women to claim their share in the Torah and begin to do the things a Jew was created to do. If necessary we must agitate until the scholars are willing to see us as Jewish souls in distress rather than as tools with which men do *mitzvot*. (1983, 17)

Similarly, Rachel Biale argues against abandoning the halakhic framework. Her book, *Women and Jewish Law*, is dedicated to providing women with some knowledge of Halakhah, so that they can begin to understand it, and to have impact upon its future development. As she argues, "only those who explore the historical roots of the Halakhah and master its logic may become part of its future growth" (1984, 266).[23]

Irigaray concludes her "Questions" with another reference to *The Song of Songs*, and, through this, uses the love song to frame her essay. For her it represents the period when feminine cultures were being eclipsed. It evidences the separation between woman and the feminine divine as well as the division between the "nations of women and of men" (1991, 117). However, as we saw earlier, *The Song of Songs* retains vestiges of that other time, when women were full subjects—that is, when they were equal lovers.

> But the Song of Solomon bears the trace of the woman as lover *(l'amante),* for it says, and repeats: "do not awaken (my) love until *she* please." She, the lover, remains a subject in the act of love. (1991, 117)

Do Jewish thinkers also find in *The Song of Songs* the possibility for healing which Irigaray perceives? While they do not see it as alluding to a time before the monopolizing of divine power by the masculine, feminist Jews do utilize it as both model and legitimation for their concerns. *The Song of Songs* demonstrates for them that there are streams within the Jewish tradition that both recognize the spiritual quality of erotic love, and find in this love a metaphor for the passion experienced in the relationship to God. They also praise it for its portrait of mutuality between a woman and a man.

Norma Joseph writes that "the *Song of Songs* illuminates the Lover image with embodied metaphors and erotic passions that redeem human sexuality while giving depth to the exhilarating power of loving God" (1992, 170).

The strength of this text is seen by Judith Plaskow to lie primarily in its power to speak of the importance of sexuality for interpersonal and communal life.

> The *Song of Songs,* because it unifies sensuality, spirituality, and profound mutuality, may offer us the finest Jewish vision of what our sexual relationships can be, a vision that at the same time points to the transformation of our common life. (1991, 206–207)

Marcia Falk presents many elements of the feminist Jewish critique and reconstruction in her book, *Love Lyrics from the Bible: A Translation and Literary Study of The Song of Songs.* While this manuscript is not ostensibly a feminist statement—it was written as a doctoral translation and literary study of a biblical text—Falk's interest and play with the text prefigure some of her later feminist expressions. She emphasizes the mutuality between the lovers in the poems, drawing upon Buber's philosophy of "I and Thou." In taking great care to identify places in which the woman lover is speaker—in fact, to italicize her words—the perspective and desire of the woman is highlighted. Falk critiques earlier interpreters who regarded the author of the whole text as necessarily a man, and who ignored the descriptive and imaginative quality of female desire (1982, 85). She also insists that current stereotypes of male and female love not be forced into this ancient song. At the end, part of the reason that drew her to this text is readily apparent. She writes

> Sexist interpretation of the *wasf* [which in her words, is "a kind of poem or poetic fragment that describes through a series of images parts of the male and female body" (1982, 80)], and of the Song in general, is a striking example of how the text can be distorted by culturally biased reading. To interpret the Song authentically, we must shed the cultural blinders that make what is foreign seem strange. It may even turn out that this ancient text has something new to teach us about how to redeem sexuality and love in our fallen world. (1982, 86–87)

The substantial and passionate exploration of fundamental features of Jewish life and thought, especially the interrogation of monotheism, demonstrates the outstanding quality, as well as the diversity, that typify feminist Jewish thought.[24] It seems to me that no other field of contemporary Jewish philosophy has as much to contribute as does feminist Judaism to the renewal of a vital Jewish thought in our time. The possibilities of such a renewal in terms of Jewish religious language will be pursued in the following chapter, in which a dialogue among Rosenzweig, Levinas, and feminist Jewish thinkers will be crafted.

Finally, I hope that, in bringing to light some of the major persons and features of the feminist Jewish critique, a dialogue among feminists and other Jewish philosophers will be encouraged. As previously indicated, this has not been the case to date as the monologue of male Jewish thinkers among themselves continues unabated. In this, they have failed to respect what Irigaray demands in the name of ethics—that is "to leave the woman her face, and even to assist her to discover it and to keep it" (1991, 114).

CHAPTER 4

Color II—A Dialogue:
Toward an Inclusive Religious Language

This chapter will explore the resources for speaking/writing of God that emerge when the critique and insights of feminist Jewish thinkers are brought together with the themes and lessons of Franz Rosenzweig and Emmanuel Levinas. It is important to emphasize again that feminist Jews are not a monolithic group, neither in terms of the foci of their critique, nor the conclusions drawn.

Judith Plaskow, Lynn Gottlieb, Sylvia Fishman, Rita Gross, and Marcia Falk have been particularly interested in issues concerning religious language and experience, and it is these thinkers who will be among the primary dialogic partners. The specific concentration of this dialogue means that many subjects that were discussed in the preceding chapter will not be explored here. It is certainly worthwhile to pursue other features of what I have earlier identified as the feminist Jewish critique, Irigaray's questions, and also the possibilities of a response from Levinas. However, in the context of this book's program, I will limit the dialogue to questions about religious language and experience.

In the title of this chapter is the word *dialogue*. What justification is there for the use of this term, and for the play with this metaphor? First, I see this discussion as a new and different moment in *my* dialogue with contemporary Jewish thinkers. In the last chapter, I tried to be very circumspect with my comments, listening as attentively and openly as possible to the variety of feminist voices. Now, I would like to explore, with the aid of Rosenzweig's and Levinas's insights, some of the powers and problems that I see in their work.

Second, the metaphor of dialogue alludes to a type of open exchange that would facilitate the emergence and testing of new directions in Jewish religious language. As I envision this exchange among the thinkers to whom I have already referred, there would be moments of agreement, times when one participant or another is brought to expand his or her initial position, and also periods in which a warning, or even a clear "No!," might be voiced. Three dimensions of the feminist Jewish critique will constitute the parameters for this interchange:

1. The necessity for feminine or female pronouns and metaphors in speaking of God,
2. The ways that feminist insights expand religious experience and expression, and
3. The critique of monotheism.

Is such a dialogue possible? The most fruitful type of dialogue in terms of revealing—and even sharpening—significant areas of agreement and disagreement and in terms of fostering the new through a process of challenge and extension requires that some important assumptions and concerns be held in common. Rosenzweig, Levinas, Plaskow, Gottlieb, Fishman, Gross, and Falk do share views about the nature and ramifications of religious language. All of these thinkers affirm the importance of the phenomenon of religious language in the lives of humans. They believe that our speaking about God reflects, as well as directs, the ways in which we understand ourselves and interact with other persons.

As discussed in the first two chapters, Rosenzweig and Levinas find that it is impossible to fully examine the nature of the human or the interhuman without utilizing religious categories and story. Rosenzweig called upon religious *midrash* to explore the powers of speech, especially the ways in which persons are transformed by this divine/human creation. The face-to-face encounter is, for Levinas, one area in which religious story emerges. In addition, there is a carefulness in their use of religious language which supports the underlying assumption about its serious ramifications in terms of the life among humans.

Rosenzweig forcefully protests against speaking about God and humans when the little word *and* is missing. If God were only an aspect of the self, God could not act upon the self nor command it to do something beyond what the self itself desires (1970, 198). Among other consequences, if God were within oneself, what meaning could there be to speak of God's commandment to love the neighbor? Similarly, Levinas repudiates any discourse that links the self and God. In Levinas's words, God can rise to "his supreme and ultimate presence as correlative to the justice rendered unto men" (1988, 78), because God is "the other who turns our nature inside out, who calls our ontological will-to-be into question" (1986, 25).

The feminist argument for the necessity of fostering the use of feminine pronouns and metaphors presupposes that religious language deeply effects our self-understanding and interactions with others. This presupposition is forcefully voiced by Judith Plaskow, when she writes that "the equality of women in the Jewish community requires the radical transformation of our religious language" (1983, 229). Rita Gross also explicitly points to this understanding when she writes that "if it is daring, degrading or alienating to speak of God using female pronouns and imagery, that perhaps indicates something about the way women and the feminine are valued" by the community (1992, 168). More positively, Lynn Gottlieb finds that "When women speak of God She, we can finally picture ourselves created in God's image" (1995, 22). Fishman believes that, by addressing both the male and female "aspects of the Godhead," the Jewish community is able to "reclaim and celebrate what is female as well as male" (1993, 242). Additionally, such efforts as those of Marcia Falk and Lynn Gottlieb to compose new blessings that refer to the divine in terms of the activity of creation and the world of nature are motivated by the concern to feature and celebrate the natural dimension of human existence. In essence, the group of feminist Jews who are reworking Jewish language about God believe that they are rectifying some of the distorted ways in which women see themselves, relate to others, and are seen and treated by men within the Jewish community.

Is such a dialogue necessary? Perhaps an anecdote will illustrate the necessity that I feel, and the naturalness that I find in initiating this dialogue. In the earliest drafts of the second chapter of this book—"Rosenzweig and Levinas: On Anthropomorphism, the Holocaust, and God's Presence"—I consistently used the pronouns "Her" and "She" to refer to God, particularly in terms of Rosenzweig's discussion of biblical anthropomorphisms. I knew, of course, that Rosenzweig did not use female pronouns, but I felt it was natural for me to use them when I tried to illuminate his understanding.

My latest reworking of that chapter, however, incorporates the critique of two of my colleagues—Barbara Galli and Norma Joseph—who objected to the use of female pronouns in the context of explaining the ideas that Rosenzweig presented in his essay. They believed that introducing such metaphors without a thorough justification was too radical of a departure from Rosenzweig's thought. However, I still hold—and will now explain—that as a commentator who seeks to illuminate the meaning of Rosenzweig's text for our time and place—particularly in the context of the recognition of the significant insights of feminist Judaism—there is a fundamental need to use female pronouns and metaphors. I believe that without these changes, the result would be terribly limiting, and, indeed, a betrayal of Rosenzweig's insights.

ROSENZWEIG AND THE USE OF
FEMALE PRONOUNS AND METAPHORS

Rosenzweig acknowledged in his review of the article on anthropomorphism that appeared in the *Encyclopedia Judaica* that theological experiences—that is, the experience of God and its description—must be open to critical analysis and critique. In his words, "the necessity for critical examination and consideration of collected experiences is for theology no different than it is for every other science" (1937, 528). This statement opens the way to raising questions about our current descriptions, and I direct this inquiry to the issue of using feminine or female pronouns and metaphors in describing these experiences. My grounds for deciding upon the authenticity of such usage will be taken from the principles that Rosenzweig enunciates in the essay.

Events of Encounter

First, Rosenzweig defined genuine "theological experiences" as "experiences of meetings," which refer not to the nature of God nor to something about humans, but to "an event between the two" (1937, 528). Thus, the first criterion for the authentic use of feminine pronouns and metaphors is that persons must experience events in which God is met as a female or woman.

The argument of many feminist Jews meets this criterion—that is, feminist Jews and others maintain the necessity for female God-language, because this reflects the way in which God is met or encountered. Marcia Falk's statement contained the core of this argument, when she affirmed, "feminist Jews in our time are taking back the power of naming, addressing divinity in our own voices, using language that reflects *our own experiences*" (1989, 128) [Emphasis added]. Sylvia Fishman's reference to Amy Eilberg's encounter with "the feminine God" who was found "in the midst of caring for my infant daughter" dramatically joins the emergence of this innovative religious language to a specific experience of the divine (1993, 177). The new liturgical creations voice the ways in which groups of women experience the encounter with God. From the *Siddur Nashim*, as Judith Plaskow describes it, we have

> Addressed as the "blessed and glorified, exalted and honored, magnified and praised . . . Holy One, blessed is She," she was also a Mother birthing the world and protecting it with her womb:
>
> Blessed is She who spoke and the world came to be. . . .
> Blessed is She who in the beginning, gave birth. . . .
> Blessed is She whose womb covers the earth.
> Blessed is She whose womb protects all creatures. (1991, 137)

Metaphors are Anthropomorphic

Second, all the metaphors that Rosenzweig explores for discussing the divine side of the meeting are naturally—given that "Anthropomorphism" is the abbreviated title of the article on which he is commenting—personal ones. In his essay, Rosenzweig notes that the Bible states that God "hears, speaks, gets angry, loves" (1937, 528). In chapter two of this book, the absolute necessity of such personal metaphors for Rosenzweig's overall philosophy was treated.

We have seen that there are some differences in how feminist Jewish philosophers and theologians look at the question of personal pronouns and metaphors to refer to God. While this issue will be explored later in this chapter, it is clear that those who speak of "God-She" are using language as anthropomorphic as are those who speak of "God-He."

Follow Biblical Precedents

Third, in his "On Anthropomorphism" essay, Rosenzweig did not propose the use of just any anthropomorphic metaphors for God. The lines by Rosenzweig quoted add a reference to the Bible to the statement that theological experiences are experiences of meetings. He writes that "the Bible offers the best guide precisely to this" (1937, 528). Thus, it is important—if not absolutely necessary—for the Bible is a "guide," that there be biblical support for the use of any pronouns and metaphors that are suggested.

The view that the Bible is a foundation or guide for our understanding of God is not foreign to feminist Jews, including those who speak of God as "She." For many of them, the changes in religious language which they are seeking are not seen as a break, but as an expansion and flowering of what is found within the Jewish tradition and its sacred texts. This position is most forcefully put by Sylvia Fishman, who focuses on the metaphor of God as a mother.

She discusses two biblical precedents for this, both occurring in the book of *Isaiah*. In the first she notes that "Isaiah tells the Jewish people that God undergoes all the stages of gestation in the process of revitalizing the Divine relationship with them" (1993, 178). Isaiah (46:3–4) says, according to Fishman,

> Listen to me, Oh house of Jacob, and all the remnant of the house of Israel, You that are born from within my belly, you that are carried from inside my womb; I remain the same into old age, and even when my hair grows white I will carry you; I created you, and I will bear you, I will carry you, and I will deliver. (1993, 178)

The second example—*Isaiah* 66:12–13—is used during the ritual cel-ebration of the New Moon, and, in it, "God tells the Jewish people that He will provide nurture like that provided by a mother who nurses her baby and caresses it on her knees" (1993, 178–179). Fishman's commentary on these passages underscores the idea that, in utilizing the metaphor of God as a mother, as "She," Jewish women are both connecting with their own expe-riences and maintaining a continuity with the tradition. She finds that

> When Jewish women draw on their own deepest experiences and dis-cover the maternal aspect of Godhead in their prayers . . . they are not making a break with the past. When they lift their voices in prayer, they are building on the legacy of the past. (1993, 179)

Judith Plaskow also refers to the limited references to God as a woman in the text of the Bible (1991, 124). In addition to one of the examples that Fishman discusses, Plaskow mentions the very interesting example of *Isaiah* 42:14, in which Isaiah found that, by speaking of a woman in travail, he could best describe God's pain and Her special way of crying out. The metaphor also gave him the means to describe God's giving comfort in the face of Israel's suffering through an allusion to that unambiguous and incontrovert-ible example of a mother's comfort.

All of Isaiah's examples are reflexive. They do not state, "and She said," but they do legitimize the practice of speaking/writing as if or like God is a mother or a woman giving birth. Of course, because Rosenzweig insisted that the anthropomorphisms are statements about the way in which God is encountered, and not about the essence of God, all metaphors must have this "as if" or "like" character. In the language of the Rabbis, the term for this is *k'b'yakhol* (as it were).[1] God, in these illustrations from Isaiah, may only be like a woman, but, in other places in the Bible, God is also only like a man.

In fact, Rosenzweig uses the metaphor of God as mother in *The Star*. The metaphor occurs in the context of his description of the way that the soul, transformed by God, endures in God's love. He writes that "The soul is at peace in the love of God, like a child in the arms of its mother" (1972, 171). There is an obvious similarity between the language that Rosenzweig uses and the statements by the prophet Isaiah. Neither the metaphor nor the simi-larity to Isaiah is surprising, because the prophet is one of the most important traditional sources that Rosenzweig uses in *The Star*. Although Rosenzweig does not follow the metaphor with the pronoun of "She" for God, the free-dom he felt to play with the image of God as mother is impressive in the context of the present lines of our inquiry.

Guard Against a Reification of Images of God

Fourth, at the end of his review of the *Encyclopedia Judaica* article, Rosenzweig spoke of the protection from polytheism that biblical anthropomorphisms afford. He contended that polytheism results from the "consolidation of a genuine present revelation of the real God to a lasting image of God" through "resisting the ever-new will of God's revelation" (1937, 533). The multiplicity of the anthropomorphisms thus guard against a reification of images of God that would prevent God from being encountered in new ways, according to God's will.

This insight finds support in the discussions of feminist Jewish thinkers who criticize the Jewish tradition's reliance on only one set of images—in this case male images—as always appropriate to express the divine/human encounter. Rita Gross, for example, almost repeats Rosenzweig's insight about polytheism as the reification of a set of images. She identifies as "unrealistic, self-aggrandizing, and fundamentally idolatrous" the claim that only male images correspond to the true reality of the divine (1983, 235).

Ensure God Can Be Met

Fifth, part of the significance of the biblical anthropomorphisms is that their variety and multiplicity act as a pledge to guarantee that God will always be able to find a path to us. Rosenzweig put this idea in another way when he wrote that the Bible affords

> . . . a boundless trust in His unboundable powers, always, and every moment, to meet our and all creation's momentary bodiliness and spirituality, bodily and spiritually, in the body and in the soul. (1937, 530)

Thus, the anthropomorphisms in the Bible teach us to trust that there is no dimension of our lives into which God cannot penetrate.

The addition of the rich vocabulary of female metaphors to current God/language tremendously extends the possibilities of seeing, finding, hearing, and experiencing God in our everyday lives. This is one of the main reasons that these new metaphors have been offered. As Plaskow wrote, "the overwhelming majority of Jewish feminists . . . are trying to enrich the range of metaphors Jews use in talking about God" (1991, 150). Falk directly links the requirement for the variety of images to the multidimensionality and variety of our experiences. She urges Jews to create a *"multiplicity of images,* as many as are needed to express and reflect the diversity of our individual lives" (1989, 129).

It is particularly this feature of Rosenzweig's understanding of Jewish religious language—that the multiplicity of images provides a model for allowing the ever-new will of God to reach us in ever-new ways—that points beyond itself to the necessity of being augmented by feminist insights. The addition of female pronouns and metaphors expands the possibilities of our religious lives. The rejection of them, on the other hand, would curtail, even decimate, the ways in which God can be, in Rosenzweig's understanding, met.

In Rosenzweig's statement that the biblical anthropomorphisms provide us with a "boundless trust in His unboundable powers" to meet us, we confront an invaluable insight that stands in diametrical opposition—for us who read it today—to its form. However, I am not suggesting a critique of Rosenzweig himself. He lived, as we all do, within the particular horizons of his time and place. What I am suggesting is that for us reading his work today, within the context of our particular time and place, a contradiction appears.

The vivid anthropomorphisms are the guarantee that God is able to meet us at any time and in any way that is required. Their boldness—which is an affront to many who believe that God can only be discussed abstractly or in terms of the *via negativa*—is important to Rosenzweig precisely for this reason. Yet, in the face of this, their gift, stands the single pronoun, "His." As such, the "His" limits. It tells us, and reminds us, of ways in which God cannot be met, as well as of aspects of our lives that are bereft of the divine. For it is only as both "His" and "Her" unboundable powers that we, today, can understand that God is fully able to meet us.

If God cannot be "She," then we no longer trust that some dimensions of our lives that beg for divine contact—dimensions alluded to by Isaiah when he spoke of Her cry for us and our being comforted by Her—are open to God's address. Thus, it is a betrayal of Rosenzweig's most fundamental understanding of the nature and powers of Jewish religious language to limit our pronouns and metaphors to "He."

In conclusion, the use of feminine pronouns and metaphors by feminist Jews is consistent with the principles concerning religious language that Rosenzweig enunciates in his review article. They refer to events of encounter and not to God Himself or Herself. They are personal, and follow biblical precedents. They guard against the reification of a single set of images of God, and they help to ensure that God can be met in ever new ways.

LEVINAS AND THE RAMIFICATIONS OF UTILIZING EXCLUSIVELY MALE GOD/LANGUAGE

The first part of this dialogue, concerning female pronouns and metaphors, juxtaposed Rosenzweig's understanding of theological experience with some of the insights of feminist Jews. The second stage of this dialogue will focus on the ramifications or consequences to individual and communal Jewish life that follow upon the exclusive use of male pronouns and metaphors for God.

As I have indicated earlier, both Rosenzweig and Levinas recognize that religious conceptions and language deeply influence the ways that we understand ourselves and live with others. However, the connection between religious language and the other is most clearly manifest in Levinas's work, especially as the underlying assumption for his view that the understanding of God found in Torah and Talmud opens us to the vulnerability of the other, or, alternately, helps us to resist every temptation to persecute or marginalize other persons. In commenting on *Isaiah* 58, Levinas writes

> we are told . . . that the religious is at its zenith in the ethical movement toward the other man; that the very proximity of God is inseparable from the ethical transformation of the social, and—notably and more specifically—that it coincides with the disappearance of servitude and domination in the very structure of the social. (1994, 5)

Levinas contends that, at the heart of Western thought, is a totalizing or self-aggrandizing impulse which has legitimated centuries of violence turned toward the other. He believes that religious conceptions and language have often been marshalled to support this history of oppression. Although he does not take up the arguments offered in the feminist critique of male God/language,[2] I see their ideas as, not only in full harmony with the deepest wellsprings of his thought, but as required for the sake of its success.

Levinas's discussion of religious language includes, as one of its primary concerns, a critique of the way in which God can be allied with oneself and with the interests of those who hold power—that is, with the official self. He passionately protests against any type of thematizing of God (1985, 106; 1989, 168). God is the Infinite and the transcendent, not a subject to be incorporated into and manipulated by philosophical systems nor the rhetoric of politics. Levinas allows the word *God* to arise only in terms of the ethical relation with another person, and the prophetic relation that overturns the self's primacy and authority in order to elicit responsibility for the other. As he writes

> To my mind the Infinite comes in the signifyingness of the face. The face signifies the Infinite. It never appears as a theme, but in this ethical signifyingness; that is, in the fact that the more I am just the more I am responsible. (1985, 105)

> Ethics is an optics of the Divine. Henceforth, no relation with God is direct or immediate. The Divine can be manifested only through my neighbour. (1990, 159)

Feminist Jewish thinkers have vigorously argued that the exclusive use of male pronouns and metaphors for God reinforces the dominance of one group over another, as well as preventing a true ethical relation among persons. The correspondence between language and communal life is summarized in Gross's reflection, introduced once before in this dialogue, that "if it is daring, degrading or alienating to speak of God using female pronouns and imagery, that perhaps indicates something about the way women and the feminine are valued" by the community (1992, 168). Plaskow reinforces this point.

> Jewish feminists have pointed out that the overwhelming preponderance of male images for God in biblical and rabbinic texts and in the traditional liturgy correlates with the normative status of maleness. Since God in the fullness of God's reality is ultimately unknowable, our images tell us more about our social arrangements—in this case the subordinate status of women—than they do about God. (1994, 69)

Male pronouns and metaphors attributed to God do not put men under the transcendent judgment of God, but uphold men in their own judgment. Feminist Jewish thinkers recognize that the male God is the apotheosis of men, the becoming infinite of the male self. Rita Gross terms this relationship "self-aggrandizing" (1983, 235). The connection between male images of God and male power is made very clear by Judith Plaskow. She has written that

> ... the images we use to describe God, the qualities we attribute to God, draw on male pronouns and experience and convey a sense of power and authority that is clearly male. (1991, 6–7)

When God is exclusively portrayed as a male, He is put into the company of males, and stands against those who are female. As we saw earlier in chapter 3, Judith Plaskow is fond of referring to the biblical statement in the book of *Exodus* (19:15), "do not go near a woman" (1991, 25). This statement is made by Moses, when he is giving instructions for the people of Israel in preparation for them to hear God at Mt. Sinai. The statement reveals the underlying symbolic identification of men and God, for, although Moses is speaking to "the people [of Israel]" it is clear that only men are being addressed. This exhortation both captures and sanctifies the notion that women must be excluded from the community when it meets its God. If noticed at all, women seem to stand as obstacles in the effort of men to experience Him.

Feminist Jews have demonstrated that the ethical force of Judaism's understanding of God actually requires the remedy of female pronouns and metaphors for God. This change in religious language will force men to see God, not just in their own countenances, but in relation to the countenances of those who stand as their neighbors and others—that is, women. Only when the Jewish community universally acknowledges that God can also be experienced as "She," will the prohibition of not going near a woman when encountering God be lifted.

Thus, the dialogue with feminist Jews, and the introduction of some of their insights about male imagery, is a necessity for Levinas's work. They have shown that the dominance of male imagery in the Jewish tradition subverts the central claims which Levinas makes for the radical ethical meaning of Judaism's understanding of God. When images for God are exclusively male, the relationship between men and God is no longer indirect, and the face of the other (woman) does not manifest the presence of God but prevents access to that presence. Listening to the views of feminist Jews brings Levinas closer to his goal of showing how the voice of God stands in judgment of the self, and in company with the poor, the widow, the orphan, and the stranger.

EXPANDING RELIGIOUS EXPERIENCE AND EXPRESSION: THE BODY AND THE NATURAL WORLD

The next stage in the dialogue between Rosenzweig, Levinas, and feminist Jews will focus on two issues that the latter raise in their attempt to expand the possibilities of contemporary Jewish religious experience and expression. They eloquently describe the ways in which our understanding and relationship to God can be affected by exploring the body and the natural world, sexuality, and erotic love. There will be a more dialogic tone to the exchange between thinkers in terms of these issues. We will again find areas in which feminist Jews critique and supplement important themes in the work of Rosenzweig and Levinas. However, we will also detail moments when conflict arises, and no clear resolution is forthcoming. In this, as in real dialogue, success is not measured only in terms of agreement, but also in terms of the clarification of significant divergent experiences, understandings, and commitments. Both results—agreement and disagreement—provide meaningful resources for contemporary Jewish religious language.

A prominent theme in feminist Jewish reflection is the need to acknowledge our bond to the natural world, and our embodied condition, which represents the essence of that bond. Much of the work of Judith Plaskow discusses the importance of recognizing that nature is the ground of human life. She speaks of humans as "participants in a broad and complex web of life all of which is sacred" (1991, 145). Further, the "fear and rejection of our embodied condition, particularly the female body" (1983, 245) as expressed in the Jewish tradition is a crucial focus in Rita Gross's thought. She, in particular, sees the devaluation of the body as a symptom of a wider refusal to acknowledge ourselves as part of the natural realm of existence, which includes both birth and death.

Significant strands of this Jewish feminist philosophical and cultural critique are shared by Rosenzweig and Levinas. For example, the very first words of *The Star*—"Concerning Death"—express Rosenzweig's passionate as well as systematic repudiation of modern philosophy's mind/body dualism with its attendant dismissal of the body. Rosenzweig writes

> All that is mortal lives in this fear of death . . . But philosophy denies these fears of the earth . . . Why should philosophy be concerned if the fear of death knows nothing of such a dichotomy between body and soul, if it roars Me! Me! Me!, if it wants nothing to do with relegating fear onto a mere "body?" (1972, 3)

Further, the important role that the category of creation (and redemption—which is between humans and the world) plays in this work reaffirms the human tie to the natural universe. This is an accurate statement, although it must also be said that Rosenzweig has a deeper interest in the transcendent dimension of human existence, first introduced by the category of revelation.

Levinas's phenomenological method depends on the acknowledgement and analysis of humans as embodied. The corporeality of the self and the other, and the different features of sensibility are prominent in his work. In *Otherwise Than Being*, one finds that

> It is because subjectivity is sensibility—an exposure to others, a vulnerability and a responsibility in the proximity of the other . . . that a subject is of flesh and blood, a man that is hungry and eats, entrails in a skin, and thus capable of giving the bread out of his mouth, or giving his skin. (1981, 77)

However, Levinas's work does not focus on the relation to the natural world. The ethical relationship, that is, the infinite responsibility to the other, completely overwhelms an interest in the tie between humans and the natural universe.

It is the role of the body and the natural world as part of religious experience and expression that is important in the context of this book. In what ways do the subjects of our study agree and supplement each other, and to what extent is there conflict and critique? Feminist Jewish philosophers have seen the body and the bond with the natural universe as pregnant with literal and symbolic significance for religious experience. The new *brachot* composed by Marcia Falk are the most vivid examples of the omnipresent effort to connect "the divine with the realms of nature and humanity" (1989, 135). Some of the blessings give religious recognition and expression to life-cycle events of women. Falk, along with Lynn Gottlieb (1995, 135–143) and others, believe that the celebration of the body and nature through the community's religious language furthers the recognition of the place of the human within the cycles of natural existence.

Is our relationship to the natural world an important element in discussions of religious life by Rosenzweig and Levinas? For Rosenzweig, as indicated earlier, creation is a fundamental category. He speaks of it as the first revelation and as the basis for all individual religious experience (1972, 139). However, its religious meaning is eclipsed by the category of revelation, or, as he puts it in *The Star*, "We put it [the concept of creation] in the context of revelation" (1972, 139). I would suggest that the emphasis on creation as one dimension of our religious experience as long as it does not over-shadow the dynamics of revelation—does not stand as a threat to Rosenzweig's overall concerns. Consequently, there does not seem to be a necessary conflict between feminist concerns and Rosenzweig's views, although it also is not clear to what degree they usefully supplement each other.

The link of humans to the natural world is not a prominent feature in Levinas's oeuvre. Again, in fact, I believe it would stand as an obstacle to the fundamental interests of his work. The transcendence of the other, to the self and everything else, along with the radical ethical orientation of the relation to the other, cannot be furthered by the language of humans as part of nature.

Is our embodied condition important in Rosenzweig's and Levinas's discussions of our religious lives? At least it can be said that they do not insist that religious experience is somehow disembodied. For example, as examined in chapter 1 they both speak about the human face as a reflection of divine reality and presence. In *The Star,* the face stands at the climax of the discussion of Rosenzweig's understanding of the ways in which God, humans, and the world interact. In living with other persons, and in looking into the face of the other, we are reminded that we all also live before the countenance of the divine (1972, 423). Of course, the face is a central theme for Levinas in his discussions of the religious life. At times, the face of the other in his writing points to the presence of God, and, at other times, it evokes our action, which is, in itself, testimony to the divine presence.

The interests of Rosenzweig and Levinas seem to diverge in terms of going further to include or celebrate the body as a fundamental feature of religious life and experience. In Rosenzweig's discussion of biblical anthropomorphisms he praises them for ensuring us that God can be present in all areas of our life, including our bodily reality. He is making the point, I believe, that we are creatures of bodies, and that, for God to be present to us, this fact of our reality must be remembered. Once again I will refer to his statement:

God is capable of what he wills (thus even of meeting the creature from time to time in fully bodily and spiritual reality) and that the creature is capable of what he should be (thus even of fully understanding and recognizing God's self-embodying or self-spiritualization turning toward him from time to time). (1937, 532)

In light of this, I believe that Rosenzweig would be open to the efforts of feminist Jews to include our bodily reality as an integral element in religious experience. It might even be legitimate to say that those efforts would be appreciated by Rosenzweig, for they would provide more force to his view that God can be present in all the possible ways of which we have need.

Similar conclusions cannot be drawn in terms of possible appreciation by Levinas of feminist Jewish struggles to speak of the body as an indispensable element in religious experience. For Levinas, even the face is more symbol than reality in experiencing the presence of God. The face is important as it evokes in us consciousness of the categorical command which comes from God. And what does Levinas say about the physical reality of the face itself? "The best way of encountering the Other is not even to notice the color of his eyes!" (1985, 85).

In summation, there is much divergence among the voices to which we are attending in terms of assessing the relevance for contemporary religious experience of the dual recognition of humans as creatures of nature and of our embodied condition. Many feminist Jews regard these ideas as extremely important, both from the point of view of the critique of the way women are understood within Judaism, and in reference to new possibilities of religious experience. Rosenzweig and Levinas value these possible areas of religious experience differently than do feminist Jews, because of the prominence that the ethical/religious relationship to the other has in their thought. For example, unlike other modern Jewish philosophers—such as Martin Buber and Abraham Heschel—they do not regard apprehension of the natural universe as a significant vehicle for religious experience.[3] As is consistently argued in this book, the principal transforming encounter, which introduces the presence of the divine and gives voice to religious language, is the encounter between persons.

Still, we have noted significant differences in the possible responses of Rosenzweig and Levinas. The former strongly values the category of creation and seems open to introducing the fact of our embodiment into religious language and experience. The category of creation is not as important to Levinas, although the view that all persons are creatures of the divine is an element in his thought. Creatureliness has only ethical import for him.[4] Further, the recognition of our embodiment does not have any role to play in his understanding of our experience of the divine, except to the extent that one is responsible for the other's bodily or material needs.[5]

SEXUALITY AND EROTIC LOVE

Two features of human experience that many feminist Jews believe must be given more attention by philosophers and theologians are sexuality and erotic love. They have uncovered a variety of attitudes toward these in the Jewish tradition. On the one hand, the association of women with sexuality is part of the formula that ends by labeling women as "other"—in this case, limiting or excluding their participation in significant dimensions of Jewish life. Judith Plaskow found that women's "gait, their voices, their natural beauty are all regarded as snares and temptations and subjected to elaborate precautions" (1991, 191). Sylvia Fishman concluded that "Thus, women's subordinate and limited position in Jewish life was linked to their sexuality and to their perceived sexual nature" (1993, 102). On the other hand, Jewish law establishes the positive value of sexual love for its procreative result as well as in-itself (Fishman 1993, 98–99). Attempting to move beyond this ambivalence, feminist Jews have reminded us of the ways in which the erotic brings us in touch with our deepest passions and pleasures, our bodies, the body and spirit of others, and the possibilities of creating another.

Providing a place for the erotic in a philosophical anthropology is not foreign to the works of Rosenzweig and Levinas. For Rosenzweig, this is best illustrated by his detailed reference to the biblical *The Song of Songs*, which occurs at the center of the most important section in *The Star*. As have many Jewish and Christian thinkers, Rosenzweig uses *The Song of Songs* to characterize the relationship between God and the soul. However, the exchange between lovers in the poem is not taken by him as a simple religious allegory. Rather, the reality and sensuality of the love between the lovers plays a significant role in his understanding of the multidimensionality of the human. As he wrote

> Love simply cannot be "purely human." It must speak, for there is simply no self-expression other than the speech of life. And by speaking, love already becomes superhuman, for the sensuality of the word is brimful with its divine supersense. Like speech itself, love is sensual/supersensual. (1972, 201)

The treatment of the caress in the chapter "Phenomenology of Eros" in *Totality and Infinity* exemplifies Levinas's deep regard for the sensual in his discussion of human nature. The analysis of such features as sensuality, desire, and voluptuosity is used by Levinas to indicate that the erotic is a primary dimension of the interhuman. However, he finds that the erotic also points beyond itself to something else. Characteristic of this treatment is his statement:

I love fully only if the Other loves me, not because I need the recognition of the Other, but because my voluptuosity delights in his voluptuosity, and because this unparalleled conjuncture of identification, in this *trans-substantiation*, the same and the other are not united but precisely—beyond every possible project, beyond every meaningful and intelligent power—engender the child. (1988, 266)

In all, sensuality and sexuality are central to Levinas's understanding of persons. He writes, emphasizing that human sexuality demonstrates the essential need that each of us has for another—the other, "sexuality in us is neither knowledge nor power, but the very plurality of our existence" (1988, 277).

Once more, it is both more intriguing and germane to this dialogue to pose the question of whether these thinkers regard, or might possibly consider, sexual love as an appropriate vehicle for religious experience and understanding. If sensuality and sexual love are taken as important matters for a philosophic anthropology, it would not be surprising that religious thinkers declare the relevance of erotic love for the relationship with God. Certainly, feminist Jews—such as Judith Plaskow and Rita Gross—are committed to portraying erotic love as a revered approach to the divine. Plaskow writes of offering our sexuality "to God in the experience of full spiritual/physical connection" (1991, 205), and Gross tells of bringing sexuality to the surface "as a significant metaphor for imaging . . . the divine-human relationship" (1983, 245). Additionally, Norma Joseph wrote of "the power of human love as a vehicle for *expressing and experiencing* God's love" (1992, 170).

In his use of *The Song of Songs* to speak of the interaction of God and soul, Rosenzweig seems to open the way to understanding the erotic as a means for religious encounter. He writes

Thus it is not enough that God's relationship to man is explained by the simile of the lover and the beloved. God's word must contain the relationship of lover to beloved, the significant, that is, without any pointing to the significate. . . . Man loves because God loves and as God loves. (1972, 199)

While these lines are not absolutely clear, it appears that Rosenzweig regards the love between persons as resulting from and mirroring the love between God and humans. Following this, it should be possible to affirm that, in loving the other—and it is precisely that sensual love of *The Song of Songs* which is being explored by him, one learns about (and experiences?) the love of God. At any rate, it is incontestable that the erotic is not being rejected by Rosenzweig as a vehicle for religious experience.

This issue can be examined from a more general point of view in terms of Rosenzweig's overall philosophical system. Rosenzweig believes that full human life is blocked off within the person whose only relationship to God is as creature to Creator. Revelation, God's second contact with humans, opens persons up to a life of speech and love in the world. Rosenzweig also asserts that God's revelation to the individual can arise or often arises through the love of the neighbor. The person who is remade by God's love is commanded to turn to others, through the love of neighbor, in order to extend this divine love. The process of extension is termed by Rosenzweig as redemption, and as it appears in *The Star*,

> Thus redemption originates with God and man knows neither the day nor the hour. He only knows that he is to love, and to love always the nighest and the neighbor. (1972, 241)

For Rosenzweig, the interhuman is a place where divine love appears. It appears, precisely, through the love of the neighbor. Rosenzweig sees this loving in terms of the commandment to love the neighbor, which does not immediately bring to mind erotic love. Still, if one takes even the most skeptical or narrow reading of his lines about human and divine love that were written as commentary to *The Song of Songs*, the view that physical love and intimacy between persons could be regarded as a vehicle for religious experience appears to be in harmony with the character of his thought. While this might again be a case in which insights from feminist Jews would go beyond Rosenzweig's specific reflections, I believe that it is equally true that this extension is not a matter of distortion but of fulfilment.

Levinas offers an important protest against viewing the erotic as a vehicle for relationship to God. While he does insist that God be linked with the relationship to the other, for him this is an exclusively ethical relation. God enters as the person finds the self overturned and taken hostage by the moral imperatives that are placed upon the self. He writes

> The uniqueness of the chosen or required one, who is not a chooser, is a passivity not being converted into spontaneity. This uniqueness not assumed, not subsumed, is traumatic; it is an election in persecution. (1981, 56)

This description of the ethical relationship between persons, which includes the notion or metaphor of persecution, is much different from what we are accustomed to in identifying the erotic relation. Mutuality, not one-way moral imperatives, is the hallmark of erotic love. With sexual intimacy the self is given pleasure and support by the other. In erotic love the boundary between the other and self, even the integrity of the other might be overcome. In addition, it is not disparaging, but accurate to say that there is always some egoism in erotic love. In Levinas's words, "love does not transcend unequivocably [sic]—it is complacent, it is pleasure and dual egoism" (1988, 266). In all, Levinas sees a fundamental tension between eros and ethics.[6]

There is a final feature of this discussion about expanding religious language and experience that should be addressed. In quoting Rita Gross a few pages earlier, I left out a segment of her statement about the ways in which sexuality can be used as a metaphor within our religious language. She held that, "once we begin to speak of deity in both female and male terms, sexuality reemerges as a significant metaphor for imaging both *intradivine relating* and the divine/human relationship" (1983, 245); [Emphasis added]. She suggests that the "intradivine" might provide another object of reflection that is available when sexuality is introduced into our religious imaging and experience. This idea is not, in fact, without precedent in the history of Judaism. It can be found in some Kabbalistic literature.[7]

However, I find that both Rosenzweig and Levinas would strongly challenge this new direction, or the "intradivine." For both of them, religious language explores the encounter with the divine, and not the nature of the divine itself. Rosenzweig's essay most vehemently makes this point. He affirmed that the biblical anthropomorphisms were "assertions about meetings between God and man," and that "God is never described" (1937, 528). Levinas's insistence that the ultimate meaning of religious language points to the ethical realm dispels any illusion that we can speak of the divine itself. He wrote "It is our relations with men . . . that give to theological concepts the sole signification they admit of" (1988, 79).

Actually, the notion that feminine metaphors could be useful to speak of the "intradivine" is not repeated by other feminist Jews, except in the context of allusions to the Kabbalah. Judith Plaskow states a view that appears very often, when she writes that "God in the fullness of God's reality is ultimately unknowable" (1994, 69). Even Gross at other times emphasizes the inability of religious language to directly describe the Ultimate (1983, 235).

I believe that the failure of other thinkers to follow Gross's suggestion—as well as the objections voiced by Rosenzweig and Levinas—stem from the understanding that, to speak of "intradivine relating," extends language beyond what it can legitimately address, and also subverts the link between our language about God and our relations to others.

In summation, the dialogue among Plaskow, Gross, Gottlieb, Fishman, Falk, Rosenzweig, and Levinas has issued in areas of agreement and disagreement. There appears to be a fundamental agreement about the necessity of female pronouns and metaphors for speaking of God. Jewish feminists have arrived at this conclusion because of their understanding that this change will both incorporate women's religious experience into the tradition and result in women being fully seen as Jews by the community. Rosenzweig's agreement rests on his concern to expand Jewish religious experience, and on his conviction that God's voice must continue to find us in all the dimensions of our lives. In our dialogue, Levinas's acceptance of this position is based upon his recognition of the social and ethical consequences of religious language, and his commitment to welcoming and giving to the "other."

We have heard divergent voices in terms of the issue of the role of nature, the body, and erotic love in religious understanding and expression. Many of the feminist Jews whom we have studied affirm all of these possible areas of religious experience. They value these as efficacious in overcoming dualisms that they see pervading Jewish life, and in sanctifying one of the most powerful areas of human relationships. We have found that, in the main, Rosenzweig supports these efforts. In particular, the possibility that erotic love might provide a vehicle for religious understanding, and experience seems to extend some of his own, perhaps somewhat latent, views. Levinas's protest stems from his passionate commitment to ensuring that the ethical relations between persons is not subverted.

The major differences that we have seen about religious language arise from important and compelling insights. On the one hand, there are the reflections about the divine dimension of our most intimate ways of relating with others. On the other hand, there is Levinas's insistence that our religious experience and expression must never dilute the integrity and transcendence of the other, the moral responsibility we have for others, and the barrier that must remain in separating self from God. I hope that some of the powers and limits of both of these positions have been illuminated.

THE CRITIQUE OF MONOTHEISM

The next stage in this dialogue will focus on the challenging and creative critique of monotheism that is contained in the writings of some feminist Jews. Feminist Jewish topi that I have aligned in terms of this issue are: the possibility of cleansing monotheism of the components of exclusion, domination, and dualism; the value of transcendence, God as person, and the Goddess; and the roles of mysticism and Jewish law.

In progressing through the various elements in this critique, some of the most important features of Jewish religious experience and language will be

examined. Feminist Jews have analyzed Jewish monotheism, as if to ask—
and it is Luce Irigaray's question—whether it is a revolutionary, liberating,
religious orientation, or an enslaving religious ideology, the primary value of
which is supporting male power and interests. There can be no more fundamental and significant turn in our dialogue about contemporary religious
language than the pursuit of this challenge. However, it is necessary to reit-
erate the observation that feminist Jews present a diversity of views, a variety
of voices. This is especially evident when the topic of the critique of monotheism is being examined.

One of the features of Jewish monotheism that is criticized is that of
exclusion. Some feminist Jews have argued that the traditional image of God
wrongly excludes some persons—that is, women—and their experiences from
the circle of the sacred by legitimatizing only male language and experience.
Judith Plaskow enunciates this view.

> Our language about divinity is first of all male language; it is selective
> and partial. . . . The images we use to describe God, the qualities we
> attribute to God, draw on male pronouns and experience and convey a
> sense of power and authority that is clearly male. (1991, 6–7)

Feminist Jewish critics believe that this feature of exclusion in Jewish
monotheism can be corrected. The principle point is incisively formulated by
Marcia Falk, who writes

> It would seem . . . that the authentic expression of an authentic mono-
> theism is not a singularity of image but an embracing *unity* of a *mul-
> tiplicity of images*, as many as are needed to express and reflect the
> diversity of our individual lives. (1989, 129)

It is important to record the manner in which the argument for correct-
ing the exclusion of persons and experiences is made. Marcia Falk holds that
"monotheism means that, *with all our differences*, I am more like you than
I am unlike you," and that "If we are all created in the image of divinity, the
images with which we point toward divinity must reflect us all" (1989, 129).
Rita Gross takes a different direction, insisting that the "inherent limitations
of any theological or religious language" require us to reject any single or
particular set of (male) images as mirroring the true reality of the divine
(1983, 235).

I believe that Rosenzweig's attitude toward the issue of exclusion would
mirror his projected position concerning female pronouns and metaphors.
Whether Rosenzweig would sympathize today with the view that traditional
Jewish religious language has excluded women and women's experiences, he

would still value the remedy that is offered. He appreciated the wide range of anthropomorphic metaphors in the Bible—which include female metaphors unnoted by him—because the very fact of their multiplicity demonstrates all the ways in which God can be met and experienced. He could easily agree with the conclusion of Falk, that the multiplicity of images deepens the possibilities of our religious experience and does not threaten monotheism. Monotheism means, in Falk's terms, that there is a unity underlying the multiplicity. I find that Rosenzweig would fully concur with this view.

However, both Rosenzweig, and Levinas would probably contest the rationales that are sometimes used to support the argument for expanding the repertoire of images. I do not believe that the discussion of the limitations of language that is provided by Gross would appeal at all to Rosenzweig. Remember that he dismisses arguments about theological experience that rely on suppositions about the "inadequacy of language" and the "limitation of thought" in his article on anthropomorphism (1937, 528). He ardently approves of the multiplicity of biblical images which reflect the wide panorama of experiences, and, I would guess, of persons having those experiences. Rosenzweig emphasizes that each of the anthropomorphisms has the power to illuminate another of the avenues that God has chosen to interact with us. Consequently, in a dialogue with feminist Jews, Rosenzweig might well propose that our understanding of monotheism is furthered through an appreciation of the divine/human powers that flourish in words, rather than by a notion of the limits of language.

Another feature of Marcia Falk's line of reasoning for the multiplicity of images of the divine should be addressed. She argues that "the images with which we point toward divinity must reflect us all" (1989, 129). Actually, there are a number of feminist Jews who promote the use of feminine metaphors for God because they believe that these will demonstrate that women also participate in the divine reality. Lynn Gottlieb, for example, finds that by drawing upon the language of the *Shekhinah*, women will create a path that enhances the "ability to see God in ourselves" (1995, 26).

Levinas might find an unintentional impetus toward exactly what Gross labels as "unrealistic, self-aggrandizing, and fundamentally idolatrous" (1983, 235) in reflections already discussed that support creating images of divinity reflecting "us all" and finding a language that facilitates seeing "God in ourselves." Levinas's work inculcates a sensitivity to the idea that divinity should not reflect me or us. He would probably also dispute the idea that religious language should, as Falk puts it, "express and reflect the diversity of our individual lives" (1989, 129), because it is only the ethical relation with the other that he saw as germane to our religious experience. In all, Levinas constantly argues that the real protection against idolatry and self-aggrandizement is the bond between the other/the neighbor and God. When the language of "God reflecting us" is allowed, then the way is paved for the apotheosis of that special, inescapable "us," as in those who hold power in the community or society.

I could imagine Levinas contending that, by featuring, in the context of religious life and language, what we share or what is the same between us, we unintentionally align ourselves with the divine, and separate off those who might be different and outside. Falk does underscore that "we are all created in the image of divinity" (1989, 129), but I think that here Levinas might find that the language of "share" and "same" threatens the fullness of the "all." Such "alls" are always very fragile!

A second aspect of Jewish monotheism—which some feminist critics identify—is the language of domination and dualism. They have argued that attributes such as lordship and kingship might condone the domination of some individuals and groups over others, including men over women and Jews over non-Jews. The discussion of the relationship between monotheism and dualism is similar. When God is seen as dominating, and, at the same time, portrayed as having male attributes, then there is a sacred dualism between those who stand on the side of the holy and those who stand outside.

Neither Rosenzweig nor Levinas would appear to be disturbed by metaphors of lordship and kingship. For Rosenzweig these metaphors reflect not divine attributes, about which we can know nothing, but the manner in which God is met. Thus, he surely would argue that there are times when God is encountered, or called upon, as lord or king, and that Jews should utilize the resources provided by the Bible to express such experiences. He might add, however, that the metaphors of kingship and lordship do not stand alone, but are part of the vast array of metaphors that reflect the diverse moments in our dialogue with God. When the issue of transcendence is taken up, I will explore what I see as Levinas's position in terms of these metaphors.

Both Rosenzweig and Levinas would criticize the dualism that sometimes appears within Jewish God/language, and they would regard its purging as a significant step. I believe that Rosenzweig would appreciate the argument that, by allowing only male images of the divine, the inferior image and social position of women is sanctified. As I said before, he was very sensitive to the way in which God/language impacts our everyday self-understanding and action. Levinas's agreement with this critique would arise from his concern for the terrible consequences of any identification of God with the self or the same—that is, with those who hold power.

One of the paramount issues concerning monotheism that feminist Jews raise—that of transcendence—is of the utmost consequence for Jewish religious life. They have endeavored to reformulate traditional language in order to both reflect and fashion their religious experiences by portraying God, as in Marcia Falk's terms, not just as a force out there, but as something that dwells within or is immanent (1989, 130). Lynn Gottlieb speaks of this immanence in terms of seeing "God in ourselves" (1995, 26). Plaskow explains this initiative as "attempting to link the reimaging of God to a new vision of community, feminists repeatedly choose metaphors that picture divine power not as something above and over us but in and around" (1991, 140).

I would anticipate that both Rosenzweig and Levinas would very strongly oppose the proposal to eliminate notions of transcendence from the understanding of God. One pivot for the former's reply would probably be in terms of metaphors and meetings. The God within the self or the community cannot be met. These descriptions of God's immanence would, thus, stand in opposition to Rosenzweig's carefully formulated view of the nature of religious language. They would subvert what he regarded as the "law of biblical style"— that biblical anthropomorphisms do not describe the divine but the way in which God is encountered—which he valued because this acts as a pledge for the possibility of hearing God's continually new voice.

Rosenzweig's second objection against jettisoning the feature of transcendence—or speaking of immanence in terms of "dwelling within"—might be drawn from his critique of Idealism. He powerfully protested what he saw as its reduction of God to the self. Nothing is more important for Rosenzweig than the notion of separation, and the corresponding word "and." In this regard, Rosenzweig wrote in "The New Thinking"

> To have cognition of God, the world, and man, is to know what they do or what is done to them in these tenses of reality, and to know what they do to one another or what is done to them by one another. And here we presuppose that these three have separate existence, for if they were not separate, they could not act upon one another. If in the "deepest core" the other were identical with myself, as Schopenhauer asserts, I could not love him, for I should be merely loving myself. (1970, 198)

As Rosenzweig indicates, if the element of transcendence is rejected, then the entirety of Judaism's passionate language about our love of God and God's love for all persons must also be eliminated. Without a notion of transcendence, which, minimally requires an understanding of separation, the love of God degenerates into a variety of self-love, whether in the singular or the plural.

Levinas's rejection of notions of divine immanence would be equally vehement, but for other reasons. As I have repeated a number of times, the intense opposition between the individual's love of the self, and all that it can identify with itself, and the demands of ethics is the catalyst for Levinas's philosophic critique. Levinas holds that it is natural for the self or a powerful group to align itself with God. Unfortunately, the language of immanence—especially the idea that God dwells within ourselves and our community, even without any pretensions of exclusivity—fortifies this alignment.

The most secure protection from individual and communal self-aggrandizement which is realized and sanctified by God—*Gott mit uns*—is through, as Levinas states it, the optics of ethics. God is always on the side of the weak, the vulnerable—namely, the neighbor. She is never with oneself. God does not pulse through me, but confronts me and obligates in the name of the other. Such obligations put the self in judgment, the very opposite of comfort.

In reply to these insights, it would neither be out of character nor unjust for feminist thinkers to remind us that women are exactly those outsiders who have been excluded throughout the course of Jewish history from any real connection with the divine. They might continue that the language of divine immanence is a necessary correction for this history. Women are strengthened, and the community is healed through the understanding that God dwells within each of us—including women—and within all of us as a whole.

Levinas's reply can be anticipated. The bonding of self and God can not be permitted, even for the sake of what appears as an action of correction. To sanction this bond would encourage the misuse of religious authority, whether by those who have always held power, or those formerly on the outside.

I wonder whether the utilization of both female and male pronouns and metaphors in religious language might prevent historical abuses that feminist Jews have discussed, as well as guard against the possible misuse of the language of immanence. This is in agreement with Sylvia Fishman's observation, in a somewhat different context, that "utilizing balanced, gender-specific imagery" provides for an "effective, sensitive, and meaningful use of language" (1993, 240).

Because the language of both female and male persons is required to explore and express our encounters with God, it is clear that God is not the same as any of us. In light of Jewish history, there is no doubt that it is a great corrective for men to use the language of God as female. It might additionally be important for women to sometimes use the language of God as male.

What of the experience of immanence? Many feminist Jews believe this validates the desire to fashion a religious language that includes the notion of immanence. In Martin Buber's classic text about the dialogue with God, *I and Thou* (1970, 134), he once replied to those who had experiences of immanence and wanted the legitimacy of these experiences to be accepted. Buber's response—which could just as well be spoken by Rosenzweig in the context of this dialogue—was that, while there might be a real experience behind the feeling of immanence, there could be other ways of interpreting that experience—ways that retain the integrity of both God and the self.

Feminist Jewish critiques of the element of divine transcendence do not always replace it with the notion of immanence. Sometimes the argument against transcendence is offered in terms of some other opposition. For example, Amy Eilberg has contrasted "the transcendent God of command and demand, of judgment of those who fail in their commitments . . . with the other dimension of God, the feminine God, for whom love and nurturing are of ultimate value" (Fishman, 177). However, the questioning of the notion of the transcendent God, and the view that transcendence must clash with images of closeness, is not shared by all feminist Jewish thinkers. Sylvia Fishman points to stories of biblical women that demonstrate that God can be experienced as transcendent as well as in ways that are "immediate" and "personal" (1993, 241).

Here, Rosenzweig might offer a response that is most appropriate. His reply to views such as those of Eilberg are not difficult to anticipate, and it would correspond to what Fishman has already been quoted as saying. Rosenzweig held that the Jewish community has never insisted that God is only transcendent. Jewish liturgy establishes what every believer knows in her or his heart—that God is both the God out there and the God close to His/ Her creatures. Rosenzweig writes of this in one of his notes to the poetry of the medieval Jewish poet and philosopher, Judah Halevi. In this case, the poem is titled "The Far-And-Near One."

> This hymn is assigned to that section of the morning prayers consisting mostly of hymns. . . . and it is animated by one particular thought. But it is the last thought that human thinking can grasp, and the first that Jewish thinking grasps: that the faraway God is none other than the near God, the unknown God none other than the revealed one, the Creator none other than the Redeemer. (1995, 204)

Another key issue that emerges from the feminist critique of traditional Jewish monotheism concerns the exclusivity of the language of God as person. It is not that feminist thinkers—such as Marcia Falk and Judith Plaskow— wish to abolish or exorcise the metaphor of God as person, but that they believe its exclusive use distorts our understanding of the human. In particular, they hold that the human relationship to nature is undercut or left without essential religious expression. Falk finds that

> . . . as long as we image divinity exclusively as a person, whether female or male, we tend to forget that human beings are not the sole, not even the "primary," life-bearing creatures on the planet. (1989, 132)

Plaskow writes

Anthropomorphic images must thus be supplemented by a second kind
of language that can evoke the creative and sustaining power of God
present throughout the world and in ever-widening circles of
relation. . . . Images of God as fountain, source, wellspring, or ground
of life and being remind us that God loves and befriends us as one who
brings forth all being and sustains it in existence. (1991, 164–165)

Julie Spitzer appears to agree with Falk and Plaskow, although she does
not highlight images of God as tied to nature. She believes that many of the
problems that feminist Jews have with the language of the divine would
disappear if God were simply spoken of using noncorporeal and nonhuman
terms (Fishman 1993, 239).

It is impossible for me to conceive that either Rosenzweig or Levinas
would be in sympathy with this direction in the dialogue about contemporary
religious language. One of the major conclusions of chapter 2 of this book
was that the metaphor of God as person is the sine qua non for their religious
language. The excitement that the biblical anthropomorphisms evoke in
Rosenzweig reflects his belief that only the story of God as person allows us
access to experiences of the mutuality of God's and our meeting, loving, and
trusting. Grounded in nothing less than the Bible itself, this language was
regarded by him to be as important as the Law and the Prophets in the history
of Judaism. His immutable confidence that revelation endures as an ever-new
reality in Judaism is sustained by the words, "God is capable of what [s]he
wills . . ." (1937, 532).

The metaphor of God as person is equally essential to Levinas's religious sensibility, although he does not directly address this question. His
understanding of God who commands responsibility for the other is grounded
in the notion of the personal God. Levinas's approach to the extremely difficult question of the Holocaust also establishes the necessity of this notion
for his thought. Our passionate life of demand, reproach, and crying out to
God, even the image of Her hiding Her face, requires this linguistic and
conceptual foundation. Levinas relates that, in the intimacy of suffering, God
becomes "my God," but this is only because God shares, in the way that
persons share, our suffering.

Rosenzweig and Levinas would seem to agree with the judgment of
Rita Gross that for many feminist Jews

. . . almost everything that makes the Jewish religious enterprise dis-
tinctively *Jewish* becomes non-sensical without the metaphor of a divine Person in a covenant relationship of mutual responsibility and love
with human persons. (1983, 236)

There is no difficulty in verifying Gross's statement. Many feminist Jews regard the metaphor of God as person to be extremely important. For example, Norma Joseph has written that

> ... it is necessary to use personal language about God. I find no other way to think, communicate or believe. For me, the possibility is not merely an item of philosophic preference but, rather, a religious necessity. (1992, 114)

Sylvia Fishman supports this view by discussing the centrality of gender images for Jewish worship. She holds that

> Gender, like ritual, is basic to human life and experience, and humans experience life not as disembodied intellectual and spiritual entities, but as physical, sexual beings. Eliminating gender from prayer language impoverishes it and robs it of power and immediacy. (1993, 242)

Finally, it is important to note that, at the same time that Plaskow expresses her position in the quotation earlier cited about broadening religious language beyond the anthropomorphic, she demonstrates the truth of Gross's contention about the impossibility of escaping the language of God as person. Plaskow ends her statement by alluding to God's loving and befriending us, which are aspects of a relationship that requires the language of persons (1991, 165; 169).

What of the issue of the Goddess? I find that Plaskow's statement accurately laid out the parameters of this discussion, when she held that feminist Jews do not see themselves as proposing a new divine entity. Thus, she agrees with Ellen Umansky that feminist Jewish thinkers must be careful in addressing the Goddess so that She will not be seen as a "separate and idolatrous Being" (1989, 191). Plaskow believes that those who speak of the Goddess "are trying to enrich the range of metaphors Jews use in talking about God" (1991, 150). Outlining the way in which the issue of the Goddess might be understood within the context of this enrichment, Gross envisioned a three-stage process. The first stage is the "simple insertion of female pronouns." The second is the breaking of "stereotypes of the feminine." The third, which utilizes the specific language of the Goddess, is the restoration of "dimensions of the deity" (1983, 246).

The replies that I have formulated for Rosenzweig and Levinas in earlier stages of this dialogue already provide resources for what I see as their attitudes toward this issue. Both Rosenzweig and Levinas would undoubtedly find the language of Goddess as dangerous and offensive, unless it is made clear—as it has been, in my view—that feminist Jews are not talking about a distinct and separate being. However, I have found that Rosenzweig would support the enrichment of our religious language by use of female pronouns and metaphors and by stories about the ways in which we meet Her, all of which uncover new dimensions of our religious lives. What I believe are the limits of his support have also been suggested, especially in terms of the issue of immanence.

There is a sustained interest in the use of mysticism, often channelled through the image of the Shekhinah, as a resource in the quest for new images of the divine as well as for new religious expressions. Susannah Heschel has remarked that the "interest in female images of God is leading to greater exploration of the Jewish mystical tradition" (1983, 217). This attraction to mysticism can also be explained in terms of intuitions shared by some feminist Jews that this feature might further the reintegration of women into the community and foster a deeper appreciation for human sexuality. Still, as was discussed in chapter 3 not all feminist Jews believe that mysticism is a helpful resource for religious language. For example, as much as Lynn Gottlieb focuses on the language of the Shekhinah, she states that she cannot agree to place "Jewish mysticism as the principal way into Jewish spirituality and theology" (1995, 7). Rather, she turns to "women's stories, poems, prayers, and archaeology as well as Jewish legends as sources for reimaging the Mystery" (1995, 7).

Mysticism was not a topic toward which either Rosenzweig or Levinas took a positive position.[8] In *The Star,* Rosenzweig portrayed mysticism as a temptation that could obstruct the individual's obligation to love the neighbor and redeem the world. He writes

> Loved only by God, [the mystic] man is closed off to all the world and closes himself off. . . . This thoroughly immoral relationship to the world is thus utterly essential for the pure mystic . . . (1972, 207–208)

Levinas's attitude toward mysticism in "Loving Torah More Than God" is diagnostic of his consistent view. He contrasts the Jewish relationship to God that is mediated by reason and the obligations of justice found in the Torah, to any "emotional communion" with God, or to a direct contact with God (1990, 144–145).

What brought Rosenzweig and Levinas to oppose mysticism as a stream of religious experience? It is the insight that mysticism as the passionate and direct experience of God can easily bring a person to ignore anything else, especially his or her responsibilities to others. Levinas seems to feel that such an all-encompassing experience might easily engender an alignment of self and God, which itself destroys the link between God and the other.

Is their view accurate? This is difficult to decide. On the one hand, Rosenzweig himself utilized mystic concepts in *The Star*, while, at the same time, criticizing the mystic experience.[9] On the other hand, feminist Jews often include statements about immanence in their arguments for the use of mysticism. I have referred to Lynn Gottlieb's translation of Shekhinah as "She Who Dwells Within." Judith Plaskow states that the Shekhinah image includes an "understanding of God's power as immanent in the world" (1991, 140). In light of the affinity of the language of mysticism with the language of immanence, the scepticism of Rosenzweig and Levinas appears to be perspicacious as well as consistent with their overall understanding of the nature of authentic religious language and experience.

The last question to be explored in the feminist critique of monotheism is the understanding of God as law-giver. In her attack upon the image of God as "dominating Other" (1991, 128) and her reflection about the "compatibility of feminism and law" (1991, 73), it is Plaskow who most directly takes up this line of inquiry. While I do not think that it is accurate to suggest that Plaskow's position represents those of many other feminist Jews, it is important to pursue this matter, especially in terms of the issues that it raises.

Many feminist Jews have noted, more generally, the bifurcation between ethics and women. God's commandments, ethics, and the realm of responsibility, especially as defined by Halakhah, have been seen by them to be handed over to men. Cynthia Ozick, as one illustration, has detailed the way in which women are excluded, debarred, demoted, and demeaned by Halakhah. Her discussion of Jewish women's expulsion from the realm of responsibility is formulated in terms of "not being a juridical adult" (1983, 125).

It is not difficult to postulate that Rosenzweig and Levinas might come to acknowledge the feminist view that, when God is exclusively portrayed as male, and His major attribute is justice, then women are banished from the ethical. As I have previously argued, they could well concur with the use of female pronouns and metaphors as the remedy for this banishment. Together, the dialogue participants could agree that when God, as She, commands, it would be impossible to suppose that only men are being addressed. Through the use of both female and male metaphors, in conjunction with the understanding that God is the God of mercy and justice, *rahamin* and *din*, the bifurcation or banishment of women evaporates.

There is, however, more to Plaskow's challenge. How important is it to Rosenzweig and Levinas that God commands? In his writings, Rosenzweig has demonstrated the importance of this dimension of the relationship to God many times. His famous correspondence with Martin Buber concerning revelation and the law provides one example of the centrality of Jewish law for him.[10] Although he affirmed that the primary content of revelation was revelation itself, he held that it was only in the experience of listening and responding to the law that its revealed character could be decided. Rosenzweig described the nature of this Jewish experience of law in terms of *Gebot* or commandment, and not *Gesetz* or law. Law is, for him, a dynamic vehicle for the individual's relationship to God, and its appropriation comes as one uncovers the personal meaning of the individual laws, as one finds the law addressed to him or her—that is, as one hears in the law the voice of God. Further, he believed that the answer that one gives to God's law/commandment has cosmic consequences. For Rosenzweig, it is precisely in responding to God's fundamental command—love of the neighbor—that the individual and the community fulfills its responsibility for the world's redemption.

The experience of God's commanding presence is no less significant in Levinas's work. In the face-to-face relationship with another, a trace of God emerges. It is that God who commands that "Thou shalt not kill!," and that God who calls upon us to care for the poor, the orphan, the widow, and the stranger. In his own unexcelled way, Levinas has written

> The first word of the face is the "Thou shalt not Kill." It is an order. There is a commandment in the appearance of the face, as if a master spoke to me. However, at the same time, the face of the Other is destitute; it is the poor for whom I can do all and to whom I owe all. And me, whoever I may be, but as a "first person," I am he who finds the resources to respond to the call. (1985, 89)

In this instance we have discovered a significant disagreement about the appropriate direction for fashioning contemporary Jewish religious language. Although, not many feminist Jews fully assent to Plaskow's position, there are some who find the notion, or language of God as lawgiver, to be without reverberation in their religious experience. As opposed to this, Rosenzweig and Levinas have provided new ways for Jews—even those who do not find many aspects of traditional Jewish law meaningful—to understand and experience God's commanding voice in their life with others.

CONCLUSION

Where has this dialogue brought us in terms of our speaking/writing of God? It has uncovered areas of agreement, in which insights build upon each other and open up new horizons of religious language and experience. It has equally exposed differences in understanding, and conflicts between primary visions of our life with other persons and experiences of God.

The dialogue with feminist Jewish thinkers—primarily with Judith Plaskow, Sylvia Fishman, Lynn Gottlieb, Rita Gross, and Marcia Falk—along with Franz Rosenzweig and Emmanuel Levinas, has reaffirmed the two principle dimensions of the connection between our relationships with others and the encounter with God.

First, we have heard, as it were, many thinkers attest that the relationship to God emerges from the life with others. Levinas sees this exclusively in terms of the ethical relationship to the other. The face of the other evokes the subject to acknowledge the commandment not to kill, and unveils a sense or trace of the divine. For Levinas, there is no other access to God, except in terms of the other. Rosenzweig appears to broaden Levinas's understanding by speaking of the love of neighbor as the embodiment of both the experience and the expression of God's love. One contribution of feminist Jews, which we found to be in harmony with Rosenzweig's intuitions, lay in their witness to the relationship to God as it arises from the physical love between persons.

Second, we have seen that the ways in which we speak of and experience God deeply affect the relationship to other persons. Rosenzweig's attack upon the mystic, who turns away from the world in order to experience God in intense seclusion, is one illustration. Levinas's fervent critique of those who seek to align God with the self is another. The analysis and critique of the effects of religious language and conceptions on individual and communal life reaches a crescendo in the work of feminist Jews. In their writings the deleterious consequences of the singular male image of God is documented, and the liberating outcomes of transformed religious language is envisioned.

We have found that, from both standpoints—the religious dimension of the interhuman, and the individual and social consequences of the religious imaginary—the language of God as female is absolutely required. The dialogue has brought out that the language of God as "She" is a necessary extension of some of Rosenzweig's most basic views about religious experience. Female pronouns and metaphors also reinforce Levinas's censure of the appropriation by the powerful of the divine, and of the use of God to sanctify violence toward and oppression of the other.

In other words, I have consistently argued that Rosenzweig and Levinas could appreciate the feminist critique of their work, if it were presented to them. They could, I believe, concede the need for changes in their religious language, in light of their own principles. Among these principles are the command to love the neighbor and be responsible to her. Another is their awareness of the ways in which religious language could either support or obstruct such love and responsibility.

There also appears to be agreement—especially among Rosenzweig and some feminist Jews—about the overall task of expanding religious language and experience. These thinkers are aware of how language contours our religious experiences. Many of them seek to ensure that religious language will retain its power to reflect and nourish our deepest relationships, especially those of love and responsibility. In terms of this projected dialogue, the great division occurs when Rosenzweig and Levinas object to areas of expansion in which, they feel, the integrity of either God or the Other is put into question.

The depth of this dialogue, I believe, testifies to the centrality of religious language in the life of the Jewish community. Speaking and writing of God are not arcane activities. They are among the most vital attempts to demonstrate Judaism's relevance in our time.

Finally, this dialogue should be seen as one contribution to the ongoing discussions about Jewish religious practice and language. Other readings of this material—as well as other voices—are necessary if we are to fashion a truly inclusive Jewish religious language.

CHAPTER 5

Judaism and Religious Pluralism:
Faith and Mystery

The recognition of the world as religiously pluralist[1] has been an important factor throughout modern Jewish history. Although limited, the Enlightenment's commitment to religious toleration was one of the catalysts that gave rise to Jewish Emancipation in Central and Western Europe in the latter part of the eighteenth century.[2] From that time, Jewish thinkers have addressed the issue of the relationship between Judaism and other religions with varying interest and cogency. What is termed interreligious dialogue—that is the face-to-face encounter of philosophers, theologians, and representatives of the different religious traditions—has accelerated since World War II. The dialogue has also coalesced and intensified the challenge to Jewish thought which the inescapable recognition of pluralism poses. This chapter will survey some of the principal responses that have been formulated by twentieth-century Jewish philosophers. A question, which has both a descriptive and prescriptive dimension provides the overall perspective for this review: How has (and should) Jewish religious reflection been (be) effected by interaction with persons of other religions?

This inquiry is guided by the insights and lessons that have emerged from the earlier chapters. It is, in my view, a necessary extension of that work. We have come to recognize the impact of the interhuman realm upon our understanding of God, and, conversely, that our religious language deeply influences the ways in which we see and treat others. This has been the foundation for the explorations of Franz Rosenzweig's attention to the commandment to love the neighbor, Emmanuel Levinas's testimony about the ethical call of the other, and the multifaceted feminist demand for a more inclusive religious life. The relationship to persons who hold faith positions that are not Jewish constitutes a further feature of the reflection upon the religious dimensions of the encounter with others—in this case, our concrete life among a variety of neighbors.

Again, although many contributions to contemporary Jewish philosophy have ignored or treated in a peripheral way the challenge of religious pluralism, this is impossible for us. The hallmark of our overall inquiry into speaking/writing of God has been the appreciation for the religious imperative of our responsibility for the neighbor and stranger. Our lives with persons of other traditions raise two questions that must be ultimately addressed: And what do we owe the other? And what can we learn from the other?

This examination continues the parameters of study that have, throughout this book, guided this inquiry. The literature on the historical interaction between Jews and non-Jews, as well as on interreligious dialogue, is vast.[3] This study of Judaism and religious pluralism will take twentieth-century Jewish reflection as its exclusive data. We are interested in the way in which modern Jewish philosophers of the last century have spoken about the relationship between Judaism and other religious traditions. The concepts, categories, and literature from the Jewish tradition that have directed the historical interaction with non-Jews for two thousand years—such as the obligations to the *ger toshav* (the biblical stranger or resident alien) and the implications of the Noahide Laws (the seven laws that were regarded by the Rabbis as given to all humans following the divine covenant with Noah), will not be explored in their own right.[4] They will be discussed only in terms of their use by the modern Jewish philosophers of our study. Consequently, the conclusions drawn at the end of this chapter must be seen as tentative. By themselves, they are not meant to constitute a final statement about the nature of Jewish recognition of and obligation to non-Jews. They are suggestions, and merely one voice in a dialogue about contemporary Judaism that must include many other voices. Particularly necessary are studies of the interaction between Jews and others that seriously struggle with traditional Jewish sources.[5]

Furthermore, this survey is schematic, rather than exhaustive. A number of different and diverse axes will be employed to assemble and assess the ways in which modern Jewish thinkers have thought about the implications of religious pluralism. The chosen axes illuminate the basic options or patterns of response, as well as continue the central lines of inquiry of this book. We will look at three standpoints that characterize the basic positions in terms of the nature and goal of pluralism; philosophers of dialogue or the interhuman—namely, Levinas, Rosenzweig and Buber; the role of feminist Jewish thought; the meaning of recognition of the other; justifications for pluralism; the challenge of pluralism to the notion of election; and the impact of the Holocaust.

The first section—three standpoints—will offer a preliminary classification that broadly sketches the major viewpoints of modern Jewish philosophers concerning pluralism. This will be followed by a more detailed analysis of the positions of philosophers who have been the subjects of earlier chapters in this book, such as Emmanuel Levinas and Franz Rosenzweig, along with a discussion of Martin Buber, and feminist thinkers. The sections on recognition of the other, justifications for pluralism, and the challenge to the notion of election explore the ways in which Jewish religious thought has already been affected by the encounter with members of other religious traditions. The short section on the impact of the Holocaust will examine the manner in which reflection on this event has brought some Jewish philosophers to new insights about interreligious life. The chapter's conclusion focuses on the faith and mystery that guide dialogue, as well as the questions concerning what is owed to the other and what can be learned from the other, drawing together and crystallizing primary insights about Jewish religious language that are detailed in this chapter.

THREE STANDPOINTS

There is significant diversity in the definitions of religious pluralism, and the goals of dialogue offered by modern Jewish thinkers. In order to begin to provide an orientation to this material, a schematic that isolates and categorizes the understandings of the nature of pluralism and its goals will be offered. Three standpoints will be outlined here, although this is not to suggest that there might not be other valuable ways in which to characterize and analyze the variety of individual views.

The first standpoint brings together those who see pluralism in terms of each group's right to live out its relationship to the divine in its own way, and without interference. In this instance, dialogue is limited to common secular or moral concerns.

The second position sees pluralism as an environment that is grounded in mutual acknowledgement and even esteem. It is held that interreligious dialogue can—and even should—have a positive effect on the development of faith.

The third standpoint defines pluralism in terms of a level of interaction in which mutual transformation is the norm. From this perspective, dialogue is a process by which new religious truths can be uncovered and appropriated by traditions.

The widely recognized rabbinical authority, Joseph B. Soloveitchik, has outlined a view of pluralism in an essay called "Confrontation" and published in 1969, that has had great impact upon modern Jewish thinking. The bold title of the essay accurately conveys both the tone and content of the exposition. Representing the minority religious community, Soloveitchik pleads for Christians to respect Judaism's separateness and independence or, in his words, "the right of the community of the few to live, create, and worship God in its own way, in freedom and with dignity" (1969, 25). In his view, interaction between members of different faith communities should not extend beyond "secular orders"—that is, it should be limited to concerns about "the general welfare and progress of mankind . . . in combatting disease, in alleviating human suffering, in protecting man's rights, in helping the needy, et cetera" (1969, 20–21). Soloveitchik does not actually use the term *pluralism* to speak of the relationship between communities, but rather describes a side-by-side living in an atmosphere of "religious democracy and liberalism" (1969, 23) or "liberal convictions and humanitarian ideals" (1969, 25).

The argument which Soloveitchik presents for this view of religious confrontation/cooperation appears to me as being three-fold. First, differences between persons and communities must be respected because of each person's "inalienable rights as a human being, created by God" (1969, 21), as well as the rights and freedoms guaranteed by democracy. Second, the impossibility of cooperation beyond the secular order is a consequence of the ontological separation of faiths. For Soloveitchik, there are no grounds for comparison, no common language, and no theological interaction among faith communities. As he writes

> The word of faith reflects the intimate, the private, the paradoxically inexpressible cravings of the individual for and his linking up with his Maker. It reflects the numinous character and the strangeness of the act of faith of a particular community which is totally incomprehensible to the man of a different faith community. (1969, 23–24)

The notion that each faith is incomprehensible to another, and its message incommunicable to another, is the leitmotiv of the essay.

Third, Soloveitchik believes that a natural correlate of religious commitment is the belief in the ultimate and exclusive truth of one's "eschatological expectations" and the singular utility of one's "system of dogmas, doctrines and values" (1969, 19).

Soloveitchik's standpoint has been taken as a significant point of departure for modern Jewish reflections on pluralism.[6] Many thinkers are in substantial agreement with the principles of this view, which were accepted in February 1964 as a guide for inter-religious discussion by the leading Orthodox institution in the United States, the Rabbinical Council of America.[7] A similar position was briefly put forth by Arthur Hertzberg in 1987. In response to a statement by the important Vatican spokesman, Cardinal Joseph Ratzinger, Hertzberg wrote

It is thus clear now beyond any doubt that no dialogue that has any
theological content can be conducted between the two communities
[Jewish and Roman Catholic]. . . . Jews should continue to discuss with
Catholics a whole host of *social and even political problems* in which
both communities are involved. . . . Jews and Catholics are comrades
in the quest for social justice. (Cited in Lubarsky 1990, 1)

There is much strength in this first position. Soloveitchik is enthusiastic
about the necessity for tolerance, and envisions this in terms of respecting the
integrity of each religious tradition. However, toleration, separation, and
noninvolvement do not entail a lack of concern for the lives of persons in
other traditions. Moral action—whether seen in terms of the general welfare
of humans or the quest for social justice—is regarded as essential to the life
of Jews among others.

A second position sees pluralism as a form of religious interaction that
both includes and goes beyond collaborative social efforts by members of
different communities. Abraham Heschel, who devoted much of his life to
interfaith cooperation, is a good representative of this stance. In the essay,
"No Religion Is an Island," first published in 1966, he affirms that pluralism
is more than a matter of acknowledging that persons of other traditions have
a right to be different. Its essence is "reverence" for other traditions and even
"mutual esteem" (1990, 350). Within this understanding, Heschel sees the
goal of pluralism as the reciprocal deepening of faith—that is, the mutual
intensification of life before God and with others.

While Heschel speaks of the ways that every religion is affected by
others, his principal interest in the essay "No Religion Is an Island" is to
explore Jewish/Christian relations. In this context, he writes that

The primary aim of these reflections is to inquire how a Jew out of his
commitment and a Christian out of his commitment can find a religious
basis for communication and cooperation on matters relevant to their
moral and spiritual concern in spite of disagreement. (1990, 347)

The inclusion of "spiritual concern" already signals a major difference from
the understanding of pluralism as offered by Soloveitchik.

Although Heschel describes four dimensions of religious life that make
up the relationship to God, his essay on Jewish/Christian cooperation focuses
on faith—that is, what he identifies as "inwardness" or that "fear and trembling" that is the core of religious subjectivity. Here he believes that much
can be shared among persons of different traditions, such as personal witness,
insights, confessions of inadequacy, and striving (1990, 348). It is also in
terms of this sphere of inwardness that one can help the other—in fact, that

one has the duty to help. He sees the fulfillment of this duty through such ventures as

> ... trying to overcome hardness of heart, in cultivating a sense of wonder and mystery, in unlocking doors to holiness in time, in opening minds to the challenge of the Hebrew Bible, in seeking to respond to the voice of the prophets. (1990, 351)

Thus, Jews and Christians can work to open each other to the presence of God, to God's search for humans, and to the common struggle against the alienation and nihilism that pervade modern life.

How does Heschel support his contention that the focus of dialogue can be extended to the realm of faith? He offers what might be taken as evidence that Jewish faith has been positively affected by persons from another tradition. Heschel's statement represents perhaps the most eloquent argument for the position that envisions pluralism in terms of learning about the life before God from those of other traditions. He writes

> No honest religious person can fail to admire the outpouring of the love of man and the love of God, the marvels of worship, the magnificence of spiritual insight, the piety, charity and sanctity in the lives of count-less men and women, manifested in the history of Christianity. Have not Pascal, Kierkegaard, Immanuel Kant or Reinhold Niebuhr been a source of inspiration to many Jews? (1990, 351)

Like Soloveitchik, Heschel spoke of the need for the separation of traditions, for respecting differences, and he valued cooperation in the realm of social action (1990, 348). Yet, he also finds that Christian thinkers have profoundly affected Jewish thought, and he believes that religious inwardness can be deepened through interreligious dialogue. The person of faith can recognize, respect, and learn from the ways that those in other traditions stand in fear and trembling before the divine presence. In fact, Heschel's last book, *A Passion for Truth*, is a fervent testimony to the impact that the reflections of the nineteenth century Danish-Christian, Soren Kierkegaard, as well as the Hasidic masters, the Besht and the Kotzker Rebbe, had on his own, intense wrestling with faith and despair.[8]

Finally, Heschel's vision rests on a particular understanding of religious truth. While he affirms that the significant theological differences between religions should not be covered over, he regards as false expressions of re-ligious self-righteousness and claims of exclusive proprietorship over truth. There are two reasons behind his rejection of self-righteousness and exclusiv-ity. First, he insists that humility is the foundation for both faith and honest religious reflection. Second, he believes that the fullness of God's truth is beyond all human understanding, and that the divine voice, while one, necessarily reaches us through a variety of expressions (1990, 353–354).

In the essay "Pluralism and Biblical Theology," the contemporary philosopher David Hartman augments the understanding of pluralism as presented by Heschel. For him, pluralism entails the acknowledgement that persons of other religious communities express viable or authentic faith stances. At one point he writes that "each should walk before God in the way that He taught it" (1990, 253). Hartman discusses both the communal and the individual dimensions of pluralism. He combines the belief in the right of different communities to understand and respond to the divine in their own ways with a recognition of the authenticity of the life of faith as lived out by persons from these different traditions. This latter dimension is apparent in his statement that it is possible to recognize the "dignity and conviction" (1990, 248) of those with whom one disagrees. However, as is the case with all of the other Jewish philosophers whom we have examined, Hartman is reticent to offer a judgment about others' specific theological positions.

Hartman shares with Heschel the view that the encounter with persons of other faith communities can be a positive force in the growth of the Jew's inner life. However, he does not detail all of the dimensions that are found in Heschel's exposition, for it is primarily in terms of the development of humility that he describes this effect. As Hartman sees it, the dialogue with others is "spiritually redemptive," for, in his words "There is nothing more efficacious for restoring humility to the human spirit than confronting people of dignity and conviction who disagree with you" (1990, 248).

In the essay, "Pluralism and Revelation," Hartman continues the basic lines of his discussion. He writes of both a "dignified other" and of the need for "acknowledging the existence of other faiths in their own right" (1990, 254). In terms of the beneficial effects of encountering the other, he adds one more insight—that of enhancing "our covenantal creature consciousness" (1990, 254). For him, this means, first, that through dialogue Jews can deepen their appreciation for the basic goodness of persons in the "eyes of God"— that is, the "ontological worth" of all (1990, 260).

Second, he notes that the challenge of meeting persons of other faiths— especially in the context of the Jewish state and the city of Jerusalem— deepens our understanding of the nature of historical life. We are reminded that history is the arena of the temporal and the limited, not of the eternal and the infinite. Through such encounters, we can more fully appreciate the inescapable limitedness or "particularity" of each community's life in history (1990, 260). This appreciation of particularity brings into question the absolute certainty and universal claims of every religious community.

A third understanding of pluralism has recently been presented by Sandra Lubarsky in her text *Tolerance and Transformation*. While it is too early to record the response to her position, I have not come across previous statements that were as extensive as hers. Lubarsky delineates a maximal view of pluralism—at least of its goals—and her views are important for this.

Lubarsky designates her stance as "veridical pluralism" (1990, 2). It focuses on the assertions about truth found in religious and nonreligious traditions. The stance of veridical pluralism holds that truth is ultimately one and coherent, despite the limited ways in which persons attend to that truth, due to their cultural, historical, and social particularity. "Transformative dialogue" is the process by which individuals and communities transcend their limited and conflicting views of the truth. Thus, for Lubarsky, the goal of dialogue is to "correct, enlarge, restate and/or reform our knowledge" (1990, 2).

In this view, dialogue among communities must go beyond efforts at ameliorating social inequities and suffering, and the development of the individual's life of faith through the contact with others. Its goal is to arrive at the truth in the highest form possible—or, in Lubarsky's words, to "*make the truth our inheritance, regardless of its progenitors*" (1990, 2 [Her emphasis]). Following this, theological affirmations and doctrinal conflicts are not, as they often are, put aside, even by proponents of the second standpoint. They become the foci of dialogue. She believes that dedication to truth need not be in conflict with one's faithfulness to a particular tradition, thereby acknowledging the existence of an issue that pervades discussions of dialogue, the tension between commitment to one's community and tradition, and openness to the other.

The justification, as it were, for this position has already been intimated. First, there is the supposition that truth is one and coherent. There might be many ways to express a single truth, and there are different dimensions of truth, but there is also a unity and overall coherence to it. As an illustration, Lubarsky writes that, both the Jewish view that there is a God, and the Buddhist view that ultimate reality is devoid of a God or gods, cannot be true. However, dialogue does not lead to the decision that one of these understandings is true and the other false. Lubarsky holds that the insights of each of these stances can "serve to correct" the other, and, ultimately, be "integrated in such a way that the self-consistent wholeness of reality is preserved" (1990, 14).

Second, Lubarsky finds that the insights of the natural and social sciences, as well as academic disciplines such as history, have demonstrated that no community can claim exclusive possession of the truth or possession of the truth in its absolute form. The knowledge of the historical interaction among communities, and the changes that each tradition has undergone over time, undermine all claims to exclusivity or absolutism.

Third, she holds that faithfulness to Judaism in fact requires us to dialogue about and seek the truth.

> It is precisely the Jewish commitment to God, who is present through-out the world as a loving and communicative parent, that calls for a Jewish affirmation of veridical pluralism. Openness to others is open-ness to God. In the twentieth century, responsiveness to God takes the form of responding, openly and seriously, to the claims of other faiths. (1990, 12–13)

Thus, I have presented three views of pluralism that diagram some of the options found in the literature of modern Jewish philosophers.

As we have seen, the first standpoint envisions pluralism in terms of tolerance for difference. While some critics may see in this option a minimalist definition of pluralism, this position lacks neither integrity nor passion. Soloveitchik teaches that faith—which is that unique link between a particu-lar community and God—is best respected when the outsider acknowledges it as impenetrable.

The strength of the second standpoint comes through in terms of the quality of the interaction with others that is portrayed. The plea for pluralism is not made on the basis of toleration. It rests on experiences of the ways in which the life of faith has been enriched through the contact with others of piety and insight. Abraham Heschel offers a statement which is nothing less than a testimony to the invaluable impact on Jewish faith of such Christian thinkers as Kierkegaard and Niebuhr.

The third standpoint portrays pluralism in terms of the mutual striving for truth. Truth is one, and each community can reach for it only out of the particularity of its history. Yet, the thirst for truth is so great that, through interaction, persons of different communities can transcend their past in the effort to appropriate the highest. In Lubarsky's words, "openness to others is openness to God" (1990, 12).

DIALOGUE AND PLURALISM

Let us now discuss the views of philosophers who have been the main subjects of earlier chapters of this book, namely Emmanuel Levinas and Franz Rosenzweig. A treatment of Martin Buber will be added here, because of his sustained interest in and commitment to interreligious dialogue, his discussions with Rosenzweig concerning this issue, and the basic ideas of the interhuman that he shares with the other two philosophers. All three provide important resources for understanding modern Jewish responses to religious pluralism.

Emmanuel Levinas's position in such essays as "Religion and Tolerance," "Israel and Universalism," and "Monotheism and Language" in *Difficult Freedom* mirrors some of the themes articulated by Soloveitchik. Just as Levinas's general view of the proper relationship to other persons is punctuated by the terms *separation* and *responsibility*, so is his understanding of the relationship between traditions or persons in different communities. Here, separation seems to imply that there is no place for issues of dogma and theological truth in the dialogue/relationship between the Jew and non-Jew. The words *tolerance* and *love* are used by Levinas to characterize the nature of authentic interaction. He has even described this relationship in terms of intimacy, but one that pointedly excludes the doctrinal sphere, as in the statement:

> The rabbinic principle by which the just of every nation participate in the future world expresses not only an eschatological view. It affirms the possibility of that ultimate intimacy, beyond the dogma affirmed by the one or the other, an intimacy without reserve. (1990, 176)

Levinas did not insist that truth must be suspended in such interaction. Rather, he understands truth in the religious context in terms of action. As he writes, "truth—the knowledge of God—is not a question of dogma for them [Jews], but one of action, as in Jeremiah 22" (1990, 176).

Responsibility for the other—that is, the full weight of moral consciousness, is the essence of that action which is required when facing the other. It is experienced as "an infinite demand made on oneself, an infinite responsibility" (1990, 174). Levinas believes that, in emphasizing tolerance and responsibility, Judaism works for the true universality—that is, a peace that respects difference, and avoids all the various ways by which religions have sought dominance over one another.

It is important to note that Levinas affirms that the inescapable call to responsibility and service to the other is a hallmark, not just of Judaism. It is something that unites all the monotheistic faiths. He writes

> But we who are Jews, Muslims, and Christians, we, the monotheists . . . we speak words that begin in the person who utters them, we rediscover the word that penetrates, the word that unites, the prophetic word. (1990, 180)

In discussing the common features and worldwide role of Judaism, Christianity, and Islam, Levinas significantly goes beyond Soloveitchik's discourse. He is not reticent to speak even of other positive relations. In commenting on Rosenzweig's views about the relationship between Judaism and Christianity, he has written

> But the very possibility of thinking, without compromise or betrayal, in two forms—the Jewish and the Christian, that of Christian loving kindness and that of the Jewish Torah—has allowed me to understand the relation between Judaism and Christianity in its *positivity*. I can formulate it in another way: in its possibility of dialogue and symbiosis. (1994a, 163)

The work of Franz Rosenzweig offers a number of dimensions that are relevant to our examination of modern Jewish understandings of pluralism. These include his portrait of the role of Judaism and Christianity in world history, the discussion of the individual's relationship to God that focuses on faith rather than on communal identification, and his understanding of the transformative dynamics of dialogue.

Rosenzweig presented an exclusive notion of religious truth, and not a pluralist one. However, what is distinctive of his view is that two traditions, rather than one, are included. For Rosenzweig, only two communities stand in a true relationship to God. God's revelation to the Jewish community at Sinai, and to the Christian community in the person of Jesus, are the axes of human history. Through these revelations, Jews and Christians enter the process of redemption—Jews as the eternal people continually turning back upon itself, and Christians as participants in the eternal way through which God's word is brought to all others. This portrait appears in Rosenzweig's *The Star of Redemption*.

> Only the eternal [Jewish] people, which is not encompassed by world history, can—at every moment—bind creation as a whole to redemption while redemption is still to come. The life of this people, alone, burns with a fire that feeds on itself, . . . The seed of eternal life has been planted, and can wait for the budding. (1972, 335)

> Christianity, as the eternal way, has to spread even further. Merely to preserve its status would mean for it renouncing its eternity and therewith death. Christianity must proselytize. (1972, 341)

The presentation of the historical roles of these communities in *The Star* is an essential component of Rosenzweig's overall theological system.[9] He affirms the validity of the Jewish and Christian relationships to God, but denies the truth of all other religious traditions. These he describes as humanly founded, and, at best, as in the case of Islam, of being an inferior copy of the true ones.

While Rosenzweig holds that the full religious life can be experienced only within these two communities, he does not believe that other persons are excluded from a relationship to God. The divine/human relationship did not wait upon, nor is it restricted by, the smoke and the fire of Sinai nor the suffering on the cross. Rosenzweig recognizes in the life of faith of the other—that life of turning to and responding to God—an integrity that transcends or overcomes the precariousness of the cultic means that could be employed. This position is made unmistakably clear through some sublime lines in "The New Thinking."

> No paths that lead from Sinai and Golgotha are guaranteed to lead to him, but neither can he possibly have failed to come to one who sought him on the trails skirting Olympus. There is no temple built so close to him as to give man reassurance in its closeness, and none is so far from him as to make it too difficult for man's hand to reach. There is no direction from which it would not be possible for him to come, and none from which he must come; no block of wood in which he may not once take up his dwelling, and no psalm of David that will always reach his ear. (1970, 202)

Although Rosenzweig's analysis of speech or dialogue is not directly linked to a view of religious pluralism, this divine/human act plays such a crucial role in his thought that its lessons are relevant to every discussion in which Rosenzweig's name appears. As was discussed in chapter 1, so clearly was speech at the core of all of his thinking that he labeled his philosophy as "speech/thinking." The label indicated that, even when done alone, philosophic thinking was to take its point of departure from the truths of human speech. In the context of our discussion of religious pluralism, his exploration of the phenomenon of speech illuminates the central features in all dialogue. As outlined in *The Star* (1972, 156–204), it is through speech that the separateness and integrity of the other is acknowledged, the self develops, and God's word enters.

Speech occurs between two or more persons. The other who speaks and listens is not the same as the self. Without this separation, nothing new can appear, be drawn out, or crystallize. Thus, the potency of speech is dependent on the acknowledgement that there is an inviolable integrity to the individual. In other words, through respect for the unique visions of different persons, speech becomes creative.

Rosenzweig saw the give and take of speech as a model for human development.[10] In his eyes, each person must wait upon interaction with others in order for her or his life to realize its full potential. Such fundamental features of our existence as love, trust, and responsibility can never be self-engendered. They are the fruits of that quintessential phenomenon of the interhuman realm—namely, speech. However, Rosenzweig also believed that the relationships between humans are paths of, or to, the divine, and that the growth of each person requires God's help, and God's word.

Speech is Rosenzweig's prime example of the way in which the divine is continually lifting up the human. He described speech as equally a human and divine activity (1972, 201). In terms of the latter, it is both a revelatory and redemptive instrument. God's love appears when a person turns to/speaks with the neighbor, and the process of redemption grows as each person is transformed from an isolated self into a being loved—by the neighbor—soul.

There is one further aspect of speech-thinking that is relevant to the discussion of pluralism. At one point in "The New Thinking," Rosenzweig refers to his "messianic theory of knowledge." He writes that this perspective

> . . . values truths according to what it has cost to verify them and ac-cording to the bond they create among men, [but that it] cannot lead beyond the two eternally irreconcilable hopes for the Messiah: the [Jewish] hope for one to come and the [Christian] hope for one to return; it cannot lead beyond the "and" of these final efforts in behalf of truth. Beyond this, only God can verify the truth. (1970, 206)

Rosenzweig offers two criteria to evaluate truth—passion and community. The highest truths are those that evoke the greatest passion/commitment among persons. This view is reminiscent of Soren Kierkegaard's famous statement in the *Concluding Unscientific Postscript*, through the pseudonym of Johannes Climacus, that "truth is subjectivity" (1971, 169). However—and here, all the critics of Rosenzweig's "individualism" fail to understand him—he goes beyond Kierkegaard by insisting on the equally important criterion of community. The most powerful truths bind humans together in a living reality. Rosenzweig's statement about the "bond" that truths "create among men" seems to focus, at the end of the quotation, on the Jewish and Christian communities. However, the criteria of passion and community need not, in my view, be understood solely in this context.

Rosenzweig is suggesting that the religious person, who recognizes a messianic theory of truth, or a theory of truth that arises out of God's revelation, can acknowledge the truth of the other, in terms of the other's passion—up to death, and the type of community created. However—and this is of equal importance—there is also a limit here. The religious person is unable to overcome the separation of traditions, and arrive at a common theological truth. The differences, in Rosenzweig's parlance, the "and" that stands between

Jewish hopes and Christian hopes, cannot be transcended by humans; truth is one only for God.

Rosenzweig was very serious about the need for mutual understanding through interreligious dialogue.[11] Although no single event of dialogue could fulfill all of the ideals that Rosenzweig saw in it, his famous correspondence with Eugen Rosenstock-Huessy in 1916 illustrates some of these.

Their exchange was deeply influenced by their earlier and on-going history together. Its occurrence, and progress, was not controlled by either party. In fact, Rosenzweig tried to defer it. Some critics have regarded it as the highest example of dialogue, while others see it as a failure.[12] The latter assessment can be made based only upon an expectation of some major agreement between the speakers, but true dialogue is not dependent on this. The exchange immediately went beyond the goals of religious dialogue that some Jewish thinkers set—that is, the secular realm, its problems, and possible solutions. Rather, there was a serious discussion of the truths and relationships between Judaism and Christianity by men committed to each of the traditions.

What then was the outcome? The integrity and separateness, that is the legitimate differences between the two were acknowledged. Each certainly deepened their understandings of the other tradition. The exchange had a transformative result, which is attested to by Rosenstock-Huessy in a later reflection.[13]

Finally, both thinkers came away with insights about the religious life that were to become absolutely central to their thought. For example, Rosenzweig learned about the orientation that revelation provides, and of the importance of religious calendars as a community's enacted memory/celebration of creation, revelation, and redemption.

The issue of religious pluralism was a primary concern of Martin Buber personally, philosophically, and from the point of view of his long scholarly career.[14] Buber's first academic study—his doctoral dissertation—examined the problem of individuation or becoming a full self in the work of the medieval Christian mystics Meister Eckhart and Jacob Boehme. The publication of his early examination of mystic experiences in the world religions—*Ecstatic Confessions* that first appeared in 1909, brought him extensive recognition.

My examination of Buber has three foci—the discussion of the relationship to God and the treatment of religious traditions in his *magnum opus*, *I and Thou* that was originally published in 1923; Buber's understanding of the relationship between Judaism and Christianity; and his insights into the possibilities of recognizing the religious integrity of persons of other traditions as well as those traditions themselves.

I and Thou is the foundation for all of Buber's mature religious reflection. In that work, he portrays the fundamental relational character of human life in light of the I-It and I-Thou encounters. For him, the fullest human life is realized through the I-Thou encounter with other persons, nature, spiritual productions, and, finally, God. Early in the book, Buber writes the following lines:

> The Thou encounters me by grace—it cannot be found by seeking. But that I speak the basic word to it is a deed of my whole being, is my essential deed. (1970, 62)

Although all I-Thou relations ultimately point to the "Eternal Thou," the life with other persons is the platform, and the education/discipline, through which the individual learns to say "Thou" to God. The meeting with God is available to all, and, in *I and Thou*, Buber's interest lies in the individual experiences rather than in specific religious traditions. Still, it is clear that the relationship with the Eternal Thou is alive in all religions. However, he makes a point of indicating that it can easily be obscured by dogma and cult and that no religion escapes these dangers of stagnation (1970, 162).

The treatment of "revelation" exemplifies Buber's belief that the relationship to God is available to everyone. He holds that there are no privileged religious formulae which lead to this encounter, and that no special doctrines immediately issue from it. The I-Thou relationship with the divine is not even restricted to those who use the word *God* or its equivalent. He quotes Nietzsche to the effect that " 'One accepts, one does not ask who gives' " (1970, 158). The person who emerges from the encounter with God comes away with a sense of the meaningfulness of all of life, and of his or her life in particular. This sense is accompanied by the awareness that the unique meaning of one's life must be verified through relationships with others.

There is a sometimes implicit, and sometimes explicit, critique of specific religious traditions in the text. The discussion of revelation makes a point of stating that no universal moral rules arise from the divine/human encounter, and is a reference to Jewish law (1970, 159). Buber also criticizes mystical, and especially Buddhist, notions that imply that the I-Thou relationship ultimately gives way to an experience of unity or nothingness. Thus, overall, the basic canon of Buber's philosophy of religion does not give priority to any religious tradition, and affirms the universality of the I-Thou encounter with the divine.

In Buber's wider oeuvre, there is a comprehensive treatment of Judaism, and a less extensive—but still significant—examination of Judaism and Christianity together. As is true with many subjects, Buber's understanding of these topics underwent changes as his overall thought developed and matured. His late, and thorough, examination of the two traditions in *Two Types of Faith* contrasted Jewish *emunah* with Christian *pistis*. He characterized

Jewish faith in terms of a trust in someone, based upon experience of that person, and Christian faith as the acceptance of a proposition about the object of faith. Despite the many places in this text where his preference for Judaism is strongly evident, Buber acknowledges the authenticity of Christianity. In the last chapter, he holds that each of these two traditions has something to teach to, and learn from, the other.

More important for our purposes are Buber's statements about the legitimate possibilities for, and the limits of recognition of, the other. In terms of Christianity itself, he wrote that it was an "authentic sanctuary" in which the I-Thou relationship can be found (cited in Lubarsky 1990, 95). He believed that, despite the difficulty that a religious person from one of these traditions has in recognizing the relationship to God of those who belong to the other one, some acknowledgement is possible. In his words, "We can acknowledge as a mystery that which, notwithstanding our existence and self-knowledge, others confess as their reality of belief" (1964, 183).[15]

In a letter to a Christian professor in 1949, Buber elaborated upon the dynamics of recognition, again highlighting the notion of mystery.

> I have a spiritual life in the closeness between God and me, and my physical life in the same way. I can no more believe that God permits a Christian to question this than I can believe that God permits me to question this sort of thing in a Christian. Judaism and Christianity stand together in the mystery of our Father and judge; thus, a Jew may speak of a Christian and a Christian of a Jew only in fear and trembling before the mystery of God. Only on this basis can there be genuine understanding between Jews and Christians. (Glatzer and Mendes-Flohr eds. 1991, 540)

In this statement, Buber holds that it is wrong for a person in one tradition to question the relationship to God of a person in the other tradition. Only from the standpoint of faith—that is, of "fear and trembling," can a Jew speak of a Christian and visa versa. Furthermore, when speaking of the other, the speaker must acknowledge that the "mystery of God" encompasses both of them.

In a later letter, Buber again takes up this issue. He restates his view that, to honestly speak of the other itself, constitutes a faith stance. There are no neutral standpoints in addressing the issue of another's relationship to God. Additionally, Buber reaffirms that the speaker must acknowledge the "mystery"—perhaps, that is, the reality cloaked in mystery—of the relationship of the other to God. He writes

> After all, two things matter in such things: that the speaker really be rooted in the religious reality from which he speaks and that, without

compromising the firmness of his speech, he acknowledge the mystery of the relationship of the person involved to transcendence. (Glatzer and Mendes-Flohr eds. 1991, 613)

The impact of the thought of Rosenzweig and Buber on contemporary interreligious dialogue is often acknowledged. These two Jewish philosophers, together with Levinas, raise some of the fundamental issues that such encounters must examine, as well as presenting unique insights into the powers and limits, the commitment, the respect, and the mystery that pervade serious dialogue. We will later look at their views in the context of examining the meaning of recognition of the other, as well as justifications for pluralism, and the understandings of Jewish election.

THE CONTRIBUTION OF FEMINIST JUDAISM

While the issue of religious pluralism has not been a principle one for many feminist Jews, some have seen it as a necessary correlate of their primary work. Many of these philosophers and theologians value interreligious dialogue, and are committed to notions of religious truth that recognize, as legitimate, a variety of expressions.[16] In this section, we look at two contributions that feminist Jews bring to the understanding of Jewish life with others.

One of the most distinctive contributions to the discussion of pluralism involves the contention that the attitude toward women in Judaism has important similarities with the attitude toward the non-Jew. Judith Plaskow and Drorah Setel are the thinkers who have most forcefully outlined this position. When the issue of pluralism is seen in one of its most concise forms, in the question of recognition/acceptance of difference, then the connection between the attitude toward women and toward non-Jews begins to emerge. Plaskow finds that Judaism is troubled by diversity. It not only marks off that which is different from the norm, but it valorizes this difference. In her words,

To understand more fully those aspects of Judaism that thwart Jewish acceptance of difference without gradation, we must examine further those ideas that have contributed to Judaism's long history of conceptualizing difference in terms of hierarchical separations. . . . Paralleling external differentiation were a host of internal separations that set apart distinct and unequal objects, states, and modes of being. (1991, 96)

According to Plaskow, when the male Jew is taken as normative, then both Jewish women and non-Jews are regarded as inferior. In the case of the non-Jew, it is the concept of the chosen people which establishes and reflects the superiority of the Jew. Following from this, Plaskow believes that "The rejection of chosenness, and the rejection of women's Otherness, are interconnected pieces of the wider project" (1991, 103).

Thus, the remedy to Jewish women's oppression must been seen in the context of the more expansive critique of the dynamics that require difference to be depicted in terms of superiority/inferiority. If changes can be effected so that Jews will accept non-Jews as equal, although different, then progress will also be made in accepting Jewish women as full partners in the community. Plaskow proposes that a "part/whole model" be examined as a paradigm for understanding or expressing the existence of distinct/different groups (1991, 105–107). In this view, the variety or plurality of different persons and communities is to be accepted and appreciated because of the richness each brings to the wider whole.

Another feature of the critique of Judaism by feminist Jewish philosophers and theologians relevant to the topic of pluralism concerns the ways in which religious understandings and images of the divine from other traditions can be used to augment Jewish religious language. The significance of this feature for our discussion pertains to the underlying supposition that the encounter with, and understanding of, other religious traditions extends to more than common moral concerns, or the deepening of individuals' faith. Going beyond the standpoints of Soloveitchik, and even Heschel, and coming close to that of Lubarsky, some feminist Jews find that Jewish understandings of the nature of the divine can be developed through both the study of other traditions and interreligious dialogue.

As we saw in chapter 3, some feminist Jews affirm that adapting female images of the divine from other religious traditions will deepen Jewish experiences of God's female dimension. Rita Gross has been impressed by the Hindu tradition as a source for providing images that speak of the "divine feminine who contains all opposites and manifests the coincidence of those opposites" (1983, 243). In addition, Lynn Gottlieb has described the "positive spiritual paradigms for women" that results from her use of "the Near Eastern story about the descent of the Goddess Inanna to the underworld in quest of inner wisdom" (1995, 36). Of course, there are also many feminist Jews who do not accept the need for, and reliance on, non-Jewish images of the divine.

RECOGNIZING THE OTHER

In reassessing the views already presented, let us also include a number of contemporary Jewish thinkers not introduced before by isolating and reexamining two questions that have intermittently emerged. First, what does it mean to recognize the other? Second, how is pluralism justified?

These questions go beyond the initial survey of general standpoints and individual views by directly examining the ways in which the relationship to persons in other traditions, and the reality of the plurality of traditions, affect Jewish religious language and self-understanding.

There are different types and degrees of recognition of those in other religious traditions. For our purposes, recognition is the principled respect for another, as well as the acceptance of specific obligations that arise from the relationship to the other. One type of recognition concerns the other's relationship to God, and the second involves the other's tradition itself. The first is framed in terms of the issue of authenticity of the individual's God-relationship. The second is expressed in terms of legitimacy of the other's religious tradition.

In terms of the issue of authenticity, three degrees of recognition of the other's relationship to God can be distinguished. The first—an elemental and a permanent feature of Jewish reflection—is the understanding that the other is, as oneself, a creature of God. The second degree of recognition acknowledges that the particular other stands in a vital or living relationship to God. The third understanding goes beyond the second, suggesting that there are lessons that can be learned from the other's relationship to the divine.

Almost every page of Soloveitchik's "Confrontation" refers to the idea that all persons are created by God. Further, as a consequence of this—that is, "as a human being, created by God" (1969, 21), he speaks of certain "inalienable rights," of which the right to practice one's religion without interference is the most relevant for him. This right translates, from the other side, into the obligation to allow others their own religious freedom.

Abraham Heschel provides a more expansive description of this first, elemental recognition of the other's authenticity—one which precedes and grounds other possible levels. He writes

> First and foremost we meet as human beings who have so much in common. . . . My first task in every encounter is to comprehend the personhood of the human being I face, to sense the kinship of being human, solidarity of being. . . . The human is a disclosure of the divine, and all men are one in God's care for man. (1990, 347)

Heschel does not directly designate the duty that corresponds to this understanding of human equality, but, if he did, it would probably resemble that which arises from Soloveitchik's thinking.

Another illustration of this first degree of recognition, appears in the work of Hartman. The primary concern of his essay, "Pluralism and Biblical

Theology," is with the category of creation. Hartman discusses the ramifications of this category for our relations with others as follows:

> The relational experience that grows from human awareness of Creation may be termed the "ontological relationship" to God. In the context of this relationship, divine consciousness embraces all of being inasmuch as all beings are equally creations of one God. By becoming conscious of one's own situation, the human being becomes aware of the connectedness of all being, bound together by virtue of the divine love expressed in creation. (1990, 246)

These lines indicate that Hartman also finds that equality is the basic lesson to be drawn from the notion of creation. In other words, creation means, for him, that one must treat others justly and respect their rights (1990, 251).

The second level of recognition of authenticity is not merely the acknowledgement of human creaturehood and equality, but of the present vitality of a particular other's God-relationship. There is a distinction between an understanding that all persons are God's creatures and the object of God's concern, and the view that the particular person stands in a living, authentic relationship with God.[17]

Soloveitchik's position, for example, is not clear in this regard. He does speak of "the right of the community of the few to live, create, and worship God in its own way, in freedom and with dignity" (1969, 25). However, neither this, nor anything else in "Confrontation," directly affirms or rejects the present reality of the other's God/relationship. Soloveitchik's contention that this relationship is impenetrable from the outside, might be the grounds for his reticence.

Some philosophers explicitly hold that practitioners of the monotheistic faiths have living God/relationships. Levinas says, for example, that, "Monotheism, the word of the one and only God, is precisely the word that one cannot help but hear, and cannot help but answer" (1990, 178). In another place, he reaffirms the rabbinic view that the just of all nations have a place in the world to come (1990, 176). Levinas does not qualify this, as does Maimonides, by saying that the just must recognize that the seven Noahide laws were divinely revealed. In light of this, it appears to me that one can conclude that, for Levinas, the just have authentic relationships to God—at least to the extent of meriting a place in the world to come.

Rosenzweig clearly articulates the view that non-Jews might have a direct relationship to God. Certainly, as participants in "the way," Christians are related to God, even if this is mediated through Jesus. However, at the same time that he explicitly rejects the truth/value of all religions except

Judaism and Christianity, he insists that authentic faith relationships are open to all. Rosenzweig formulates this, as we saw: "There is no temple built so close to him as to give man reassurance in its closeness, and none is so far from him as to make it too difficult for man's hand to reach" (1970, 202). Additionally, statements can be found to demonstrate that such thinkers as Heschel, Buber, and Hartman agree with Rosenzweig in that the direct relationship to God is open to all.

Going further, we have also come upon those who believe that more must be acknowledged, beyond the common creatureliness and the reality of the other's relationship to God. They hold that the faith of the other could be so alive that it can act as a transformative power. The faith of the other has the potential to deepen one's own. Buber, along with Rosenzweig in his personal dialogues with Rosenstock-Huessy, would at least admit that the faith of a Christian can positively affect one's own. At the end of *Two Types of Faith*, Buber affirms that both Jews and Christians have things to teach each other in terms of faith.

> . . . an Israel striving after the renewal of its faith through the rebirth of the person and a Christianity striving for the renewal of its faith through the rebirth of nations would have something as yet unsaid to say to each other and a help to give one another—hardly to be conceived at the present time. (1961, 173)

Most eloquently, as we have seen, Heschel found that the life of inwardness can be shared among persons of different religions, and that modern Jews have been inspired by the insight, piety, charity, and sanctity of the lives of Christians (1990, 351). Heschel actually extended this mutuality beyond Christians, saying, "The purpose of religious communication among human beings of different commitments is mutual enrichment and enhancement of respect and appreciation" (1990, 352). We have also found that Hartman believes that the faith of others, who might be neither Christian nor Muslim, can enhance the Jew's relationship to God.

The issue of legitimacy—the second type of recognition of the other—concerns, not the individual's God/relationship, but the neighbor's religious community or tradition. There is a distinction between affirming that another stands in relation to God, and affirming the legitimacy of his or her tradition as a path toward transcendence. The latter aspect is more complex. Among other reasons, many Jewish philosophers have seen a fundamental difference between the legitimacy of Christianity—and perhaps Islam—and that of the nonmonotheistic, or so-called "pagan," religious traditions.

Jews in the West have had the longest period of engagement with Christianity. Even more importantly, outside of the state of Israel, modern

Jewish philosophers have lived with Christians and envisioned dialogue particularly, or even exclusively, with that tradition in mind. As was indicated, most of the preceeding discussion about the deeper dimensions of recognition of the individual's God/relationship was focused on the Christian. Still, the idea of recognition of the other as a creature of God is not exclusive to Christians, and even the view that the faith of the other can deepen one's own is not necessarily limited, as we have seen, by Heschel and Hartman to the Christian or Muslim.

Many Jewish philosophers do not believe that there can be a recognition of the legitimacy of other religious traditions. It seems to me that this is Soloveitchik's position. Although he concentrates on the confrontation with Christianity, the broad legitimacy issue is clearly addressed. He affirms that each community's beliefs are exclusive, and their eschatological expectations are "unyielding" (1969, 19). Additionally, as noted, he believes that the essential experiences undergone within faith communities are incommunicable to those outsiders.

> It [the word of faith] reflects the numinous character and the strangeness of the act of faith of a particular community which is totally incomprehensible to the man of a different faith community. (1969, 23–24)

However, we have also come across theological stances that affirm the legitimacy of Christianity, and sometimes Islam. Rosenzweig provides the most detailed view of the recognition of the legitimacy of Christianity. In *The Star*, he describes Judaism and Christianity as twin forms of authentic religious life and sketches the world/historical role of each community. Buber also explicitly spoke of Christianity as an "authentic sanctuary," comparable to Judaism, in his examination of the two types of faith (cited in Lubarsky 1990, 88). Heschel has written that Jews "ought to acknowledge the eminent role and part of Christianity in God's design for the redemption of all men" (1990, 351). Leo Baeck also saw Christianity as separate and legitimate.[18]

Other philosophers focus on the three monotheistic faiths, often in the context of the repudiation of idolatry, especially its modern varieties. Levinas, for example, has written of the three that, "Each of these spiritual families taught universalism to the world, even if they did not always agree on matters of pedagogy. Our essential fates look kindly on one another" (1990, 178). In the wake of the Holocaust, and the continued necessity to testify against the forces that led to it, Emil Fackenheim has affirmed the legitimacy of the three traditions. He wrote that individuals of these traditions not only witness to "the One God" but also stand in a "living relation to him" (Morgan ed. 1987, 236).

Going further, some Jewish philosophers contend that there are a great number of legitimate religious traditions. The expansive quality of Buber's view can be well understood in contrast to Rosenzweig's position. Buber did not share Rosenzweig's philosophy of history that gave special place only to Judaism and Christianity, and rejected other religious traditions. The disagreement is illustrated by a discussion about paganism that appears in an exchange of letters between the two.[19] Rosenzweig wrote that there are no individual pagans. He meant by this that no one stands outside a relationship to God. Still, he held that the notion of "pagan religions" (Glatzer and Mendes-Flohr eds. 1991, 273), and of religious traditions that have no place in the divine plan, was a viable element in his religious understanding. Buber responded that the "Taoist is no pagan" (Glatzer and Mendes-Flohr eds. 1991, 275)—that is, that other traditions cannot be condemned as illegitimate religious approaches to God. For Buber, the category of paganism could be applied to persons in any tradition. In his words, anyone who practices magic, in whatever tradition "enters the realm of paganism" (Glatzer and Mendes-Flohr eds. 1991, 275). Buber's respect for the legitimacy of other religious traditions is also apparent in *I and Thou*. Even when he argues against some of the primary doctrines of a tradition—as he does with Buddhism—Buber still views the tradition as legitimate.

Hartman provides another example of those who affirm the variety of humans' religious communities. He wrote that "Buddhism, Hinduism, Christianity, Islam, and Judaism are distinct spiritual paths, they bear witness to the complexity and fullness of the infinite" (1990, 248), and, again, that "each should walk before God in the way that He taught it" (1990, 253).

JUSTIFYING PLURALISM

An essential aspect of the modern Jewish philosophical discourse about religious pluralism involves the ways in which pluralism is justified. This justification often blends together traditional resources, philosophical notions from modern religious reflection, and insights into the contemporary social and political environment in which Jews live. Thus, the justification discourse is one example of the manner in which Jewish thought responds, through both continuity and innovation, to the challenge of religious pluralism. It reflects, in microcosm, the three-fold nature of modern Jewish philosophy: the obligation to the past, the commitment to present Jewish communities, and the encounter with modernity.

The following treatment of justification, in harmony with the methodology of the chapter as a whole, is not exhaustive, but endeavors to identify some of the options taken by different twentieth-century thinkers. Among the most common patterns of justification are references to traditional Jewish concepts and categories, allusions to the limited nature of every tradition, revelation, knowledge, and language, along with remarks about the special situation of living in the modern world.

There are a number of traditional concepts that Jewish thinkers draw upon in order to present the argument for pluralism. There are important references to the notion of the seven Noahide laws, and to the category of the *ger toshav*—that is, the stranger or resident alien referred to in the Bible— which have been the foci for discussions of the relations between Jews and non-Jews for almost two millennia. However, in addition to these sources, there is mention of the basic notion of the covenant, and, even more frequently, the creation stories in the Bible. In terms of the latter, modern Jewish philosophers allude to both the general contention that sees all persons as God's creations, and to the more specific story of the universality of the indwelling divine image.

How do arguments justifying basic toleration of those who are different, as the first dimension of authenticity, utilize traditional categories? Leo Baeck, Emmanuel Levinas, Eugene Borowitz, and Joseph Soloveitchik utilize a combination of notions.

Baeck tied the general respect that every person owes to the other to the universality of the Noahide covenant. He writes

> A Noahide, or son of Noah, is every inhabitant of the country, regardless of his belief or nationality, who performs the most elementary duties of monotheism, humanity and citizenship. Every Noahide, according to this ordinance, is entitled not only to toleration, but also to recognition. (1970, 198)

However, Baeck does not, in this context, entertain either the recognition that the other is in an authentic relationship to God, or that the tradition of the other is a legitimate vehicle toward the divine.

Eugene Borowitz equates the toleration and respect due to all persons to the biblical command of "universal human dignity" (1991, 185). He finds the grounds for this dignity in a variety of biblical notions, including the understanding that all persons are created in God's image, and the command concerning the treatment of the stranger. However, the doctrine of the Noahide covenant plays the most important role in his discussion. This he designates as "the even more daring assertion that God has an ongoing partnership with humankind" (1991, 185).

Levinas speaks of this general tolerance in terms of the Bible's commandment in regard to the treatment of the stranger. For him, this "welcome given to the Stranger which the Bible tirelessly asks of us" is not one teaching among others, but "the very content of faith" (1990, 173).

Finally, the category of creation is prominent in the thought of Soloveitchik. He justifies the respect or toleration that is owed to a person of another tradition in terms of "one's inalienable rights as a human being, created by God" (1969, 21).

The argument for recognizing a second degree of authenticity—that persons of other faiths might have a vital relationship to God—takes up a complex of forms in the thought of modern Jewish philosophers. As already noted, Levinas appears to ground the universality of the relationship to God on the rabbinic idea—derived from the covenant with Noah—that the "just of every nation participate in the future world" (1990, 176). Borowitz also looks to the covenant with Noah. In both cases, they do not refer to the God/relationship, but to a person's ultimate salvation. However, I am drawing the conclusion that such ultimate salvation would not be possible without a prior God/relationship.

The concept of the covenant with Abraham, with its promise that all nations will be blessed through God's covenantal partner (*Genesis* 12: 3), is the platform for many discussions of pluralism in general, and the authenticity of the other's relationship to God in particular. Elliot Dorff finds that this covenant is a relevant resource for modern Jews, demonstrating two universal dimensions within Judaism. In this context he speaks of the idea that "God can and does relate to all people," albeit in different ways, and that the biblical promises for the end of time clearly encompass "universal peace, prosperity, goodness, and fulfillment" (1982, 497–498).

Finally, Hartman refers to the category of creation to discuss the universality of God's relationship. He writes, as we have seen, of God's love for all persons that emerges from an awareness of creation (1990, 246).

It is revealing that the two philosophers who so strongly contend that others have a relationship to God—Rosenzweig and Buber—actually do not present arguments. Rosenzweig confidently writes "There is no direction from which it would not be possible for him [God] to come" (1970, 202); and Buber holds that "Extended, the lines of relationships intersect in the eternal You" (1970, 123). The universality of the relationship to God is just taken for granted by these thinkers. This is true, even for Rosenzweig, who contests the truth value of other traditions, except for Christianity. It seems to me that these philosophers are basing themselves on a modern sensibility that, at least in their eyes, could not possibly question the understanding that opens the way for every person to have an authentic relationship to God.

How is the case for the recognition of the legitimacy of other traditions argued? A variety of answers appear here, partially dependent on the differences in the extent of recognition granted—that is, whether it is to Christianity, to the monotheistic faiths, or to all traditions. It seems that some thinkers take the legitimacy of Christianity as not requiring an argument. Certainly, this is the way that Christianity appears in Rosenzweig's *The Star*.

Heschel's discussion is more complex. On the one hand, he does not justify the recognition of Christianity, although he does discuss the elements that the two faith communities share. In this connection, he refers to

> . . . a commitment to the Hebrew Bible as Holy Scripture. Faith in the Creator, the God of Abraham, commitment to many of His commandments, to justice and mercy, a sense of contrition, sensitivity to the sanctity of life and to the involvement of God in history. (1990, 348–349)

On the other hand, Heschel—as well as a number of other thinkers—places the mutual recognition by these two religious traditions against the background of the unprecedented nature of the modern world. Heschel sees the connection between the two traditions in terms of their common opposition to modern nihilism. The understanding that both Jews and Christians face a common challenge is very important to him. He offers that "Jews and Christians share the perils and the fears; we stand on the brink of the abyss together" (1990, 345).

David Novak also cites a modern challenge as justifying the mutual recognition of the Jewish and Christian traditions. He argues that, "Jews and Christians might have a new sense of relationship because the predominately secular civilization is a threat to both Judaism and Christianity" (1989, 9). Still, as indicated by the title of Novak's book—*Jewish-Christian Dialogue: A Jewish Justification*—he does not take the legitimacy of Christianity as being self-evident. In a carefully constructed argument, Novak draws upon and traces the development of the notion of the Noahide covenant as the basis for his granting legitimacy to Christianity. In fact, the importance of the Noahide laws as a guide for all Jewish discussions of pluralism is forcefully put by Novak. He writes

> Any Jewish constitution of the status of non-Jews, if it is to find a genuine place for itself in the ongoing tradition of Judaism, must constantly and consistently refer to the doctrine of the Noahide laws. (1989, 26)

Emmanuel Levinas includes Islam with Judaism and Christianity through allusion to both the biblical heritage and to their common mission. The one God has called all three communities to teach of the responsibility which members of these communities have for every human (1990, 178–180).

When recognition of other traditions, beyond Christianity and Islam, is proposed by modern Jewish thinkers, it is obvious that reference to a common biblical heritage is insufficient. I was initially surprised that an understanding of the limits of our relationship to God is so frequently the foundation of the argument for this extensive recognition of other religions. Repeatedly, there is reference to the limits of each tradition, as well as of our knowledge, language, and paths to and service of God.

Some reference to the limitations of human historical experience in the face of the infinite nature of the divine is present, for example, in the writings of Buber, Heschel, Hartman, and Borowitz.

To backtrack somewhat, Buber uses this discourse at one point in his discussion of Judaism and Christianity. He argues for respect, which is more than toleration, between the faiths, because "we are united in our feeling that our Father's house is differently constructed than our human models take it to be" (1963, 40).[20]

A perennial leitmotiv in Heschel's work is the contrast between the finiteness of human approaches to or understandings of God and the infinite glory of the divine. This appears in his discussion of Judaism—once describing the Bible as in itself, a midrashic response to revelation (1966, 185), as well as his general affirmation of religious pluralism. He has written, "the majesty of God transcends the dignity of religion," and more extensively,

> The ultimate truth is not capable of being fully and adequately expressed in concepts and words. The ultimate truth is about the situation that pertains between God and man. . . . Revelation is always an accommodation to the capacity of man. . . . The voice of God reaches the spirit of man in a variety of ways, in a multiplicity of languages. One truth comes to expression in many ways of understanding. (1990, 353–354)

The limited nature of all experiences and understandings of revelation is a key component in Hartman's defense of pluralism. He specifically contests the view that revelation is exclusive to a particular tradition and a "source of absolute, eternal, and transcendent truth" (1990, 248). In speaking of the finite nature of all that pertains to the human, he both supports Judaism's commitment to the Sinai encounter, and allows for God's interaction with others. As he sees it,

> Revelation in history is always fragmentary and incomplete. Divine-human encounters cannot exhaust the divine plentitude. Revelation expresses God's willingness to meet human beings in their finitude, in their particular historical and social situation, and to speak to them in their own language. (1990, 247)

The radical particularization of history eliminates the need for faith communities to regard one another as rivals. . . . But if Revelation can be separated from the claim of universality and if a people of biblical faith can regain an appreciation of the particular that characterizes the divine-human encounter, then pluralism can become an integral part of biblical faith experiences. (1990, 252)

Central to Borowitz's rejection of the "imperialistic assertion of the primacy of the particular," is his allusion to the limits of any understanding of God. He actually takes this as a "fundamental principle" of non-Orthodoxy. In his words,

Jews who are not Orthodox believers should take seriously the fundamental principle of non-Orthodoxy, that our human insight into religious truth, while great enough to stake our life on, is always limited and not absolute. Those whose piety differs from ours may therefore well have another true if similarly limited sense of the Ultimate, and thus we must be practicing religious pluralists. (1991, 192)[21]

Finally, it is important to note the manner in which Heschel augments his discussion of the limits of human and historical experience. In harmony with his view that people of different faiths can profoundly help one another, he expands the discourse about particularity to include an understanding of interdependence. Most of the writers working with the notion of particularity are deeply concerned to turn the separateness and independence of individual faiths into an absolute principle. However, Heschel finds this to be parochial. For him, "no religion is an island," which means that advocates of pluralism must become aware of the ways in which communities interact and affect one another (1990, 345).

THE QUESTION OF ELECTION

As we have seen, the works of modern Jewish philosophers reflect some of the ways in which living and speaking with persons from other religious traditions have affected Judaism. Jewish thinkers have extended the recognition of the other beyond earlier parameters set by the tradition, and they have explored new ways of conceiving of history and our contact with the divine in the context of justifying this life and recognition. Religious pluralism has affected Jewish thought even more directly—and perhaps substantially—by challenging one of its cardinal notions, that of election.

Many contemporary Jewish thinkers have explicitly remarked that there is at least an apparent tension between the notion of election—that is, the understanding that God initiated and established a unique covenant with the Jewish people—and our contemporary pluralist environment.

Hartman begins his essay, "Pluralism and Biblical Theology," in the following manner: "It has often been felt that scriptural revelation and divine election are incompatible with religious pluralism" (1990, 243). He sees the heart of the problem not as a matter of monotheism, but as "the claimed uniqueness of divine revelation and election" (1990, 244).

Dorff also acknowledges that the traditional notion of election is the source of a serious uneasiness among contemporary Jews. While affirming that the covenant "does not entail exclusivity or triumphalism in Judaism," he concedes that

> It is not easy, though, to balance a sense of appreciation and pride in being God's Covenanted people and following God's preferred way with the firmly held belief that, as God's creatures, all people are the object of His concern and eligible for His favor. (1982, 483)

Finally, under the heading of "Chosenness, Hierarchy, and Difference," Judith Plaskow remarked that the concept of election, and of "chosenness" in her vocabulary, necessarily entails an unacceptable statement of privilege "in relation to those who are not chosen" (1991, 100).

A few decades earlier, Mordecai Kaplan—and today, Judith Plaskow—concluded that, in light of our lives with others, the concept of election/chosenness must be rejected. Kaplan wrote that chosenness was "objectionable as barring the way to peace and harmony among religions and making for self-righteousness and cant" (1946, 20).[22] His replacement of this concept with that of "peoplehood" was in harmony with other changes to Jewish religious thought that he sought, including the excision of supernatural revelation and the erasure of the metaphor of God as person. He believed that Jews should see their religion and culture/civilization as expressions of the history and life of the Jewish people. Thus, this people's religion is distinct, while not differing in nature, from the religions and cultural expressions of other peoples.

As has already been mentioned, Plaskow's critique of chosenness/election is given a powerful and singular perspective by her feminist Jewish framework. She believes that, in essence, the concept of chosenness masks a claim for superiority. Chosenness is diagnostic of the overall and systematic way in which difference is treated in Judaism. Difference is not just marked off. There is always an accompanying hierarchy and valuation. Plaskow contends that feminist Jews must confront this pervasive treatment of difference, by suggesting a way in which persons' distinctiveness can be acknowledged without privileging some and attacking others. In her words

> If Jewish feminism is to articulate a model of community in which difference is acknowledged without being hierarchalized, it will have to engage the traditional Jewish understanding of difference by rejecting the idea of chosenness without at the same time denying the distinctiveness of Israel as a religious community. (1991, 97)

Plaskow also offers a remedy that recognizes that there are always differences in any group/community, or between communities. However, it positively responds to these differences, by viewing distinctive elements as a necessary and enriching feature of any wider whole.

Most modern Jewish thinkers have explored the possibilities that reside in the concept of election rather than summarily discarding it in reacting to pluralism. For many of them, election testifies to Israel's vocation. It is seen as a specific call or summons, not as a category that implies something about the nature of Jews. In this light, election is sometimes seen as something that other peoples can appropriate, if they endeavor to live out the ideal to which Israel is devoted. For other thinkers, the prima facie tension between election and pluralism is overcome through an analysis of the religious role of the particular in human history.

The most extensive treatment of this concept is found in a work by David Novak, *The Election of Israel.* He sees election as the central category for Jewish religious life and thought, as he writes

> So the ultimate answer to any question of Jewish identity is theological, the one that points to the factors of election and covenant, the one that points to God's relationship with his people. More specific answers, legal or otherwise, will have to be consistent with this ultimate answer in order to be truly cogent. (1995, 5)

However, Novak believes that "the classical doctrine of election" needs to be reexamined—or, in his words, retrieved. He argues that, starting with Spinoza, modern Jewish thinkers have eroded or undermined this doctrine, especially by eliminating the notion that the transcendent God actively chooses Israel. With the help of Rosenzweig—whom he also criticizes—and philosophy, Novak reaffirms an understanding of election that retains this divine relationship to a particular people as well as the universal dimension of the doctrine.

Rosenzweig saw Jewish election in terms of divine vocation, of Jews accepting and living out God's law. He wrote that, through Jewish law, "the passive state of a people being chosen and set apart is changed into the activity on the people's side of doing the deed which sets it apart" (Glatzer ed. 1970, 243). Rosenzweig also believed that the unique role of Israel in history, as well as the Christian mission to all peoples, would continue as long as human history itself endured.

Buber understood election as a reminder of the responsibility to act as a model for others. Israel was the first people to understand that the relationship to God was the basis for the totality of community or national life. As a nation of priests, Israel was enjoined to establish justice as a principle in every realm. When the people lives up to this ideal, it stands as a model for others. One of the most powerful statements of Buber's view of election is found in his famous essay, "Hebrew Humanism," originally published in 1942. In it, he insists that election is not a matter of the people's superiority, nor its glorious future. It is a demand.

> Israel is chosen to enable it to ascend from the biological law of power, which the nations glorify in their wishful thinking, to the sphere of truth and righteousness. God wishes man whom he has created to become man in the truest sense of the word, and wishes this to happen not only in sporadic instances, as it happens among other nations, but in the life of an entire people, thus providing an order of life for a future mankind, for all peoples combined into one people. (1973, 461)

Levinas belongs to that group of philosophers who explain the meaning of election in terms of *vocation* and *model*. He does not see Israel's vocation as a matter of some special characteristic nor as something in which others cannot participate. The vocation is one of absolute responsibility for the other. Thus, Israel is chosen to embody that which is a demand for everyone. It takes upon itself a duty to which all persons are subject. This responsibility can only be taken up, not transferred to another. In his incomparable words

> The idea of a chosen people must not be taken as a sign of pride. It does not involve being aware of exceptional rights, but of exceptional duties. It is the prerogative of a moral consciousness itself. It knows itself at the centre of the world and for it the world is not homogenous: for I am always alone in being able to answer the call, I am irreplaceable in my assumption of responsibility. Being chosen involves a surplus of obligations for which the "I" of moral consciousness utters. (1990, 176–177)

David Hartman, Elliot Dorff, and Abraham Heschel are examples of those who concentrate on the relationship between the particular and the universal to explore the meaning of election.

Hartman does not see the Jewish notion of election as implying that God cannot have special relationships with other peoples. He distinguishes between the ways that creation and revelation are understood. The God of creation has a general relationship to all persons. However, within history, God can only work through particulars. He writes

> Election represents a particularization of God's relationship to human-kind by way of divine involvement in history, but *without* implying that there can be only one exclusive mediatory of the divine message. Consequently, theologians who claim that worship of the universal God is incompatible with election are making a "category mistake." The universal God is the God of Creation. It is God as the Lord of history Who enters into specific relationships with human beings and Who may be perceived in a particularistic manner. (1990, 252)

Dorff discusses the notion of election in terms of the universalist and the particularist elements that permeate both Jewish and Christian self-understandings. The recognition that God relates to all persons is an expression of universalism. Particularism is evidenced in the understanding that God relates to humans through the finite realms of history and community. Together, these strains indicate that the historical experience of God by one group should not be taken as cancelling out the experience of others. In his words,

> The particular way in which God relates to each group may be different, and it is inevitable that people will feel that their own way is best, but that should not produce the conclusion that other ways are necessarily bad, ineffective, or inauthentic. It may well be that God wisely entered into different forms of relationship with different peoples to fit the traditions, talents, and sensitivities of each group. (1982, 497)

Finally, Heschel is aware of the challenge of pluralism to the concept of election. He, too, explains this concept in terms of particularity. He does not question that the Jewish people has been sought out by God. However, he leaves the way open for God's approach to others. In one discussion, he cites the Prophet Micah.

> The Jews do not maintain that the way of the Torah is the only way of serving God. "Let all the peoples walk each one in the name of its god, but we will walk in the name of the Lord our God for ever and ever" (Micah 4, 5). (1990, 357)

PLURALISM AND THE HOLOCAUST

Two prominent contemporary Jewish philosophers—Emil Fackenheim and Irving Greenberg—have found that the event of the Holocaust emerges as a catalyst for addressing the issue of pluralism. For Fackenheim, the Holocaust challenges both Judaism and Christianity, as well as the relationship between the two. Since 1967, Fackenheim has devoted the majority of his prolific writings to analyzing these challenges and the possible responses. As has already been noted, he has suggested that the Holocaust necessitates Jewish recognition of Christianity and Islam. In his words,

> But since the experience of Nazism and of Christian opposition to Nazism (which goes back to my adolescence), I have been convinced that there is now a need for Jewish recognition that the Christian (and the Mohammedan [sic]) not only affirms the One God but also stands in a living relation to him. Where to go from here I cannot say. (Morgan ed. 1987, 236).

Fackenheim has not actually been able to go much further. He believes that Jewish-Christian dialogue might creatively open up new perspectives, but he has been, on the whole, disappointed by the realities of that process (Morgan, ed. 1987, 235–240).

For Irving Greenberg, the Holocaust is a reorienting event that brings into question both the regnant values of modernity and those antipluralist elements in all religious traditions. The secular world can no longer be taken as absolute, because many of its prominent features—the notion of progress, the promise of science and technology, certain "universalist norms," and the value of individualism—not only failed to prevent but actually furthered the horrifying murder.

Greenberg insists that in order to further the task of redeeming the secular, religious traditions must be carefully examined. Elements that threaten the respect for others cannot be allowed to remain embedded within religions. In his words,

> Thus, Jews, Christians, and others must challenge every aspect of their traditions that overtly or covertly degrades others or nurtures hatred and thus reduces solidarity . . . If the commandments of God lead to collaboration in genocide or weakening of the capacity to resist it, then God, as it were, must be challenged. This challenge would be testimony for God, whereas acquiescence to degradation would be testimony against God. (1982, 76–77)

The effect of the Holocaust on religious thinking must also extend, according to Greenberg, to the repudiation of "religious triumphalism," and of the discourse that seeks to bestow divine authority upon any specific community (1982, 78).

CONCLUSION: ENTERING INTO DIALOGUE—
WHAT IS OWED TO THE OTHER?;
AND WHAT CAN BE LEARNED FROM THE OTHER?

In the following pages, let us draw together and extend some of the insights offered by modern Jewish thinkers that, throughout this chapter, have been reviewed concerning the challenge of pluralism. Let us also explore the nature of the stance that makes recognition possible, what is owed to the other, and what has been learned from the encounter.

A number of philosophers realize that one of the primary ways in which the encounter with the other influences Jewish understanding emerges from the very act of entering into dialogue. The nature of the stance, as it were, that precedes and grounds recognition or that allows the possibility of making statements about the authenticity of another's God/relationship, and about the legitimacy of another religion as a true path of/to the divine, needs to be illuminated. Statements about another's relationship to God must come from and are an aspect of one's own faith. Yet, statements about the other refer to religious experiences and realities that are not known first-hand by the one making the statement. Thus, to speak of the religious life of the other, requires *faith* but also an appreciation for *mystery*. The first is the prerequisite. The second refers to what must be left unknown and unsaid about the other.

Rosenzweig, Buber, and Heschel are examples of those who understood that recognition of the authenticity/legitimacy of the other's religious life could arise only from a prior religious commitment. Rosenzweig's presentation of *The Star*, as well as the discussion of the "messianic theory of knowledge," presuppose such a faith commitment. Buber insisted that it was vital, in the context of religious dialogue, that "the speaker really be rooted in the religious reality from which he speaks" (Glatzer and Mendes-Flohr eds. 1991, 613). Heschel was also adamant that the "*pre-requisite of interfaith is faith*" (1990, 350 [His emphasis]). He added that "Interfaith must come out of depth, not out of a void absence of faith. It is not an enterprise for those who are half learned or spiritually immature" (1990, 350).

Faith that is sensitive enough to recognize the faith of the other is also necessarily aware of the limits of language and understanding. Recognition cannot mean that the other's relationship to God is transparent to the outsider. Such a view would also imply that one could completely comprehend/appropriate the other's God/relationship into one's own system. Soloveitchik argues in the strongest terms against the attempt to appropriate the religious life of another for both moral reasons and because "the act of faith" is "totally incomprehensible" to the outsider (1969, 23–24). None of the other Jewish philosophers whom we have examined would substantially disagree with him.

Buber eloquently spoke of faith and mystery together. I have already quoted part of a longer statement of Buber, which is

> After all, two things matter in such things: that the speaker really be rooted in the religious reality from which he speaks and that, without compromising the firmness of his speech, he acknowledge the mystery of the relationship of the person involved to transcendence. Only on the basis of such an attitude, which to be sure is necessarily founded on paradox, can faith and humanity coexist in our world. (Glatzer and Mendes-Flohr eds. 1991, 613)

Finally, David Novak also brings together the necessity of an intimate experience of one's own tradition and an awareness of the hiddenness of the other's in his discussion of the parameters of Jewish/Christian dialogue. He writes

> The authentic relationship between Jews and Christians in the dialogue is a relationship between persons whose faith is already nurtured from within their own religious communities. No matter how visible the life of that singular religious community is to others, it can never be for an outsider what it is for an insider. For that life can be directly understood only by one who has made a total commitment to be one with that historical community. (1989, 114)

Thus, in drawing upon one's religious experiences, and demanding both an openness to difference as well as a sensitivity to the mystery of the other's religious life, the first effects of encounter or dialogue appear.

We have come across a number of statements about the obligations that arise from the encounter with a person from another religious tradition. As Levinas might put it, the relationship to the other immediately impinges upon our self-understanding, and shapes our actions by bringing to the fore what is owed. We will discuss this question by reviewing the nature of the recognition that is owed to the other, and the consequences drawn from this by different modern Jewish thinkers. Although many would not agree with my conclusions, I find that a convincing case is made by modern Jewish philosophers for insisting that we owe to others both the recognition of the authenticity of their relationship to God, and the legitimacy of their religious tradition.

An almost omnipresent dimension present in the discourse on pluralism by modern Jewish philosophers was the fundamental recognition of the other as a creature of God. This was also explained in terms of the basic worth and equality of all persons in the face of the divine. From this was taken the requirement of universal justice and the obligation to allow persons the freedom to worship God without interference. Under this rubric, it appears that Soloveitchik also included the obligations to work for the general welfare of all persons, as well as to join together with others in this pursuit.

Is the Jew obligated to acknowledge that persons of other traditions have a viable relationship to God? Many of the Jewish thinkers whom we have examined agree that this level of recognition is necessary. They seem to find it impossible to suggest that only the Jew has a viable relationship to God.

Rosenzweig and Buber recognize that persons from other religious traditions can be in an authentic living relationship to God. For both of them, not only is this relationship available to everyone, but they also insist that no paths can ensure its achievement. Rosenzweig expressed this by saying that no Psalm of David is guaranteed God's ear. Buber, for his part, saw the potentialities of an I-Thou relationship at all times, but also knew of the way in which this relationship is sometimes hindered by religious establishments.

Some Jewish thinkers believe that the recognition of other persons' lives of faith is possible or necessary, because Jews do have experiences of the faithfulness, conviction, or religious inwardness of those in other traditions. Heschel's discussion of the way some modern Christians have taught Jews about inwardness is a vivid example of this experience. Fackenheim would include the experience of Christian opposition to Nazism as justifying the idea that both Christians and Muslims stand in a living relation to God.

Is this recognition limited to those who are monotheists—that is, to Jews, Christians, and Muslims? Both Buber and Hartman would not limit recognition to persons from monotheistic traditions. Certainly, the former was able to experience the depth of faith expressed in lives and writings of persons from many of the world's religions. Along with his appreciation for the mystery that enshrouds all religious life, Buber's openness to every name by which the Ultimate is named resounds forcefully.

What follows upon this recognition of authenticity? In a general way, one is obligated to acknowledge, respect, and treat seriously the other's religious experiences. More specifically, we might consider Heschel's contention that we are responsible for helping the other in the core of that person's religious subjectivity. In his words, the purpose of "interreligious cooperation" is the helping of one another "to search in the wilderness for well-springs of devotion, for treasures of stillness, for the power of love and care for man" (1990, 359). In Heschel's view, dialogue must be extended to the sharing of the nature of our religious lives for the benefit of us both.

The next step is the question of the recognition of other religious traditions. What is required of the Jew today? Many modern Jewish philosophers realize that we must match, and then go beyond what traditional Jewish sources have allowed, which, at a maximum, have acknowledged the legitimacy of Christianity and Islam.[23] The vitality and historical role of Christianity and Islam are seen by a number of Jewish thinkers—including Levinas—as requiring them to acknowledge these traditions. None of these philosophers—except Lubarsky—expect, or would encourage, the narrowing of doctrinal disagreements, but they also do not believe that recognition implies this.

Many believe that all religious traditions must be recognized. Modern Jewish thinkers—including some who are Orthodox—seem to find that other faiths must be recognized in their own right. This means that traditions must be heard, and not judged or acknowledged, on the basis of their inclusion under one or another Jewish rubric, such as that of the Noahide laws.

There are a number of arguments given as a basis for allowing other traditions to be validated in their own terms. For example, philosophers such as Buber, Heschel, Hartman, and Borowitz argue in terms of the particularity, or limitedness, of all historical experience in the face of the infinite fullness of the divine. They would affirm that, in Heschel's terms, "The voice of God reaches the spirit of man in a variety of ways, in a multiplicity of languages" (1990, 354). It is also important to note the point made by feminist Jews, who suggest that, only in recognizing the multiplicity of human religious lives, will the diversity within the Jewish community itself be accepted.

Despite the obligations that arise from the recognition of the authenticity and legitimacy of the other, are we left with any criteria to use if we find that some religious practices within another tradition are abhorrent and must be contested? This is a complex and important issue, and one that is beyond the scope of the present study. Still, one initial criterion can be mined from the material discussed here.

This criterion is moral, and not doctrinal, and is made possible because of prior Jewish commitments. From a Jewish faith position, and in terms of our common status as creations or creatures of God, we can/must respond when the dignity of the other is at stake. We have the obligation to say "No!" when actions are done within any community that negate the infinite worth that the Jewish traditions gives to all human life.

Levinas used such terms as the transcendence and infinity of the other to indicate that the neighbor is fully beyond appropriation by anyone, and that there is an absolute injunction against violating that dignity and worth.

Soloveitchik indicates an important element of this dignity when he refers to the freedom of all persons to practice their religion.

How is Lubarsky's contention that dialogue should alter the different partners' doctrines concerning ultimate reality to be assessed? It does not appear to me that other Jewish philosophers agree with this position. They would find that such transformations might jeopardize that integrity and separateness—that is, the legitimate differences between traditions. Furthermore, I believe that it goes beyond the prerequisites of dialogue—namely, faith and mystery, that we have also discussed. Religious claims or doctrines about ultimate reality arise from the particular experience of religious communities. Jews can speak only from their own faith experiences, and they must respect the mystery of the other's experiences. In light of these considerations, a judgment about the doctrinal claims of other traditions—which is the prerequisite for coming to agreement about them—appears to me to be an inappropriate feature of interreligious dialogue.

However, this does not mean that the religious truth of the other cannot be understood or assessed. Not the nature of the claim but the power of the truth can, to some extent, be known. As noted earlier, I believe that, by extending Rosenzweig's notion of messianic truth, some criteria to understand this power of truth can be uncovered. Although Rosenzweig focused on the Jewish and Christian communities, and their "two eternally irreconcilable hopes," his theory that "values truths according to what it has cost to verify them and according to the bond they create among men" (1970, 206), can be stretched to ground a way of assessing religious truth. The criteria for valuing truth—namely, passion and community—need not be limited to two communities. They can, to some extent, be recognized by an outsider. Their absence can also be noted. Truths that do not bring people to stake much on, or which pit persons against each other, can rightly be said to lack authentic power. In all, Rosenzweig provides a set of criteria to enable the committed person to recognize the power of the truth of another, while acknowledging the impossibility of affirming the ultimate validity or truth/content of that truth for herself or himself.

What are the nature and limits of the dialogue that this overall examination of recognition entail? We are obligated to speak about and work with others for the general welfare of all humans. Dialogue should include exchanges of the ways that the life before God, and with others, is experienced for the benefit of all partners. Doctrinal statements are a part of dialogue. They are important because they help us to understand the other in their own terms. Their power can be assessed—at least the human dimension of it. However, the mystery of the particular relationship to God from which such statements arise precludes the possibility of seriously assessing the truth/content of such affirmations. Dialogue must also respect the separateness and integrity of each community, or what Soloveitchik understood as the metaphysical otherness of community (1969, 21). Despite this, dialogue cannot exclude critical words, when either side believes that the dignity of humans is not being respected by those in the other community.

To conclude this chapter, let us reexamine the ways in which Jewish religious life and reflection are affected by the pluralist encounter. This could be expressed through yet another question: What can we learn from the other?

First, entering into dialogue, in which authenticity and legitimacy are vital concerns, requires that one speaks from—and, thus, fosters the exploration of and learning about—the depths of one's own religious life. Dialogue draws upon, makes visible, puts at stake, and extends what has been experienced and understood within one's community.

Second, the encounter with others teaches us about the limits and particularity of our own religious experience. Hartman spoke of this understanding of limits in terms of the deepening of that important religious emotion, humility. Our religious language should reflect this humility, at least to the extent that any form of religious triumphalism is exorcised.

Third, in a related way, we can see that the notion of election has been reworked in response to pluralism. Jewish thinkers discuss election in terms of the particularity of the Jewish vocation. They conclude that openness to the other does not require that the concept of election be jettisoned. Election is part of Israel's mystery. However, our sensitivity to the mystery of the experiences that inhere in other traditions—which is another distinct lesson—means that we can not claim that God's election of the Jewish people is an exclusive one.

Fourth, as Heschel explained, the dialogue with persons from other traditions deepens Jewish faith in still another way. While doctrinal claims might separate such persons, elements of religious inwardness or subjectivity can be shared and mutually developed. This is that "fear and trembling" to which Heschel referred. From dialogue, we can learn of and exchange insights about common challenges in our time, as well as about authentic faith responses.

Fifth, the discourse about pluralism reminds us of our moral duties to alleviate suffering and all the conditions that jeopardize the dignity and worth of other persons.

Sixth, as mentioned under number three, dialogue develops a sense of the mystery of the other's relationship to God. It could similarly develop a respect for the mystery in which all of us stand.

Seventh, and lastly, the encounter with others brings to life the realization of the richness of the world's religious traditions, and thus, of the infinite fullness and love of the divine. The effect of this might be to add a sense of thankfulness for the other—especially, for the other as different—to our religious reflection and language.

Pluralism challenges Jewish faith and reflection. As a real challenge, it necessitates a complex of responses—that is, changes. I hope that we have come to see that this challenge—as well as those discussed in earlier chapters—brings to Judaism treasures that it probably can not otherwise discover. These discovered treasures emerge, and continue to emerge, from the life with others—that life of faith and mystery, commitment and openness, and steadfastness and responsibility.

Conclusion:
On Witnessing to the Divine Presence

It is not by superlatives that we can think of God, but by trying to
identify the particular interhuman events that open
towards transcendence and reveal the traces where God has passed.
—*"Dialogue with Emmanuel Levinas" in* Face to Face with Levinas

The Jewish philosophers whom we have examined testify to the power and meaningfulness of that religious language, born out of the life with others, to nourish Jewish life and thought. In order to better assess the adequacy of this language to orient the Jewish community, two questions must be addressed.

First, is the discourse about God's presence in connection with the encounter with others responsive to contemporary challenges to religious meaning, or is it a reversion to an unreflective fundamentalism? Second, to what extent is the relation to others an authentic Jewish vehicle for religious language and experience?

These expressions of religious language do not ignore the intense challenges to religious meaning that have punctuated the lives of all moderns. Perhaps the greatest challenge to the significance and vitality of contemporary religious language, at least for Jews, reverberates from the Holocaust. The discussion of the ramifications of the Holocaust by such philosophers as Emil Fackenheim, Richard Rubenstein, Arthur Cohen, Irving Greenberg, and others has detailed the extent of this threat.[1] Notions of God's providential direction of history, as well as Israel's covenant with God, seem to have been shattered in the wake of the murder camps. However, this is not the only test of Jewish religious language that has appeared in the modern period. Secularism—that is, the view that everyday experience together with the findings of science define the contours of reality—threatens to dissipate every encounter with the divine into a mere feeling.[2] If, following secularism, such encounters are reduced to hallucinations, or some type of isolated subjective sensations, then the concept of revelation has been unequivocally undermined. Feminist Judaism contests the depiction of God as male, as well as the exclusivity, dualism, hierarchy, and even the metaphor of God as person that many feminists believe have been the staple of the traditional discourse of monotheism. Finally, as we have seen, the religiously pluralist nature of the contemporary world puts into question every group's claim of divine election.

RESPONDING TO CONTEMPORARY CHALLENGES

Jewish religious language that features the life with others both reflects and responds to this contemporary situation.[3] Levinas's discussion of the God who is found within by the person who takes up Torah in the struggle for justice is a poignant response to the Holocaust. This is also evident in the concluding statement of his essay, that "loving Torah even more than God means precisely having access to a personal God against Whom one may rebel—that is to say, for Whom one may die" (1990, 145). Rosenzweig's refrain about trust in God, oneself, the tradition, and the community arises from a deep encounter with the secular world. He insists that God's presence is not cut off today. However, his is not just a language of assurance or certainty. Rosenzweig knows that there are moments of silence, and, equally significant, he discerns God's presence not in extraordinary interventions, but in the love of the neighbor.

We have noted the first tentative steps in the response of Jewish religious language to the required transformations outlined in feminist Jewish criticisms. Furthermore, we found that the language of God's presence was deepened and extended both through the addition of female pronouns and metaphors, and the revisioning of the divine/human relation in light of the erotic and nature. Finally, the awareness of the plurality of religions is bringing Jewish philosophers to consider new obligations of recognition, as well as to articulate a sensitive understanding of election in terms of the Jewish vocation among others.

Thus, this way of speaking of the divine presence in terms of the interhuman is not a withdrawal from religious reflection. Jewish philosophers have turned to this language precisely because it provides a sophisticated portrait of features of the human that are overlooked in the modern Western secular, scientific, and philosophic discourses. While persons who belong to different religious traditions might have other ways to speak of the nature of human life, this pattern of religious language is an inescapable instrument for Jews. Rosenzweig believed that the changes engendered by speech, and through love, were quintessential to human development. Furthermore, he found that the depth of these transformations testified to God's presence. Speech and love are divine gifts that remake individuals who are imprisoned in the cage of the self into persons capable of participating in the address and response that establish all human life. For Levinas, the very nature of subjectivity—that is, the essential characteristic of being a person—involves being obsessed, even to the point of possession, by responsibility for the other. In the face-to-face encounter, Levinas found the means to describe the nature, consequences, and religious features of this obsession. He spoke of that trace of the divine which is manifested through the ethical response to the other's face.

Feminist Jews have utilized the language of the divine to express some fundamental truths of us all, including that our bodies are not mere tools, that we are profoundly connected with the cycles of nature, and that human differences should be appreciated as contributing to the richness of all. Additionally, living among those of other religious traditions has cultivated elements in Jewish religious language that highlight both the universal and particular features of human life. Jews share with all others the dignity of being God's creatures, each one created in the image of the divine. However, in terms of historical existence, persons live distinctive lives in communities. Jewish philosophers have expressed the first—universal dimension—in terms of creation, and the expected messianic redemption. They have expressed the second—the element of particularity—through such concepts as revelation, election, and the history of the covenant.

JEWISH CONTINUITY AND INNOVATION

In what ways is this language of the encounter with others truly Jewish? Throughout this book, I have sought to indicate that my reading of modern Jewish philosophy is just one interpretation—an interpretation that invites other commentators and other readings. Additionally, I have noted that a conclusive judgment about some of the major changes suggested here that concern issues raised by feminist Judaism and religious pluralism cannot be made without the addition of both more voices and detailed studies of the Jewish tradition. However, I have also claimed that this reading of modern Jewish philosophy, and the conclusions reached through it, provide authentic avenues for contemporary Jewish religious language. We can substantiate this claim by looking at both the ways in which this language draws upon the Jewish past, and the extent to which it provides something new.

Rosenzweig's and Levinas's examinations of the relation between persons drew consistently upon Jewish sources. We have already intensively explored Rosenzweig's small writing on anthropomorphism. According to him, this biblical feature provides the justification for utilizing the language of human relations to speak of the encounter with the divine. In this connection, it is also important to recall Rosenzweig's daring statement that attributed to these anthropomorphisms a role in Jewish survival equal to that of the Law and the Prophets. Rosenzweig utilizes other strands in the Bible in discussing the divine dimension of the meeting between persons. His interpretation of the divine/human love poem, *The Song of Songs*, is the keystone of *The Star* in it's entirety. From it he takes the conviction that human love draws upon and leads to God, as well as the understanding of the divine dimension of speech. Finally, Rosenzweig believed that the basis for all commandments was the dual commandment to love—that is, the command to love God through the loving of the neighbor.

Levinas cites the Bible as well as other traditional sources, particularly in his Jewish writings, in his discussions of the way in which the interhuman realm "open[s] towards transcendence." The obligation that the individual has to the other is detailed, according to Levinas, in the biblical command to care for the stranger, orphan, widow, and the poor. He explains central aspects of the face-to-face relation in terms of the commandment, "Thou shalt not kill." His extensive corpus of lectures on and interpretations of Talmudic tracts constantly reaffirm the major lesson in all of his writings—namely, the priority of ethics with its insistence on the inescapable answerability of the self for the other. Because Levinas believes that a knowledge of Talmudic literature is a sine qua non of authentic Judaism, the importance of this lesson for contemporary Jewish life and thought cannot be exaggerated.

The claim of feminist Jewish thinkers upon the Jewish community is based in many ways on the tradition itself. The demand for equality and full participation, they believe, is derived from the Torah's own insistence on justice. The discussions about female pronouns and metaphors look to the real, if infrequent, use in the Bible. Furthermore, the interest in love and the erotic as instruments for religious experience finds a model, once again, in *The Song of Songs* as well as in the often unappreciated literature of Jewish mysticism.

Traditional Jewish concepts and categories play an integral role in the discussion of religious pluralism. Many Jewish philosophers explore such concepts as the *ger toshav*, and the Noahide laws, in order to understand Jews' relations to non-Jews. Those probing the obligations concerning recognizing others turn to biblical pronouncements about the way in which the stranger was to be treated, as well as to the range of Jewish reflections on the meaning of creation, revelation, redemption, and the covenant. Thus, the use of religious language to explore what is owed to persons in other religious traditions is certainly nourished and directed by traditional antecedents.

Yet, despite the role of Jewish sources in these discussions of religious language and the relation to others, the new, and innovative nature of much of these examinations cannot, and must not, be ignored. In light of the challenges to Jewish religious language that have appeared throughout the modern period, it would be impossible for this language to retain vitality unless it included the innovative. In other words, the significance and power of contemporary Jewish religious language must be measured, not only in terms of its fidelity to the past, but also in terms of its ability to respond to our unprecedented modern or postmodern times. To offer one way of looking at what these times require of Judaism, let us explore the daring and perspicacious thought of the contemporary philosopher Irving Greenberg.[4]

In the essay, "Religious Values After the Holocaust: A Jewish View," Greenberg assesses the impact of the Holocaust upon secular values, Christianity, and, particularly, Judaism. He finds that the extensively choreographed, and precisely executed, murder of six million Jews puts into question such pivotal secular features as the positive correlation between increasing human power and progress, "the universalist orientation of modern culture—its mindset to operate by rationalized, universal categories rather than by personalized and particularist relational categories" (1982, 69), and the overarching value of individualism. While Greenberg does not believe that modernity must be condemned as an aberrant path in human history, he insists that its presuppositions and values must be revised in order to eliminate extreme tendencies and to forge a new balance between universalism and particularism (1982, 70–71).

Greenberg continues to value the secular world's enhancement of human life, but he recognizes that secularism's excesses can only be controlled through religious/transcendent sensitivities and imperatives. He speaks of a "holy secularity" which draws upon one's religious tradition to contest the apotheosis of the secular world as well as the triumphalist elements in all religions. In his words, "Holy secularity focuses on the re-creation of the image of God and of a society that nurtures this human dignity" (1982, 77).[5]

Greenberg's most radical comments, however, are directed toward the effects of the Holocaust upon basic features of Jewish self-understanding. He finds that traditional beliefs in, and understandings of, God's covenantal providence must be reformulated, because there was no divine intervention at that crucial hour. This monumental deficiency suggests, in his eyes, "the absence of a covenantal partner or a breakdown of covenantal responsibility" (1982, 71). Yet, as we have already heard, Greenberg does not profess a Judaism bereft of the transcendent, because it is precisely the sense of the transcendent, and the ultimate moral values secured by it, that must check all those dangerous modern human pretensions to the absolute.

In order to gauge a satisfactory response to the Holocaust, Greenberg puts this event into the wider context of Jewish history. He believes that there are some parallels between it, and two other epochal challenges—namely, the destructions of the First and Second Temples. Each time, in response to the earlier shattering events, Jews rethought the nature of the covenant and God's presence, rather than repudiate the transcendent altogether. The second destruction, for example, brought Jews to see their relationship to God in terms of an equal partnership, rather than as one where God was conceived of as the mature, active partner, and humans were the passive dependents. When God's direct intervention failed to appear, the Rabbis emphasized humans' freedom of action and ultimate responsibility for their own world.

The Holocaust marks another step in the development of the relationship between God and the Jewish people, and the expansion of the sphere of human responsibility. The covenant with God is now a voluntary one, according to Greenberg. The Jewish obligation to abide by the terms of the covenant has been rescinded, because of God's absence during the Holocaust. However, in lieu of the legal contract, a new relationship has been established through Jewish loyalty. Greenberg cites the growth of Jewish life in North America, and the emergence of the modern state of Israel, as evidence of a new Jewish dedication to the covenant. Furthermore, the development of both of these Jewish communities has been predicated on the wider understanding that human duty must increase, even as God's intervention in the world is less manifest.

Two implications of the new model of "voluntary covenant" are especially important in Greenberg's eyes. First, he details major changes in Jewish institutions as well as conceptions of God's presence in the following statement:

> Just as prophecy and the temple were too "sacramental" and overt for the post-Destruction era, so the rabbinate and synagogue may be too "sacred" for a post-Holocaust era. The covenant will be acted out with God becoming the "silent" partner, present, sharing in the pain and joy, but essentially calling on the human to take full responsibility for the fate of humanity and for coming (or bringing) of redemption. However, this will be *called* a human response. The explication of "what doth the Lord require of thee" (KJV) may come from more secularized speakers—perhaps writers, artists, professors, politicians. Paradoxically again, the secularization will shift the consciousness of God's presence from the more limited number of sacred settings to an almost universal presence; that is, secular settings will be the focus of religious activity. Prayer will be expressed in actions and/or will be the prayer of the strong: that is, it will be silent, less pleading, less repetitious and flattering to the Divine. (1982, 83)

Second, Greenberg finds that the new covenant will be "pluralist and multiform" (1982, 84). In particular, a new equality between Jewish men and women is required. In his words, the "call for religious equality . . . is an attempt to raise them [women] to a new level of full human responsibility and religious testimony" (1982, 84).

There is an obvious but still profound correspondence between the previous summary paragraph of Greenberg's views about the shape of post-Holocaust Judaism, and Jewish philosophical understandings of the role of religious language in the life with others presented in the preceding chapters of this book. Greenberg holds that religious experience will no longer be restricted to a "limited number of sacred settings" consecrated by the tradition, such as the synagogue. Rather, through the impact of secularization, there will be a shift in "the consciousness of God's presence . . . to an almost universal presence; that is, secular settings will be the focus of religious activity." This is precisely the change indicated by the philosophers who speak of God's presence in terms of the interhuman, and is also suggested by this study of responses to religious pluralism and feminist Judaism. For Rosenzweig and Levinas, every place where the neighbor is met, or the face-to-face meeting occurs becomes the preeminent setting for the encounter with God. The examination of interreligious dialogue focused on one arena for such an encounter. Jewish philosophers recognize that this dialogue with others is grounded in both faith and mystery. Whenever it takes place, there is an opportunity for God's presence to be evoked and shared. Feminist Jews have further amplified the settings for experiencing God's presence by speaking of the erotic life and the tie to nature.

Greenberg characterizes the human response to God's presence in ethical/religious terms. The encounter with God does not lead persons to some "other" world, but directs them into this world in the deepest ways. It demands that persons "take full responsibility for the fate of humanity and for the coming (or bringing) of redemption." Correspondingly, Levinas insisted that it was, through the face-to-face relation, which is the ethical relation par excellence, that a trace of God appears—namely, that God who commands us not to kill, and calls us to be responsible for others. For Rosenzweig, the divine imperative to love the neighbor meant that the individual always stands under the obligation to turn toward those who stand closest and to speak. He regarded the fulfillment of the love command as integral to the process of redemption. In fact, Rosenzweig believed that the person who turns toward the neighbor was the primary, if not the exclusive,[6] agent of redemption (1972, 213–215).

An awareness of the ethical import of religious experience and language is also behind the efforts of feminist Jews to correct traditional God/language. They understand that the place of women within the Jewish community cannot be transformed unless the language about God reflects women's lives and experiences. The seemingly simple endeavour to foster the use of female pronouns and metaphors stands, in this light, as a revolutionary,

transformative moment in Jewish history, redressing what many see as millennia of oppression and exclusion. Whenever God is called upon as "She,"
the full participation of women in the life of the Jewish community is significantly furthered.

The relation with persons in other traditions constitutes another sphere
in which Jewish philosophers feel that they are responding to a divine calling.
The concern to acknowledge the authenticity and legitimacy of the religious
lives of those who are different grows from the awareness that there is a
divine command to respect and help others. It must also be mentioned that
Jewish philosophers who take part in these discussions often believe that their
venture constitutes an indispensable moment in the struggle for universal
peace.

Two further aspects of Greenberg's statement are important to note.
First, despite the unprecedented post-Holocaust era, and the new covenant,
the author persists in employing anthropomorphic metaphors to speak of
God. God is portrayed as a person sharing our "pain and joy." God calls and
stands with us in a covenantal relationship, even if this calling "partner" does
not directly intervene into the realm of human history. Thus, the powers
inherent in the language of God as person, to which both Rosenzweig and
Levinas so eloquently attested, are also appreciated by Greenberg.

All three find that this language still nourishes Jewish life in our hopeful,
albeit troubled time.[7] For Rosenzweig, the anthropomorphisms of the Bible
guarantee that the divine call is "open to everybody today" (1937, 529). For
Greenberg, anthropomorphic language provides a basis to speak of God's "almost universal presence." However, it also yields the resources to reflect our
experiences as lonely sojourners. Levinas wrote of this in terms of standing
"under an empty sky," and Greenberg spoke of God as our "silent partner."

The role of the language of God as person is not as overwhelming in
the discourse of feminist Jews and of religious pluralism. A few of the former
thinkers believe that this language should be rejected, or at least augmented
with nonpersonal language. However, the majority of feminist philosophers
acknowledge the important place which it has had in the past and continues
to hold in the present. In particular, the fundamental and almost universal
demand to introduce female pronouns and metaphors for God, certainly provides evidence of a commitment to the power of this language to reflect and
support women's lives and experiences.

While the issue of anthropomorphic language was not directly raised in
connection with Jewish philosophers' thinking about religious pluralism, it
was often tangentially present. The language of humans being created in
God's image, the divine concern for the stranger, and the covenant with
Noah, exemplify the use of personal metaphors to speak of the divine. There
is more evidence for this in the depiction of the diverse ways in which the

peoples of the earth relate to the ultimate. Despite the differences between Heschel's existentialist orientation and Hartman's Maimonides-inspired work, Heschel relates that the "voice of God reaches the spirit of man in a variety of ways" (1990, 353), and Hartman that "each should walk before God in the way that He taught it" (1990, 253).

A second element featured in Greenberg's statement alludes to the new messengers/spokespersons of this post-Holocaust Judaism. He foresaw that the "explication of 'what doth the Lord require of thee' . . . may come from more secularized speakers." The Jewish philosophers who have explored the life with others as a creative source for religious language—especially the language of responsibility—clearly exemplify Greenberg's contention.

Finally, Greenberg's understanding that the voluntary covenant will exhibit a new equality between Jewish men and women is fully consonant with an omnipresent aspect of this examination of contemporary Jewish religious language. The critique and creative contributions of feminist Judaism is not an isolated matter, but both corrects and opens up some of the elemental powers of this language. In fact, the "call for religious equality" includes—but also goes beyond—what Greenberg saw as the "attempt to raise" women to a new position within the community. It signifies the elevation of all Jews, both women and men, "to a new level of fully human responsibility and religious testimony."

A Midrash

Isaiah 43:10, "You are my witnesses, says the Lord." The Rabbis interpreted this as meaning: "If you are my witnesses, I am God, but if you are not my witnesses, I am not God." [And now it must be added: without Her witnesses, both God and we are lost.][8]

Contemporary Jewish philosophers have reaffirmed and extended the lesson of the ancient *midrash*. To accomplish this, they have been compelled to describe our lives with and obligations to others. In the face of the radical challenges of modernity, they have found that this speaking/writing of God still uncovers—it even elicits—the presence of the divine. Carried by this language, they offer glimmers of hope and trust, reminding us that, only through ethical testimony to God's presence, can we prevail.

Notes

INTRODUCTION

1. These three axes for Jewish philosophy were suggested by David Hartman in a lecture in 1973. A number of different views about the nature and parameters of modern Jewish philosophy are discussed in Kenneth Seeskin's *Jewish Philosophy in a Secular Age* (1990, 1–29), and in Norbert Samuelson, ed., *Studies in Jewish Philosophy*.

2. Jacob Neusner has contrasted the perception by some that Judaism is under seige with the true challenges of living in freedom, in "Freedom's Challenge to Judaism" (1981, 30–39).

3. There is a very large literature on the nature of religious language, particularly by Christian theologians. One of the most influential thinkers is Gordon D. Kaufman. See, for example, Gordon D. Kaufman, *God the Problem* (1992).

4. See Steven T. Katz's *Post-Holocaust Dialogues* (1983), and my treatment of the work of Fackenheim and Cohen in "Can We Still Stay with Him?: Two Jewish Theologians Confront the Holocaust," (Oppenheim, 1987).

5. The relevance of *midrash* and the "midrashic framework" for modern Jewish philosophy has been the recurring interest of Emil Fackenheim. He sees *midrash* as a classic method of interpretation that allows for the contradictions that inevitably beset attempts to write about God's presence from the standpoint of Jewish commitment. Fackenheim explores this in "The Structure of Jewish Experience," in Michael Morgan's *The Jewish Thought of Emil Fackenheim* (1987, 207–222). A good introduction to the modes of rabbinic interpretation included under the term *midrash* is given by David Stern in the essay, "*Midrash*" in Cohen and Mendes-Flohr, eds., *Contemporary Jewish Religious Thought* (1987, 613–620). However, the term has also

been used by contemporary Jewish thinkers in a wider sense to mean interpretation, explanation, and even story. I will be using it in this more general and expansive way throughout this book.

6. A discussion of Buber's understanding of the life of dialogue and the sphere of "the between" is presented in Maurice Friedman's *Martin Buber* (1956, 85–97).

7. Stéphane Mosès, in commenting upon Rosenzweig's understanding of the relationships between God, the world and humans, maintains that "asymmetry is fundamental in the general economy of *The Star*," in *System and Revelation*, (1992, 101). Levinas writes, for example, in *Otherwise Than Being*, that "In proximity the other obsesses me according to the absolute asymmetry of signification, of the-one-for-the-other" (1981, 158). The importance of this notion for Levinas is discussed by Edith Wyschogrod (1972, 33), and by Robert Gibbs throughout his work *Correlations in Rosenzweig and Levinas*. A brief discussion of the differences between Levinas and Buber in this regard, along with a bibliography, is found in the present work in chapter 1, note 35.

8. See Paul Ricoeur's *Freud and Philosophy*.

9. This point—namely that "To date, feminism has made no impact on the discipline of Jewish philosophy"—is detailed in Hava Tirosh-Rothschild's article, " 'Dare to Know': Feminism and the Discipline of Jewish Philosophy" (1994, 85).

10. This lack of recognition by male Jewish thinkers of feminist Jewish philosophy parallels the treatment—until, perhaps, this last decade—of modern Jewish philosophy by Christian and post-Christian thinkers. In each case, those who have been in the majority and held power have refused to hear the voice of the other. Diagnostic of this lack of recognition by male Jewish philosophers is the absence of any reference to feminist Jewish reflection in reviews by David Novak (1990) and Kenneth Seeskin (1991) of Jewish philosophy and theology in the decade of the 1980s for the journal *Modern Judaism*.

CHAPTER 1

1. The different readings of Rosenzweig have multiplied during the last few years. Robert Gibbs briefly notes that there is a significant disagreement between his *Correlations in Rosenzweig and Levinas*, and Stéphane Mosès' *System and Revelation*. One of the most outstanding areas of disagreement appears in the contrast between Gibbs's statement that *The Star* utilizes creation, revelation, and redemption as theological concepts (1992, 19–20), and Mosès's view of them as designating religious experiences (1992, 100). Also see Wendell Dietrich's "Is Rosenzweig an Ethical Monotheist? A Debate with the New Francophone Literature," and Norbert Samuelson's "The Concept of 'Nichts' in Rosenzweig's 'Star of Redemption,' " both of which present points of departure that vary from that which is offered in the present treatment.

2. This discussion of Levinas differs from inquiries that examine him exclusively in terms of postmodern philosophic themes. A good example of such a treatment of Levinas's work is found in Mark C. Taylor's *Altarity*.

3. There is an excellent discussion of the influence of Rosenzweig on Levinas, as well as some recurring themes in their writings, in Gibbs's *Correlations in Rosenzweig and Levinas*, 23–33. Also see Richard Cohen's *Elevations*.

4. The standard treatment of Rosenzweig's life is presented in Nahum Glatzer's *Franz Rosenzweig*, 1–176.

5. For an examination of Levinas's life, and a discussion of the French-Jewish intellectual environment of the last decades, see Judith Friedlander's *Vilna on the Seine*, especially 80–91.

6. Levinas dedicated his book *Otherwise Than Being*; "To the memory of those who were closest among the six million assassinated by the National Socialists," and to millions of other "victims of the same hatred of the other man" (1981, v).

7. See Levinas's discussion of Rosenzweig's critique of philosophy in *Difficult Freedom*, 181–191.

8. Rosenzweig believed that the emergence of the Jewish and Christian communities was part of a process whereby what had earlier been latent possibilities of encounter and speech in humans had now become actual.

9. Also see Levinas, *Ethics and Infinity*, 75–76.

10. The same point—namely, that " 'ego' is the essence of the world. All the wisdom of philosophy can be summed up in this sentence"—is found in Rosenzweig, *Understanding the Sick and the Healthy*, 54.

11. Levinas's characterization and critique of philosophy are powerfully presented in such essays as "God and Philosophy" and "Ethics as First Philosophy" in *The Levinas Reader*. Also see the preface to *Totality and Infinity*, 21–30.

12. Mosès holds that the link between the state and philosophy is also very strong in *The Star*. He writes of "the theme that was to dominate in *The Star*, that of the ontological bound [sic] uniting the political system of the State . . . with the philosophical system of the Totality. . . ." (1992, 32–33). There are also two excellent discussions of Rosenzweig's view of politics and history: Alexander Altmann's "Franz Rosenzweig on History" (1988), and Paul Mendes-Flohr's "Franz Rosenzweig and the Crisis of Historicism," in his *The Philosophy of Franz Rosenzweig*.

13. See Harold Stahmer's "The Letters of Franz Rosenzweig to Margrit Rosenstock-Huessy."

14. Barbara Galli illuminates, for the first time, the importance of Rosenzweig's commentary on Halevi's poems in her book *Franz Rosenzweig and Jehuda Halevi*. She discusses the carefully crafted method that Rosenzweig employed to address both Halevi and his contemporaries (1995, 403).

15. Many commentators have looked at the significance of Levinas's innovative style. Susan Handelman, for example, has written that his work is "less 'art' than a kind of 'prophetic appeal,' for Levinas's repetitive writing style reflects that insistent call and appeal from the other which for him defines the essence of language" (1991, 180).

16. Richard Cohen discusses Levinas's "attack" upon phenomenology in the name of "the superlative positivity of the other person" in *Elevations*, 278–286.

17. Throughout this book, I detail the way that, for Rosenzweig, the love of God and the love of the neighbor are transformative and command every individual touched by this God/neighbor love to turn to others. In the second part of *The Star*, the commandment to love the neighbor is held to be incumbent upon all whom are touched by God's love, but, in the third part, the theological task of bringing God's love to the world is assigned to Christianity and not to Judaism. Thus, there appears to be a tension between the general treatment of the love of the neighbor and the specific roles given to Judaism and Christianity. However, I believe that despite this, Rosenzweig maintains that the Jew is commanded to love whomever stands the closest to him or her. Rosenzweig never explicitly states that for the Jews, the love of the neighbor cannot extend beyond the covenantal community. Statements both in *The Star* (1972, 218) and in his letters (Glatzer ed. 1970, 92) seem to imply that the neighbor is just whomever stands closest to the subject. Richard Cohen also provides a view that echoes other commentators concerning this question in *The Star* when he writes "What election requires of Jews in relation to non-Jews is concrete acts of neighborly love and the essentially anonymous works of justice" (1994, 20). There is a good discussion and critique of Rosenzweig's understanding of the love of the neighbor in David Novak's *The Election of Israel*, especially on pages 85–107.

18. In a letter of 1920, Rosenzweig relates that the self achieves some type of stability and authenticity only through extending a hand to the neighbor (1970, 92).

19. It is important to note that Levinas does not attribute to love—even the love of the neighbor—the same capacity that Rosenzweig does. On the whole, he is reticent to use the term *love* to speak of the ethical relationship. Gibbs makes this point, but also notes a change in *Correlations*, on page 184. A discussion of the tension between ethics and eros in Levinas's thought is presented in Richard Cohen's *Elevations*, especially on pages 207–208.

20. Erik Erikson, for example, places the developmental task of identity prior to the task of intimacy, in *Identity: Youth and Crisis*. Also see, B. Ables, *Therapy for Couples*, 24; and on the relationship between autonomy and intimacy, M. Scarf, *Intimate Partners: Patterns in Love and Marriage*, 20–24.

21. Rosenzweig affirms this understanding in the "New Thinking" (1937, 379). Also see Levinas's preface to Mosès's *System and Revelation*, (1992, 14).

22. Novak explains the term *metaethic* as the "transcendence of the universal by the particularity of human experience" (1995, 82). Also see Nathan Rotenstreich's

"Rosenzweig's Notion of Metaethics" in Mendes-Flohr's *The Philosophy of Franz Rosenzweig.*

23. Chapter 2 in this book explores the place of particular sacred texts in Rosenzweig's and Levinas's understanding of the relationship to God. Another aspect of this is eloquently brought out in Michael Fishbane's statement in *The Garments of Torah* that, "for Rosenzweig, the temporal path from history to redemption leads through the transformation of (scriptural) texts into empowered persons: one word at a time," on page 110. Also see the essays by Buber and Rosenzweig in *Scripture and Translation.* One expression of Levinas's appreciation for the Talmud is found in his *Nine Talmudic Readings,* (1990a, 3–11).

24. It is interesting to ask whether the use of religious stories is merely a requirement for reflection, or whether Rosenzweig and/or Levinas might believe that persons cannot fully live with others unless they see their lives as taking place within such stories.

25. Gibbs writes in terms of Rosenzweig that "a non-theological view of speech will not adequately describe intersubjective space" (1992, 58). Levinas has written that "It is our relations with men . . . that give to theological concepts the sole signification they admit of" (1988, 79).

26. While Richard Cohen's *Elevations* introduces some extensive analyses of Rosenzweig's understanding of love, it appears to me that he does not give due attention to the phenomenon of speech. This is especially evident in the chapter on Rosenzweig and Nietzsche (1994, 75–81; also 95, 101, 110). Yet, love and speech stand together, almost as synonymous, in the central part of Rosenzweig's *The Star* (1972, 201–202). Rosenzweig writes of "the wholly real employment of language [or speech] as the center-piece" of his treatment of revelation (1972, 174).

27. A central feature of Gibbs's treatment is his depiction of Rosenzweig's concern for the "speaking of language"—that is, its "practice or performance" (1992, 59).

28. This quotation was featured in an early review of *The Star* by Margarete Susman in 1923. Her review is translated in Arthur Cohen's, *The Jew,* (1980, 276–285). Rosenzweig's statement about the importance of the quotation was brought to light by Barbara Galli in a presentation at the annual meeting of the Association for Jewish Studies in December 1995.

29. For example, the divine commandments to love God and to love the neighbor unlock the self and open the soul to the world (Rosenzweig 1972, 176–177, 214–215).

30. Rosenstock-Huessy attributes to Rosenzweig the motto that, "the best things you can tell" in his letter in *Judaism Despite Christianity,* (1971, 163).

31. Rosenzweig belonged, during the period following World War I, to an informal group of thinkers—called the "Patmos Circle"—who were interested in the issue of the corruption of language in the political and academic spheres. Among these

people were Eugen Rosenstock-Huessy and Karl Barth. See Stahmer, *Speak That I May See Thee!*, pp. 121–124.

32. Richard Cohen discusses the distinction between "the saying" and "the said" in the context of Derrida in *Elevations* (1994, 155–157).

33. Edith Wyschogrod notes one of the ways in which language and the face are related in her book *Emmanuel Levinas*. She writes that "All language refers to the face which is its own 'word of honor,' " (1974, 88).

34. Richard Cohen treats the theme of "the face" in Rosenzweig and Levinas in relation to some important Jewish mystical texts in the chapter, "The Face of Truth and Jewish Mysticism," *Elevations* (1994, 241–273).

35. While Rosenzweig and Levinas share with Buber a deep concern for the dynamics of relationship, they are critical of the presentation of these in terms of the philosophy of "I and Thou." Rosenzweig did not agree with the stark opposition between the I-Thou and the I-It relationships. Levinas's main criticism of Buber is that, in proposing that the interaction of the self and other is symmetrical or mutual, the necessary shattering of the self's powerful egoism is lost. Rosenzweig's incisive one-page critique of Buber's famous book is discussed in Casper's, "Franz Rosenzweig's Criticism of Buber's *I and Thou*," in *Martin Buber: A Centenary Volume* (1984, 139–159). Levinas has written extensively about Buber: for example, "Martin Buber and the Theory of Knowledge," in *The Levinas Reader* (1989, 59–74). There is a fine analysis of Levinas's critique and Buber's responses in Robert Bernasconi's, " 'Failure of Communication' as a Surplus" (1988).

36. However, in *Otherwise Than Being or Beyond Essence*, Levinas turns to the concept of "proximity" to detail much of what he earlier speaks of in terms of the face (1981, 81–94).

37. Richard Cohen adds a helpful insight in terms of the way in which the commandment not to kill arises from the face-to-face. He writes "Only in the face of the other does the self come to feel its own natural capacities as potentially murderous. . . .'Thou shalt not murder' . . . is the very apparition of the other as other, the epiphany of the other's face" (1994, 125).

38. The biblical quotation is from *Isaiah* 57:18–19.

39. Of course, it is not just themes that help to characterize the nature of modern Jewish philosophy. Other aspects of the task of the modern Jewish philosopher are discussed in the introduction of this book.

40. There are many good discussions of the critiques that these Jewish philosophers offered. See, for example, Otto Pöggeler's "Between Enlightenment and Romanticism: Rosenzweig and Hegel," in Mendes-Flohr (1988, 107–123), and Richard Cohen's examinations of Levinas's relation to Husserl and Heidegger in *Elevations*, (1994, 133–161, 224–240).

41. Mark Taylor presents a forceful discussion of postmodernist thought in *Altarity*.

42. See Levinas's discussion of "fecundity," in *Totality and Infinity* (1988, 267).

43. There is an extensive literature on the relationship between Rosenzweig and Heidegger. Karl Löwith wrote a classic early essay, "M. Heidegger and F. Rosenzweig, or Temporality and Eternity," and there are recent articles by Steven Schwarzschild and Alan Udoff. The influence of Heidegger on Levinas is complex. See, for example, Levinas's statement in *Ethics and Infinity* (1985, 37–44), and, as noted before, Richard Cohen's discussion in *Elevations* (1994, 133–161, 224–240).

44. See my "Death and Man's Fear of Death in Franz Rosenzweig's 'The Star of Redemption' " (Oppenheim, 1978).

45. Bernard Casper presents a slightly different but illuminating angle to view Rosenzweig by taking the notion of "responsibility" as his key. The examination of the dynamics of dialogue is especially helpful. See, "Responsibility Rescued" in Mendes-Flohr's *The Philosophy of Franz Rosenzweig*.

46. For example, Galli examines one of Rosenzweig's letters to Rosenstock-Huessy in which the importance of faith as being different between the two of them is emphasized (1995, 335–336). Levinas's work is permeated with the view that only the other's infinite difference can contest and transform the self. Temporality is one of the essential dimensions of this difference. Richard Cohen contributes a very insightful discussion of the development of the theme of "temporality and alterity" in Levinas's thought. He writes

> Levinas's great insight is to have realized that the other person encountered face-to-face is not the subject's contemporary. . . . the other's time disrupts my time. . . . It is this upset, this non-integrateable insertion of the other's time into mine, that breaks up time and maintains the alterity required by a genuine or veritable time, neither the other's nor mine. (1994, 147)

47. This translation of Rosenzweig's article "On Anthropomorphism" (1937), was made by Barbara Galli. Rosenzweig's appreciation for the religious significance of anthropomorphic metaphors is a major point of departure in my *Mutual Upholding: Fashioning Jewish Philosophy Through Letters* (Oppenheim, 1992).

CHAPTER 2

1. It is important to note that Rosenzweig saw *The Star of Redemption* as a philosophic book, and regarded the new thinking itself as a new kind of philosophy (1970, 198). Levinas writes of God's relation to ethics throughout his philosophic works, including *Totality and Infinity* and *Otherwise Than Being or Beyond Essence*.

2. Gibbs speaks of the "thinning of the theological vocabulary" in Levinas's work, compared to the theological expressions of such other modern Jewish philosophers as Hermann Cohen, Buber, and Rosenzweig (1992, 23).

3. All the quotations from Rosenzweig's article in *Kleinere Schriften*, "Zur Encyclopedia Judaica: Zum Zweiten Band, Mit einer Anmerkung uber Anthropomorphismus" (1937, 525–533), appearing here are taken from a fine, unpublished English translation by Barbara Galli.

4. See Galli, "Rosenzweig Speaking of Meetings and Monotheism in Biblical Anthropomorphisms." Her commentary on Rosenzweig's essay emphasizes the importance of time in sensing the mystery of God (1993, 221).

5. The 1979 translation of and commentary on Levinas's essay was by Richard Sugarman and Helen Stephenson in *Judaism*. There is also a discussion of this essay in Susan Handelman's *Fragments of Redemption* (1991, 275–278).

I am using the translation by Sean Hand, published in *Difficult Freedom* (Levinas, 1990). Where two page numbers appear side by side, as in (142/189), the first refers to the 1990 translation, and the second to the 1976 French edition of *Difficile Liberté*.

6. Galli (1993) points out some of the ways in which more recent treatments of anthropomorphism in the Bible reassert the views that Rosenzweig critiques.

7. In this essay and elsewhere, Rosenzweig uses male pronouns to write about God. I do not believe that it is legitimate to change this usage when directly discussing a work by Rosenzweig. However, the issue of the gender of pronouns referring to the divine will be a critical feature of the third and fourth chapters of this book.

8. Nathan Rotenstreich critiques Rosenzweig's use of the term *common sense* as a foundation for his philosophic system in "Commonsense and Theological Experience on the Basis of Franz Rosenzweig's Philosophy" (1967, 353–360).

9. Rosenstock-Huessy shared Rosenzweig's view that philosophy—indeed, all academics—distrust language. Eugen sarcastically wrote in a letter to Franz about a contemporary who proved "the incomprehensibility and incommunicability of all thinking and of all language in the course of a work in three volumes" (Rosenstock-Huessy 1971, 107).

10. Fackenheim presents an illuminating discussion of the way that confidence in the ability to experience revelation has been subverted in the modern period in *Quest for Past and Future* (1968, 229–243).

11. Galli notes (1994, 71–75) that one of the determining factors in Rosenzweig's thinking about the way that the name of God should be translated in his and Buber's work on the Bible was the need to convey to his contemporaries the faith that God continued to care for them. While for Moses Mendelssohn, the notion of God's necessary existence, as "the Eternal," was primary, it was God's providence that Rosenzweig regarded as essential for his time—as it is for ours.

12. Gibbs provides the most helpful discussion of the distinction and interrelationship between Levinas's philosophic ("Greek") and Jewish ("Hebrew") writings in *Correlations* (1992, 156–175).

13. Both Rosenzweig and Levinas see the faithful person as one who takes a risk. Faith is a deep passion. It is not something that simply requires prudence. God treats persons as adults—that is, people have the freedom to believe or not believe. Rosenzweig wrote in *The Star* of God's tempting persons by making it difficult to believe

> He [God] must make it difficult, yea impossible, for man to see it [God's power and direction], so that the latter have the possibility of believing him and trusting him in truth, that is to say in freedom. (1972, 266)

14. The matter of Levinas's exclusive use of male pronouns for God will be examined in the fourth chapter.

15. The notion of God hiding His face (*hester panim*) is examined by André Neher in his article "Silence" in Cohen and Flohr, eds., *Contemporary Jewish Religious Thought* (1987, 873–879). Also see the important treatment of the history of theodicy in Jewish thought in Eliezer Schweid's *To Declare that God Is Upright* (Hebrew), (1994, 35–36). \

16. The concept of martyrdom or sanctification of God's name (*kiddush ha-Shem*) is also explored in Cohen and Flohr's *Contemporary Jewish Religious Thought*, this time in an essay by Hyam Maccoby (1987, 549–554). Schweid also discusses this (1994, 135–179).

17. In his treatment of Rosenzweig, Gibbs explores the importance of the cry—that intense questioning of God—and also the command as major poles for contemporary theology (1992, 100–101). Galli also turns to Gibbs's comments about the cry in her article on translating the name of God (1994, 63–64, 83).

18. Handelman notes the similarities between Levinas's discussion of this story of Yossel and the book of Job. She writes

> Like the biblical book of Job, this essay is a kind of affirmation through accusation, a piety on the border of blasphemy, a trial of God with Israel as accuser, prosecutor, and witness.(1991, 278)

19. See, for example, "Violence and Metaphysics," in Jacques Derrida's *Writing and Difference* (1978, 79–153).

20. As noted earlier, Levinas holds that Judaism is a religious category (1990, 144). By this, he means that it presents or represents a spirituality—that is, an ethical way relevant for all persons. Levinas explained this idea in a different way in one of his Talmudic commentaries when he wrote

> The heirs of Abraham—men to whom their ancestor bequeathed a difficult tradition of duties toward the other man, which one is never done

with, an order to which one is never free . . . So defined, the heirs of Abraham are of all nations: any man truly man is no doubt of the line of Abraham. (1990a, 99)

21. The question of the possibility of a direct relationship to God can be confidently discounted in terms of Levinas's writings, for, as he has written, "no relation with God is direct or immediate. The Divine can be manifested only through my neighbor" (1990, 159).

The matter is not as clear in Rosenzweig's work. I believe that Rosenzweig affirms the possibility of a direct experience of God. The presentation in *The Star*, in the chapter on revelation, of the love between God and humans is too powerful to rule out the direct experience of God in terms of his thought. In addition, he speaks of the mystic who is loved by God but refuses to enter into relationships with others (1972, 208). However, it appears to me that Rosenzweig speaks—perhaps for the majority of persons—of God first approaching persons through the neighbor's love and speech. It is true that the individual cannot love another person, unless God first loves him or her. However, God's love, through the love of the neighbor, is what originally awakens the soul. This is Rosenzweig's explanation of redemption, as I read *The Star* (1972, 235). It appears that Gibbs, in *Correlations*, concurs with this view, writing that "we will experience God's command to love through the voice and the words of a sensuous and probably sensual being" (1992, 99).

22. Rosenzweig recognized that there are times when the world is experienced as bereft of God's presence. Although there are moments when we feel this presence, there are other times when we cannot escape the doubts and suspicions of unbelief. He expressed this condition very eloquently in *The Star of Redemption*.

> It is the same man, disbelieving child of the world and believing child of God in one, who comes with dual plea and must stand with dual thanks before Him who gives of his wisdom to flesh and blood even as to those who fear him. (1972, 297)

23. Gibbs sees Levinas as reaffirming Rosenzweig's understanding—which is also a basic Jewish teaching—"that love is experienced as a commandment" (1992, 25). Gibbs continues, that in contrast to any sentimental view of love, both Rosenzweig and Levinas elucidate the intimate tie between love and responsibility. Also see Mosès (1992, 113–114).

24. A similar note is sounded in the famous midrashic commentary on *Isaiah* 43, 12–13, " 'you are my witnesses,' says the Lord" and "I am God," which contends that without that witnessing, there is no divine presence. See the conclusion of this book.

CHAPTER 3

1. "The Fecundity of the Caress" is a poetic, phenomenological description and explication of the transformative powers of erotic love. It does not explicitly mention Levinas's work, but proffers a critique by offering a much different vision.

2. Irigaray's position that there are significant differences between men and women places her, along with Hélène Cixous, with those whose work has been described as "gynocentric feminism." In contrast to this stream, feminists who believe in a universal human identity, and view the focus on women's differences from men as misogynist have been termed "humanist feminists." See Fraser and Bartky (1992, 5–11), for a discussion of this distinction, especially among French theorists.

3. Whitford discusses Irigaray's critical examination of Western philosophy and philosophers in her chapter, "The Same, the Semblance, and the Other" (1991a, 101–102).

4. See Levinas's crucial essay "Ethics as First Philosophy," in *The Levinas Reader* (1989, 75–87).

5. While Irigaray certainly does not identify herself as a Christian feminist, her work both critiques and draws upon Christian and post-Christian images, concepts, and values in Western culture. Particular Christian concepts, images, and associations—such as God the Father and giver of Law, the Mother/son and Father/son relationships, the Fall, and the possibility of a future age beyond both Father and Son—are integral to her oeuvre. Any analysis of her relevance for feminist Jewish thought must keep these features in mind.

6. This treatment is by no means meant to be taken as complete in terms of the literature of feminist Judaism. It illuminates some of the writings of a group of North American philosophers and theologians who take part in this enterprise. Among other lacuna, the substantial contributions of feminist Jews through the genres of poetry, liturgical writings, novels, short stories, and autobiographical reflections are not utilized here. In addition, there are obvious limitations that follow from allowing Irigaray's essay to provide/dictate the context for exploring this literature.

There is also an expanding literature by Jewish women who oppose the basic understandings and efforts of feminist Jews, but who still desire "a type of Judaism that acknowledges women's concerns as defined by women" (Myers and Litman 1995, 53). The article by Jody Myers and Jane Litman, "The Secret of Jewish Feminity," describes and critiques some of these views.

7. In *Elevations,* Richard Cohen directly—albeit, briefly—looks at Irigaray's critique of Levinas. Although Cohen offers some helpful insights into the overall approach to gender in Levinas's works, his treatment of Irigaray's questions is superficial and offensive. He brings to a close his discussion with the comment, "Irigaray is obviously serving her own feminist agenda, and is using Levinas as the usual sexist fall guy" (1994, 195). Cohen's inability to recognize that Irigaray does raise some serious questions—among them, concerning Levinas's rendering the other, but not the subject, as "feminine"—is diagnostic of the grave failure to give feminism or feminist Jewish thought any hearing in his *Elevations.*

In "Feminism and the Other," Tina Chanter is positive about Levinas's presentation of the feminine, finding that the "value of Levinas's account of femininity lies in the originality of his description of identity, and his radical reworking of the concept of Otherness" (1988, 50). Other discussions of the feminine in Levinas include another essay by Chanter, "Antigone's Dilemma" (1991), and one by Catherine Chalier, "Ethics and the Feminine" (1991).

8. In the essay, "Sexual Difference," Irigaray wrote that "sexual difference is one of the important questions of our age, if not in fact the burning issue" (1991b, 165). Her thesis is that, unless sexual difference is recognized, women will never be seen as separate from men—that is, as subjects in their own right. They will continue to be socially and politically appropriated by men and incorporated into the male unconscious and cultural symbolic. Further, unless sexual difference becomes a fundamental category for thought and the imagination, men will persist in the denial of any and all true otherness. Irigaray views positively the recent philosophical attention to plurality, but she believes that this issue can be honestly addressed only after the acknowledgement of sexual difference. See Whitford, 1991a, 83–84.

9. Descriptions and analyses of the physical intimacy and pleasure between lovers is an important feature of Irigaray's work. She sees the act of love as providing an experience for women (and men) to rethink their imaginary, symbolic, and social existence. Irigaray is at her most visionary and utopian best when she speaks of this "amorous exchange" between persons (See Whitford 1991a, 165–168). Also, see the entire essay by Irigaray, "The Fecundity of the Caress," 1986.

10. Plaskow sees the questioning of male norms "by redefinitions of 'importance' from the perspective of women's experience" as constituting the "third or constructive phase of feminist scholarship" (1994, 67).

11. Myers and Litman found, in their survey of the literature of some Orthodox women, that the issue of *niddah* was "seen as most in need of explanation since most at odds with the modern world" (1995, 52). They refer to such writers as Tamar Frankiel, Tehilla Abramov, and Shimona Krengel, who not only focused on niddah to offer a critique of modernity, but utilized it to discuss women's special relationship to God.

12. The mother/daughter and daughter/mother relationships are important elements in Irigaray's writing, as she once called these "a highly explosive nucleus" for society (Whitford 1991, 50). Irigaray believes that these relationships have been left without representation in our society, which makes it impossible for women to have an identity independent of being-for-men. She argues that women's relationship to their mothers must have symbolic representations, including the religious dimension of this symbolic, through mother/daughter images. See "Maternal Genealogy and the Symbolic," in Whitford (1991a, 75–97).

13. Behind these lines stand a number of features of Irigaray's philosophy. She holds that, in Western culture, women are identified with nature. In denying any place for women, philosophy rejects that which concretely ties both women and men to the natural universe—that is, their bodies. The retrieval of women as subjects is linked with the acknowledgement of human embodiment and the fundamental interconnection with nature.

14. See Plaskow's discussion of Alice Walker's novel, *The Color Purple*, as an example of the connection among God, humans, and the natural world as championed by feminist thought (1991, 145).

15. Plaskow briefly reviews the history of feminist efforts to transform Jewish liturgy, from the early effort of *Siddur Nashim: A Sabbath Prayer Book for Women* of the 1970s, in "Jewish Theology in Feminist Perspective" (1994, 83).

16. The identification of women with the trilogy "animality, perversity, childhood" in patriarchal society frequently appears in Irigaray's writings. Whitford has commented that

> ... if men allow women to represent the carnal for them, they collude in keeping women in a kind of pseudo-childhood, which is both "perverse" and "animal," i.e, pre-ethical, outside the sphere of the so-called "higher" human activities. (1991a, 150)

17. Cynthia Ozick contests this view, arguing in the essay "Notes toward Finding the Right Question," that the way to change the status of women in Judaism is not by theological alterations of Jewish belief, but through sociological transformations of Jewish practices and institutions.

18. Plaskow (1991, 33) borrows the term *Godwrestling* from Arthur Waskow. See also Plaskow (1994, 78).

19. The issue of the role of goddesses in pre-Israelite religions has been explored by many historians. See, for example, the important critical writings of Tikva Frymer-Kensky, *In the Wake of the Goddesses* (1992, 9–13), and Steve Davies, "The Canaanite-Hebrew Goddess," (1986).

20. Elizabeth Grosz summarizes a number of the reasons that bring Irigaray to state that women must have their own divine. She writes

> God provides a metaphor for several concepts essential to her understanding of women's autonomous identity: first, it represents an idealized perfection, an actualization of the potential to which women can aspire; second, as a mode of situating space and time (insofar as these coordinates are God-given); third, as horizon and context of identity; and fourth, as the supreme form of an alterity which institutes ethics: one can love the other only if one also loves oneself and [a] God. (159–160)

21. A recent, fascinating, and important study of the use of gender in the symbolism of the Kabbalah is Elliot Wolfson's *Circle in the Square*. Although it is too rich and complex of a work to carefully discuss here in terms of feminist Jewish views of the image of the divine in Judaism, the argument of the final chapter does support their position about the dominance of the male image. Wolfson writes that, while the "kabbalists clearly describe the divine in terms of male and female . . . the gender polarity of God is transcended in the singular male form that comprises both masculine and feminine" (1995, xiii).

22. In the essay, "The three *genres*," Irigaray juxtaposes God's invisibility with the invisibility of "our sexual relation, our carnal act, especially through the mediation of woman" (1991a, 152).

23. Rachel Biale presents a very helpful overview of the variety of positions taken in the current discussion concerning the Halakhah's impact upon women in the "Epilogue" to her book, *Women and Jewish Law* (1984, 256–266).

24. I hope that, in juxtaposing Irigaray's philosophical work with feminist Jewish texts, some suggestions might be found about new areas and directions to be pursued by these Jewish philosophers and theologians.

CHAPTER 4

1. Fackenheim describes this term in the following manner:

> . . . the term "as it were" (*k'b'yakhol*) is a fully developed technical term, signifying, on the one hand, that the affirmation in question is not literally true but only a human way of speaking; and, on the other hand, that it is truth nonetheless which cannot be humanly transcended. (Morgan, 1992, 217)

2. As discussed in chapter 3, the secondary literature on Levinas and the issue of women is large and expanding. See note 7 in that chapter. While Simone de Beauvoir in *The Second Sex* did not regard his statements about women as constructive (cited in Chanter 1988, 54), others believe that his work provides a good foundation for overturning traditional notions that justify the marginalization and subjection of women.

Levinas has made comments about the feminist movement in general terms. In "Judaism and the Feminine," he rejects the view that sees women as essentially compliments to men, insisting that both men and women are full individuals or "totalities" (1990, 35). On the other hand, he has written in "And God Created Woman" that "Real humanity does not allow for an abstract equality, without some subordination of terms" (1990a, 173).

3. Buber's treatment of the I-Thou relationship with nature—which, as all such relationships, can point to the Eternal Thou—is not repeated in the work of Rosenzweig and Levinas. (See Buber 1970, 172–173). Abraham Heschel gives priority to nature as one of the "three starting points of contemplation about God" (1966, 31).

4. See Gibbs, 1992, 211; 215.

5. Levinas often emphasizes that Judaism insists that the material needs of the other must be treated as spiritual requirements thrust upon the self. See his discussion of the Talmudic concern with such issues as the length of the workday and the food that must be provided to the laborer in "Judaism and Revolution" (1990a, 100–105).

6. Richard Cohen puts this somewhat differently by writing that for Levinas, "Eros, then, stands to the fully human tasks of ethics and justice as an interlude, intermission, or vacation" (1994, 210). He also speaks of eros, or at least "erotic nudity," as a subversion of the ethical relation (1994, 208–209).

7. See Wolfson's *Circle in the Square*, especially the chapters "Erasing the Erasure" and "Crossing Gender Boundaries" (1993, 49–121).

8. For a discussion of the role of mysticism in Rosenzweig's work, see Moshe Idel's "Franz Rosenzweig and the Kabbalah," 1988. Edith Wyschogrod has commented on Levinas's use of the "*via negativa* of the mystics" in "Emmanuel Levinas and the Problem of Religious Language," 1974, 33.

9. The main focus of Moshe Idel's "Franz Rosenzweig and the Kabbalah" is the place of mystic concepts in *The Star*.

10. Part of the exchange of letters is included in Rosenzweig, *On Jewish Learning*, 1965, 109–118.

CHAPTER 5

1. For a discussion of the term pluralism see John Hick's essay, "A Philosophy of Religious Pluralism." Hick distinguishes among pluralism, exclusivism, and inclusivism. He defines pluralism as "the view that the great world faiths embody different perceptions and conceptions of, and corresponding different responses to, the Real or the Ultimate" (1989, 36). Exclusivism relates truth and salvation solely to a single tradition. Inclusivism finds some truth in other traditions in so far as they conform to one's tradition and its higher truth.

2. In *Out of the Ghetto*, Jacob Katz describes the intellectual and social background of Jewish emancipation. The limits of acceptance of the Jew into European society is discussed by Katz, as well as by Michael Meyer in *The Origins of the Modern Jew*.

3. A good introduction to some of the history of the Jewish/Christian encounter is provided by Jacob Katz in *Exclusiveness and Tolerance*, and the readings in Frank Talmage's *Disputation and Dialogue*. A more modern focus is given by Geoffrey Wigoder in the article "Ecumenism," and the chapter "Christian attitudes to Judaism and the Jews" in his *Jewish-Christian Relations Since the Second World War* (1988, 1–47).

4. There are a number of good writings on the traditional Jewish resources relevant to the issue of pluralism. These usually focus on the category of the *ger toshav* and the notion of the Noahide laws. The first refers to the treatment of the non-Jew that later commentators believed was required because of the special protection and status that the Torah gave to foreign residents or "the stranger" in Israel, expressed

in such verses as *Leviticus* 19:33–4, and *Deuteronomy* 10:19. There are different descriptions of the seven Noahide laws, but they are often listed as the obligations against committing idolatry, blasphemy, sexual immorality, murder, robbery, eating a living animal, as well as the requirement to establish courts of justice. The literature concerning these laws examines the question whether those non-Jews who uphold the covenant with Noah are righteous and deserve a place in the world to come. See David Novak's books, *Jewish-Christian Dialogue* and *The Image of the Non-Jew in Judaism*, and also Joseph Levi's article, "Stranger."

5. A good example of this is David Novak's *The Election of Israel.*

6. See, for example, Novak's discussion and critique of Soloveitchik's position in *Jewish-Christian Dialogue* (1989, 6–9); and David Hartman's essay, which will be discussed later in this chapter, "Pluralism and Revelation."

7. Soloveitchik had presented elements of his position in 1964 at a conference of the Rabbinical Council.

8. Steven Katz has written an insightful article—"Abraham Joshua Heschel and Hasidism"—on this unappreciated book.

9. There are many good treatments of Rosenzweig's presentation of Judaism and Christianity in *The Star.* For example, see Julius Guttmann's *Philosophies of Judaism* (1964, 389–397); and Novak's *Jewish-Christian Dialogue* (1989, 93–113).

10. For a more extended discussion of Rosenzweig's understanding of speech, see my *Mutual Upholding* (Oppenheim 1992, 117–138).

11. See Paul Mendes-Flohr's chapter "Ambivalent Dialogue: Jewish-Christian Theological Encounter in the Weimar Republic," in *Divided Passions* (1991, 135–140).

12. Alexander Altmann writes of his appreciation for the power of the dialogue between Rosenzweig and Rosenstock-Huessy in *Judaism Despite Christianity* (1971, 27). The exchange of letters between the two young thinkers is the substance of that book. In *Tolerance and Transformation,* Lubarsky points to Rosenzweig's "lack of commitment to the truth value of Christianity" (1990, 50). The conclusion of this chapter will argue that such a commitment to the truth value of another tradition is impossible.

13. Rosenstock-Huessy discusses this in *Judaism Despite Christianity* (1971, 171–177).

14. There are a number of essays on Buber's interest in other religions as well as his particular work on the relationship between Judaism and Christianity in *The Philosophy of Martin Buber*, edited by Paul Schilpp and Maurice Friedman; and *Martin Buber: A Centenary Volume*, edited by Haim Gordon and Jochanan Bloch.

15. Cited in Lubarsky, (1990, 95).

16. There appears to be a commitment to pluralism by such writers as Judith Plaskow, Rita Gross, Lynn Gottlieb, and others. I have had difficulty in finding specific statements to corroborate this impression, but their views of religious language and experience as well as other ideas clearly point in this direction.

17. This distinction can be found in Judaism and in Christianity. In early rabbinic thought, the pagan is seen as being created by God, but not standing in a vital nor authentic relationship to God. See the discussion of idolatry in Novak's *Jewish-Christian Dialogue* (1989, 26–41).

18. This is Lubarsky's assessment of Baeck (1990, 74).

19. The exchange is contained in Glatzer and Mendes-Flohr eds., *The Letters of Martin Buber* (1991, especially 267–282).

20. Elliot Dorff discusses this quotation in his article (1982, 493).

21. It is interesting—and I am not sure that I have seen others express it in this manner—that Borowitz finds that the understanding of the limits of the human is "the fundamental principle" of those who are not Orthodox Jews. At least in Hartman (1990, 248), we have someone who both holds this position and is Orthodox.

22. Cited in Lubarsky (1990, 110).

23. See Novak's discussion of the Jewish tradition's attitude toward Christianity and Islam in terms of the Noahide laws (1989, 26–72).

CONCLUSION

1. See note 4 to the Introduction.

2. In addition to the Holocaust, Fackenheim has explored the response of Jewish faith to secularism in the chapter "The Challenge of Modern Secularity" in *God's Presence in History* (1972, 35–66).

3. In the "Introduction" to this book, it was indicated that there has been a flourishing of Jewish religious language—and not a decline—specifically in reaction to the Holocaust. Fackenheim, Greenberg, and Cohen speak of new ways in which God's presence is experienced.

4. There is an excellent discussion of Greenberg's work by Steven Katz in "Irving (*Yitzchak*) Greenberg," in *Interpreters of Judaism in the Late Twentieth Century* (1993, 59–89).

5. Greenberg's response to the Holocaust in terms of reassessing God's presence in the world, as well as Jewish religious institutions, is strongly reminiscent of some of the prison writings of Dietrich Bonhoeffer, the Christian theologian who was

jailed and killed for his opposition to the Nazis. The parallel extends to Greenberg's term "holy secularity," and Bonhoeffer's "religionless Christianity." See Bonhoeffer's *Letters and Papers from Prison.*

6. The possible role of God in the process of redemption is beautifully probed by Rosenzweig in the section of *The Star*, titled "On the Possibility of Entreating the Kingdom" (1972, 265–275).

7. Jacob Neusner, in *The Foundations of the Theology of Judaism,* vol. 1: *God*, provides a very important analysis of the development of the notion of God, starting as a principle and premise, and emerging as a person, in the Oral Torah. His argument about the importance of the study of Oral Torah for contemporary Jewish theology is thoroughly convincing (1991, xiii–xxviii).

8. The original *midrash* from *Pesikta de-Rav Kahana* was cited by Rosenzweig in *The Star* (1972, 171). Obviously, the last sentence is my addition.

Bibliography

Ables, Billie
 1977 *Therapy for Couples.* San Francisco: Jossey-Bass.
Ackelsberg, Martha
 1986 "Spirituality, Community, and Politics: *B'not Esh* and the Feminist Recon-
    struction of Judaism," *Journal of Feminist Studies in Religion,* 2:2.
Adler, Rachel
 1983 "The Jew Who Wasn't There: *Halakhah* and the Jewish Woman," in *On
    Being a Jewish Feminist,* edited by Susannah Heschel. New York: Schocken
    Books.
Altmann, Alexander
 1971 "Franz Rosenzweig and Eugen Rosenstock-Huessy: An Introduction to Their
    'Letters on Judaism & Christianity,'" in *Judaism Despite Christianity: The
    "Letters on Christianity and Judaism" between Eugen Rosenstock-Huessy
    and Franz Rosenzweig,* edited by Eugen Rosenstock-Huessy. New York:
    Schocken Books.
 1988 "Franz Rosenzweig on History," in *The Philosophy of Franz Rosenzweig,*
    edited by Paul Mendes-Flohr. Hanover: University Press of New England.
Baeck, Leo
 1970 *Judaism and Christianity: Essays by Leo Baeck.* New York: Atheneum.
Bernasconi, Robert
 1988 "'Failure of Communication' as a Surplus: Dialogue and Lack of Dia-
    logue between Buber and Levinas," in *The Provocation of Levinas: Re-
    thinking the Other,* edited by Robert Bernasconi and David Wood. Lon-
    don: Routledge.
Biale, Rachel
 1984 *Women and Jewish Law: An Exploration of Women's Issues in Halakhic
    Sources.* New York: Schocken Books.

Bonhoeffer, Dietrich
    1959   *Letters and papers from prison.* London: Collins.
Borowitz, Eugene
    1991   *Renewing the Covenant: A Theology for the Postmodern Jew.* Philadelphia: Jewish Publication Society.
Buber, Martin
    1961   *Two Types of Faith.* New York: Harper and Row.
    1963   *Israel and the World: Essays in a Time of Crisis.* New York: Schocken Books.
    1964   "Church, State, Nation, Jewry," in *Christianity: Some Non-Christian Appraisals*, edited by David McKain. New York: McGraw-Hill.
    1970   *I and Thou*, translated by Walter Kaufmann. New York: Charles Scribner's Sons.
    1973   "Hebrew Humanism," in *The Zionist Idea: A Historical Analysis and Reader*, edited by Arthur Hertzberg. New York: Atheneum.
    1985   *Ecstatic Confessions.* San Francisco: Harper and Row.
Buber, Martin, and Franz Rosenzweig
    1994   *Scripture and Translation.* Bloomington: Indiana University Press.
Casper, Bernhard
    1984   "Franz Rosenzweig's Criticism of Buber's *I and Thou*," in *Martin Buber: A Centenary Volume*, edited by Haim Gordon and Jochanan Bloch. New York: Ktav Publishing House.
    1988   "Responsibility Rescued," in *The Philosophy of Franz Rosenzweig*, edited by Paul Mendes-Flohr. Hanover: University Press of New England.
Chalier, Catherine
    1991   "Ethics and the Feminine" in *Re-Reading Levinas*, edited by Robert Bernasconi and Simon Critchley. Bloomington: Indiana University Press.
Chanter, Tina
    1988   "Feminism and the Other" in *The Provocation of Levinas: Rethinking the Other*, edited by Robert Bernasconi and David Wood. London: Routledge.
    1991   "Antigone's Dilemma" in *Re-Reading Levinas*, edited by Robert Bernasconi and Simon Critchley. Bloomington: Indiana University Press.
Christ, Carol P., and Judith Plaskow, editors
    1992   *Womanspirit Rising: A Feminist Reader in Religion.* San Francisco: Harper Collins.
Cohen, Arthur A., editor
    1980   *The Jew.* Alabama: University of Alabama Press.
Cohen, Arthur A., and Paul Mendes-Flohr, editors
    1988   *Contemporary Jewish Religious Thought.* New York: Free Press.
Cohen, Richard
    1987   *Face-to-Face with Levinas.* Albany: State University of New York Press.
    1992   "God in Levinas," *Journal of Jewish Thought and Philosophy*, vol. 1.
    1994   *Elevations: The Height of the Good in Rosenzweig and Levinas.* Chicago: University of Chicago Press.
Daum, Annette
    1989   "Blaming the Jews for the Death of the Goddess," in *Nice Jewish Girls: A Lesbian Anthology*, edited by Evelyn Beck. Boston: Beacon Press.

Davidman, Lynn, and Shelly Tenenbaum, editors
1994   *Feminist Perspectives on Jewish Studies.* New Haven: Yale University Press.
Davies, Steve
1986   "The Canaanite-Hebrew Goddess," in *The Book of the Goddess Past and Present*, edited by Carl Olson. New York: Crossroad.
Derrida, Jacques
1978   *Writing and Difference.* Chicago: University of Chicago Press.
Dietrich, Wendell
1988   "Is Rosenzweig an Ethical Monotheist? A Debate with the New Francophone Literature," in *Der Philosoph Franz Rosenzweig (1886–1929): Internationaler Kongress—Kassel 1986*, vol. 2, edited by Wolfdietrich Schmied-Kowarzik. Freiberg/München: Verlag Karl Alber.
Dorff, Elliot
1982   "The Covenant," *Anglican Theological Review,* October 64.
1992   "Pluralism," in *Frontiers of Jewish Thought*, edited by Steven Katz. Washington, D.C.: B'nai B'rith Books.
Duncan, Erika
1983   "The Hungry Jewish Mother," in *On Being a Jewish Feminist: A Reader*, edited by Susannah Heschel. New York: Schocken Books.
Eigen, Ron, editor
1993   *Hadesh Yameinu: A Siddur for Sabbath and Festivals.* Montreal: Reconstructionist Synagogue.
Erikson, Erik H.
1968   *Identity, Youth and Crisis.* New York: W. W. Norton.
Fackenheim, Emil
1968   *Quest for Past and Future.* Bloomington: Indiana University Press.
1972   *God's Presence in History: Jewish Affirmations and Philosophical Reflections.* New York: Harper and Row.
1973   *Encounters Between Judaism and Modern Philosophy: A Preface to Future Jewish Thought.* New York: Basic Books.
Falk, Marcia
1982   *Love Lyrics from the Bible: A Translation and Literary Study of The Song of Songs.* Sheffield, England: The Almond Press.
1989   "Notes on Composing New Blessings," in *Weaving the Visions*, edited by Judith Plaskow and Carol Christ. San Francisco: Harper Collins.
Fishbane, Michael
1989   *The Garments of Torah: Essays in Biblical Hermeneutics.* Bloomington: Indiana University Press.
Fishman, Sylvia Barak
1993   *A Breath of Life: Feminism in the American Jewish Community.* New York: Free Press.
Fraser, Nancy, and Sandra Lee Bartky
1992   *Revaluing French Feminism: Critical Essays on Difference, Agency, and Culture.* Bloomington: Indiana University Press.
Friedlander, Judith
1990   *Vilna on the Seine: Jewish Intellectuals in France Since 1968.* New Haven: Yale University Press.

Friedman, Maurice
  1956 *Martin Buber: The Life of Dialogue*. Chicago: University of Chicago Press.
Frymer-Kensky, Tikva
  1992 *In the Wake of the Goddesses*. New York: Free Press.
Galli, Barbara
  1993 "Franz Rosenzweig Speaking of Meetings and Monotheism in Biblical Anthropomorphisms," *The Journal of Jewish Thought and Philosophy*, vol. 2.
  1994 "Rosenzweig and the Name for God," *Modern Judaism*, vol. 14:1
  1995 *Franz Rosenzweig and Jehuda Halevi: Translating, Translations, and Translators*. Montreal and Kingston: McGill-Queen's Press.
Gibbs, Robert
  1992 *Correlations in Rosenzweig and Levinas*. Princeton, NJ: Princeton University Press.
Glatzer, Nahum N., editor
  1970 *Franz Rosenzweig: His Life and Thought*. New York: Schocken Books.
Glatzer, Nahum N. and Paul Mendes-Flohr, editors
  1991 *The Letters of Martin Buber: A Life of Dialogue*. New York: Schocken Books.
Gordon, Haim, and Jochanan Bloch
  1984 *Martin Buber: A Centenary Volume*. New York: Ktav Publishing House.
Gottlieb, Lynn
  1995 *She Who Dwells Within: A Feminist Vision of a Renewed Judaism*. San Francisco: Harper Collins.
Gottschalt, Alfred
  1982 "Religion in a Post-Holocaust World," in *Jews and Christians After the Holocaust*, edited by Abraham Peck. Philadelphia: Fortress Press.
Greenberg, Blu
  1981 *On Women and Judaism: A View from Tradition*. Philadelphia: Jewish Publication Society.
  1987 "Women and Judaism," in *Contemporary Jewish Religious Thought*, edited by Arthur Cohen and Paul Mendes-Flohr. New York: Free Press.
Greenberg, Irving
  1982 "Religious Values After the Holocaust: A Jewish View," in *Jews and Christians After the Holocaust*, edited by Abraham Peck. Philadelphia: Fortress Press.
Greenberg, Julie
  1986 "Seeking a Feminist Judaism," in *The Tribe of Dina: A Jewish Women's Anthology*, edited by Melanie Kaye/Kantrowitz and Irena Klepfisz. Montpelier: Sister Wisdom Books.
Gross, Rita M.
  1983 "Steps toward Feminine Imagery of Deity in Jewish Theology," in *On Being a Jewish Feminist*, edited by Susannah Heschel. New York: Schocken Books.
  1992 "Female God Language in a Jewish Context," in *Womanspirit Rising*, edited by Carol Christ and Judith Plaskow. San Francisco: Harper and Row.

Grosz, Elizabeth
  1989   *Sexual Subversions: Three French Feminists.* Sydney, Australia: Allen and Unwin.
Guttmann, Julius
  1964   *Philosophies of Judaism.* London: Routledge and Kegan Paul.
Handelman, Susan
  1982   *The Slayers of Moses.* Albany: State University of New York Press.
  1991   *Fragments of Redemption.* Bloomington: Indiana University Press.
Hartman, David
  1978   "Halakhah as a Ground for Creating a Shared Spiritual Language," in *Joy and Responsibility: Israel, Modernity and the Renewal of Judaism.* Jerusalem: Ben-Zvi Posner.
  1990   "Pluralism and Biblical Theology," and "Pluralism and Revelation," in *Conflicting Visions: Spiritual Possibilities of Modern Israel.* New York: Schocken Books.
Heschel, Abraham Joshua
  1966   *God in Search of Man: A Philosophy of Judaism.* New York: Harper and Row.
  1969   *Israel: An Echo of Eternity.* New York: The Noonday Press.
  1973   *A Passion for Truth.* New York: Farrar, Straus and Giroux.
  1990   "No Religion Is an Island," in *Christianity Through Non-Christian Eyes*, edited by Paul Griffiths. New York: Orbis Books.
Heschel, Susannah, editor
  1983   *On Being a Jewish Feminist: A Reader.* New York: Schocken Books.
Hick, John
  1989   "A Philosophy of Religious Pluralism," in *Three Faiths—One God*, edited by John Hick and Edmund Meltzer. Houndmills, Basingstoke, Hampshire: Macmillan.
Hyman, Paula
  1983   "The Jewish Family: Looking for a Usable Past," in *On Being a Jewish Feminist*, edited by Susannah Heschel. New York: Schocken Books.
Idel, Moshe
  1988   "Franz Rosenzweig and the Kabbalah," in *The Philosophy of Franz Rosenzweig*, edited by Paul Mendes-Flohr. Hanover: University Press of New England.
Irigaray, Luce
  1986   "The Fecundity of the Caress: A Reading of Levinas', *Totality and Infinity*, IV: B, 'The Phenomenology of Eros,' " in *Face-to-Face with Levinas*, edited by Richard Cohen. Albany: State University of New York Press.
  1991   "Questions to Emmanuel Levinas: On the Divinity of Love," in *Re-Reading Levinas*, edited by Robert Bernasconi and Simon Critchley. Bloomington: Indiana University Press.
  1991a "The Three Genres," in *The Irigaray Reader*, edited by Margaret Whitford. Cambridge, Mass.: Basil Blackwell.

1991b "Sexual Difference," in *The Irigaray Reader*, edited by Margaret Whitford.
       Cambridge, Mass.: Basil Blackwell.
Joseph, Norma
    1992 "Response," in Michael Oppenheim, *Mutual Upholding: Fashioning Jewish
          Philosophy Through Letters*. New York: Peter Lang.
Kaplan, Mordecai
    1946 "The Chosen People Idea as an Anachronism," *The Reconstructionist*, 11.
Katz, Jacob
    1961 *Exclusiveness and Tolerance: Studies in Jewish-Gentile Relations*. London:
          Oxford University Press.
    1973 *Out of the Ghetto*. Cambridge, Mass.: Harvard University Press.
Katz, Steven
    1980 "Abraham Joshua Heschel and Hasidism," *The Journal of Jewish Studies*,
          31:1, Spring.
    1983 *Post-Holocaust Dialogues: Critical Studies in Modern Jewish Thought*.
          New York: New York University Press.
    1993 "Irving (Yitzchak) Greenberg," in *Interpreters of Judaism in the Late Twen-
          tieth Century,* edited by Steven T. Katz. Washington, D.C.: B'nai B'rith
          Books.
Kaufman, Gordon D.
    1972 *God the Problem*. Cambridge, Mass.: Harvard University Press.
Kendall, Thena
    1983 "Memories of an Orthodox Youth," in *On Being a Jewish Feminist*, edited
          by Susannah Heschel. New York: Schocken Books.
Kepnes, Steven
    1992 *The Text As Thou*. Bloomington: Indiana University Press.
Kepnes, Steven, editor
    1996 *Interpreting Judaism in a Postmodern Age*. New York: New York University
          Press.
Kierkegaard, Soren
    1971 *Concluding Unscientific Postscript* [by Johannes Climacus]. Princeton:
          Princeton University Press.
Koltun, Elizabeth, editor
    1976 *The Jewish Woman: New Perspectives*. New York: Schocken Books.
Lefkovitz, Lori
    1995 "Eavesdropping on Angels and Laughing at God: Theorizing a Subversive
          Matriarchy," in *Gender and Judaism*, edited by T. M. Rudavsky. New York:
          New York University Press.
Levi, Joseph
    1987 "Stranger," in *Contemporary Jewish Religious Thought*, edited by Arthur
          Cohen and Paul Mendes-Flohr. New York: Free Press.
Levinas, Emmanuel
    1981 *Otherwise Than Being Or Beyond Essence*. Boston: Martinus Nijhoff.
    1983 "Franz Rosenzweig," *Midstream*, 19:9.
    1985 *Ethics and Infinity: Conversations with Philippe Nemo*. Pittsburg: Duquesne
          University Press.

1986 "Dialogue with Emmanuel Levinas," by Emmanuel Levinas and Richard Kearney, in *Face-to-Face with Levinas*, edited by Richard Cohen. New York: State University of New York Press.

1987 *Time and the Other*. Pittsburg: Duquesne University Press.

1988 *Totality and Infinity: An Essay on Exteriority*. Pittsburg: Duquesne University Press.

1989 *The Levinas Reader*, edited by Sean Hand. Oxford: Basil Blackwell.

1990 *Difficult Freedom: Essays on Judaism*. Baltimore: Johns Hopkins University Press.

1990a *Nine Talmudic Readings*. Bloomington: Indiana University Press.

1992 "Foreword," in *System and Revelation: The Philosophy of Franz Rosenzweig* by Stéphane Mosès. Detroit: Wayne State University Press.

1994 *Beyond the Verse: Talmudic Readings and Lectures*. Bloomington: Indiana University Press.

1994a *In the Time of the Nations*. Bloomington: Indiana University Press.

1994b *Outside the Subject*. Stanford: Stanford University Press.

Lubarsky, Sandra

1990 *Tolerance and Transformation: Jewish Approaches to Religious Transformation*. Cincinnati: Hebrew Union College Press.

Mendelssohn, Moses

1969 *Jerusalem and Other Jewish Writings*. New York: Schocken Books.

Mendes-Flohr, Paul

1991 *Divided Passions: Jewish Intellectuals and the Experience of Modernity*. Detroit: Wayne State University Press.

Mendes-Flohr, Paul, editor

1988 *The Philosophy of Franz Rosenzweig*. Hanover: University Press of New England.

Meyer, Michael

1967 *The Origins of the Modern Jew*: Detroit: Wayne State University Press.

Morgan, Michael, L. editor

1987 *The Jewish Thought of Emil Fackenheim*. Detroit: Wayne State University Press.

Mosès, Stéphane

1992 *System and Revelation: The Philosophy of Franz Rosenzweig*. Detroit: Wayne State University Press.

Myers, Jody, and Jane Litman

1995 "The Secret of Jewish Femininity: Hiddenness, Power and Physicality in the Theology of Orthodox Women in the Contemporary World," in *Gender and Judaism*, edited by T. M. Rudavsky. New York: New York University Press.

Neher, André

1988 "Silence," in *Contemporary Jewish Religious Thought*, edited by Arthur Cohen and Paul Mendes-Flohr. New York: Free Press.

Neusner, Jacob

1981 "Freedom's Challenge to Judaism," in *Stranger At Home*. Chicago: University of Chicago Press.

1991 *The Foundations of the Theology of Judaism, vol. 1: God*. Northvale, N.J.: Jason Aaronson.

Novak, David
    1983   *The Image of the Non-Jew in Judaism.* New York: Edwin Mellen.
    1989   *Jewish-Christian Dialogue: A Jewish Justification.* New York: Oxford
            University Press.
    1990   "Jewish Theology," *Modern Judaism*, 10:3.
    1995   *The Election of Israel: The Idea of the Chosen People.* Cambridge: Cam-
            bridge University Press.
O'Conner, Noreen
    1988   "The Personal is Political: Discursive Practice of the Face-To-Face," in *The
            Provocation of Levinas*, edited by Robert Bernasconi and David Wood.
            London: Routledge.
Oppenheim, Michael
    1978   "Death and Man's Fear of Death in Franz Rosenzweig's *The Star of Re-
            demption*," *Judaism*, 27:4.
    1985   *What Does Revelation Mean for the Modern Jew? Rosenzweig, Buber,
            Fackenheim.* Lewiston, N.Y.: Edwin Mellen.
    1987   "Can We Still Stay with Him: Two Jewish Theologians Confront the Ho-
            locaust," *Studies in Religion*, 16:4.
    1987a "The Relevance of Rosenzweig in the Eyes of His Israeli Critics," *Modern
            Judaism*, 7:2.
    1992   *Mutual Upholding: Fashioning Jewish Philosophy Through Letters.* New
            York: Peter Lang.
    1996   "Feminism, Jewish Philosophy, and Religious Pluralism," *Modern Judaism*
            16:2.
Ozick, Cynthia
    1983   "Notes toward Finding the Right Question," in *On Being a Jewish Femi-
            nist*, edited by Susannah Heschel. New York: Schocken Books.
Plaskow, Judith
    1983   "The Right Question Is Theological," in *On Being a Jewish Feminist*, edited
            by Susannah Heschel. New York: Schocken Books.
    1989   "Blaming the Jews for the Birth of Patriarchy," in *Nice Jewish Girls: A
            Lesbian Anthology*, edited by Evelyn Beck. Boston: Beacon Press.
    1991   *Standing Again at Sinai: Judaism From a Feminist Perspective.* San Fran-
            cisco: HarperCollins.
    1994   "Jewish Theology in Feminist Perspective," in *Feminist Perspectives on
            Jewish Studies*, edited by Lynn Davidman and Shelly Tenenbaum. New
            Haven: Yale University Press.
Plaskow, Judith, and Carol P. Christ, editors
    1989   *Weaving the Visions: New Patterns in Feminist Spirituality.* San Francisco:
            HarperCollins.
Pöggeler, Otto
    1988   "Between Enlightenment and Romanticism: Rosenzweig and Hegel," in
            The Philosophy of Franz Rosenzweig, edited by Paul Mendes-Flohr. Hanover:
            University Press of New England.
Ricoeur, Paul
    1970   *Freud and Philosophy.* New Haven: Yale University Press.

Rosenstock-Huessy, Eugen, editor

1971 *Judaism Despite Christianity: The "Letters on Christianity and Judaism" between Eugen Rosenstock-Huessy and Franz Rosenzweig.* New York: Schocken Books.

Rosenzweig, Franz

1937 ["On Anthrophomorphism"] *"Zur Encyclopaedia Judaica: Zum Zweiten Band, Mit einer Anmerkung uber Anthropomorphismus," Kleinere Schriften.* Berlin: Schocken Verlag.

1953 *Understanding the Sick and the Healthy: A View of World, Man, and God,* edited by N. N. Glatzer. New York.

1965 *On Jewish Learning,* edited by N. N. Glatzer. New York: Schocken Books.

1970 "The New Thinking" and other writings, in *Franz Rosenzweig: His Life and Thought,* edited by Nahum N. Glatzer. New York: Schocken Books.

1972 *The Star of Redemption.* Boston: Beacon Press.

1976– *Der Mensch und sein Werk, Gesammelte Schriften.* The Hague: Martinus
84 Nijhoff.

1995 *Jehuda Halevi,* in Barbara Galli, *Franz Rosenzweig and Jehuda Halevi.* Montreal and Kingston: McGill-Queen's Press.

Rotenstreich, Nathan

1967 "Commonsense and Theological Experience on the Basis of Franz Rosenzweig's Philosophy," *Journal of the History of Philosophy* 5.

1988 "Rosenzweig's Notion of Metaethics," in *The Philosophy of Franz Rosenzweig,* edited by Paul Mendes-Flohr. Hanover: University Press of New England.

Rubenstein, Richard L.

1966 *After Auschwitz: Radical Theology and Contemporary Judaism.* Indianapolis: Bobbs-Merrill.

Rudavsky, T. M., editor

1995 *Gender and Judaism.* New York: New York University Press.

Sacks, Maurie

1995 "An Anthropological and Postmodern Critique of Jewish Feminist Theory," in *Gender and Judaism,* edited by T. M. Rudarsky. New York: New York University Press.

Samuelson, Norbert

1988 "The Concept of 'Nichts' in Rosenzweig's *The Star of Redemption,*" in *Der Philosoph Franz Rosenzweig (1886–1929): Internationaler Kongress— Kassel 1986,* vol. 2, edited by Wolfdietrich Schmied-Kowarzik. Freiberg/ München: Verlag Karl Alber.

Samuelson, Norbert, editor

1987 *Studies in Jewish Philosophy.* Lanham, Md.: University Press of America.

Scarf, Maggie

1987 *Intimate Partners: Patterns in Love and Marriage.* New York: Random House.

Schilpp, Paul, and Maurice Friedman, editors

1967 *The Philosophy of Martin Buber.* La Salle, Ill.: Open Court.

Schweid, Eliezer

1994 *To Declare that God Is Upright: Theodicy in Jewish Thought* [Hebrew]. Israel: Tag Publishers.

Seeskin, Kenneth
  1990 *Jewish Philosophy in a Secular Age*. Albany: State University of New York Press.
  1991 "Jewish Philosophy in the 1980's," *Modern Judaism*, 11:1.
Setel, Drorah T.
  1986 "Roundtable Discussion: Feminist Reflections on Separation and Unity in Jewish Theology," *Journal of Feminist Studies in Religion*, 2:1, Spring.
Soloveitchik, Joseph B.
  1969 "Confrontation," *Tradition*, 6:2.
Stahmer, Harold
  1968 *"Speak That I May See Thee!"* New York: Macmillan Company.
  1988 "The Letters of Franz Rosenzweig to Margrit Rosenstock-Huessy: 'Franz,' 'Gritli,' 'Eugen' and '*The Star of Redemption*,' " in *Der Philosoph Franz Rosenzweig (1886–1929): Internationaler Kongress—Kassel 1986*, vol. 1, edited by Wolfdietrich Schmied-Kowarzik. Freiberg/München: Verlag Karl Alber.
Stern, David
  1988 "Midrash," in *Contemporary Jewish Religious Thought*, edited by Arthur Cohen and Paul Mendes-Flohr. New York: Free Press.
Sugarman, Richard, and Helen Stephenson
  1979 "Emmanuel Levinas' 'To Love the Torah More Than God,' " *Judaism*, 28.
Susman, Margarete
  1980 "Franz Rosenzweig's *The Star of Redemption* (A Review)," in *The Jew: Essays from Martin Buber's Journal Der Jude, 1916–1928*, edited by Arthur Cohen. Tuscaloosa: University of Alabama Press.
Talmage, Frank, editor
  1975 *Disputation and Dialogue: Readings in the Jewish-Christian Encounter*. New York: Ktav Publishing House.
Taylor, Mark C.
  1987 *Altarity*. Chicago: University of Chicago Press.
Tirosh-Rothschild, Hava
  1994 " 'Dare to Know': Feminism and the Discipline of Jewish Philosophy," in *Feminist Perspectives on Jewish Studies*, edited by Lynn Davidman and Shelly Tenenbaum. New Haven: Yale University Press.
Umansky, Ellen M.
  1989 "Creating a Jewish Feminist Theology," in *Weaving the Visions,* edited by Judith Plaskow and Carol Christ. San Francisco: Harper Collins.
Whitford, Margaret
  1991 *The Irigaray Reader*. Cambridge, Mass.: Basil Blackwell.
  1991a *Luce Irigaray: Philosophy in the Feminine*. London: Routledge.
Wiesel, Elie
  1960 *Night*. New York: Hill and Wang.
  1978 *A Jew Today*. New York: Random House.

Wigoder, Geoffrey
 1988 "Ecumenism," in *Contemporary Jewish Religious Thought*, edited by Arthur Cohen and Paul Mendes-Flohr. New York: Free Press.
 1988a *Jewish-Christian Relations Since the Second World War*. Manchester: Manchester University Press.
Wolfson, Elliot
 1995 *Circle in the Square: Studies in the Use of Gender in Kabbalistic Symbolism*. Albany: State University of New York Press.
Wyschogrod, Edith
 1972 "Emmanuel Levinas and the Problem of Religious Language," *The Thomist*, 36:1, January.
 1974 *Emmanuel Levinas: The Problem of Ethical Metaphysics*. The Hague: Martinus Nijhoff.

Index